Get Updates and More on Nolo.com

Go to this book's companion page at:

www.nolo.com/back-of-book/FIFO.html

When there's an important change to the law affecting this book, we'll post updates. You'll also find articles and other related materials.

More Resources from Nolo.com

Legal Forms, Books, & Software
Hundreds of do-it-yourself products—all written in plain English, approved, and updated by our in-house legal editors.

Legal Articles
Get informed with thousands of free articles on everyday legal topics. Our articles are accurate, up to date, and reader friendly.

Find a Lawyer
Want to talk to a lawyer? Use Nolo to find a lawyer who can help you with your case.

NOLO
LAW for ALL

⚖ NOLO **The Trusted Name**
(but don't take our word for it)

"In Nolo you can trust."
THE NEW YORK TIMES

"Nolo is always there in a jam as the nation's premier publisher of do-it-yourself legal books."
NEWSWEEK

"Nolo publications…guide people simply through the how, when, where and why of the law."
THE WASHINGTON POST

"[Nolo's]…material is developed by experienced attorneys who have a knack for making complicated material accessible."
LIBRARY JOURNAL

"When it comes to self-help legal stuff, nobody does a better job than Nolo…"
USA TODAY

"The most prominent U.S. publisher of self-help legal aids."
TIME MAGAZINE

"Nolo is a pioneer in both consumer and business self-help books and software."
LOS ANGELES TIMES

8th Edition

The Foreclosure Survival Guide

Keep Your House or Walk Away With Money in Your Pocket

WITHDRAWN

Attorneys Amy Loftsgordon & Cara O'Neill

EIGHTH EDITION   AUGUST 2021

Editor   AMY LOFTSGORDON

Book Design   SUSAN PUTNEY

Proofreading   IRENE BARNARD

Index   THÉRÈSE SHERE

Printing   BANG PRINTING

ISSN: 2768-153X Print
ISSN: 2768-1548 Online

ISBN: 978-1-4133-2910-0 (pbk)
ISBN: 978-1-4133-2911-7 (ebook)

This book covers only United States law, unless it specifically states otherwise.

Please note

Accurate, plain-English legal information can help you solve many of your own legal problems. But this text is not a substitute for personalized advice from a knowledgeable lawyer. If you want the help of a trained professional—and we'll always point out situations in which we think that's a good idea—consult an attorney licensed to practice in your state.

About the Authors

Amy Loftsgordon is a legal editor and writer at Nolo, focusing on foreclosure, debt management, consumer protection, and personal finance. She edits a number of Nolo books and is the coauthor of *Solve Your Money Troubles* and *Credit Repair*. Before joining Nolo, Amy worked in foreclosure and debt collections for over 15 years She has drafted foreclosure-related training and loan servicing procedures, written manuals for collection operations, and audited completed foreclosures for compliance with applicable laws. Amy was also instrumental in preparing expert reports used in lawsuits against banks and servicers accused of mishandling collection, preforeclosure, loss mitigation, foreclosure, and REO processes. She received a B.A. from the University of Southern California and a law degree from the University of Denver Sturm College of Law. She is licensed to practice law in Colorado.

Cara O'Neill is a bankruptcy and litigation attorney in Northern California and a legal editor and writer at Nolo. She started her career as a civil and criminal trial lawyer, adding bankruptcy after the 2008 economic downturn. She also served as an administrative law judge in the automotive industry mediating disputes between automotive manufacturers and dealers and taught law courses as an adjunct professor. She earned her law degree in 1994 from the University of the Pacific, McGeorge School of Law, where she served as a law review editor and graduated Order of the Barristers—an honor society recognizing excellence in courtroom advocacy. Cara has edited, authored, and coauthored several Nolo books, including *How to File for Chapter 7 Bankruptcy, Chapter 13 Bankruptcy, The New Bankruptcy, Everybody's Guide to Small Claims Court, Solve Your Money Troubles*, and *Credit Repair*.

Table of Contents

Your Foreclosure Companion 1

Changes in the Eighth Edition 2

What You'll Find in This Book 3

1 Foreclosure: The Big Picture 5

What to Expect 7

Your Options: An Overview 8

How You Can Stay in Your House Payment Free 19

Why Foreclosure Doesn't Have to Be So Bad 20

Don't Get Scammed by a Foreclosure "Rescue" Company 21

Beware of Property Preservation Companies 26

2 Foreclosure Nuts and Bolts 29

How Much Time and Notice You'll Have Before a Foreclosure Sale 33

In or Out of Court? 37

Deficiency Judgments: Will You Still Owe Money After
the Foreclosure? 49

Taxes 50

3 Can You Keep Your House? Should You? 51

The Emotional Part of Foreclosure 52

The Economics of Foreclosure: What You Need to Know 56

When It Makes Sense to Keep Your House 62

When It Makes Sense to Give Up Your House 65

4 Working Out a Way to Avoid Foreclosure 67

Do You Have Enough Time to Work Out an Alternative
    to Foreclosure? 69

Using a HUD-Approved Housing Counselor 76

Basic Loss Mitigation Options 81

Loss Mitigation Options for Government-Backed Mortgages 90

Foreclosure Avoidance Mediation Programs 97

Hardest Hit Fund and Other Statewide Mortgage-Relief Programs 98

Special Protections for Servicemembers on Active Duty 101

Mortgage Relief for Borrowers After a Natural Disaster 105

5 How Chapter 13 Bankruptcy Can Delay or Stop Foreclosure 109

Using Chapter 13 to Keep Your House 111

An Overview of the Chapter 13 Bankruptcy Process 118

Coming Up With a Repayment Plan 118

Will You Need a Lawyer? 123

6 How Chapter 7 Bankruptcy Can Delay or Stop Foreclosure 125

How Chapter 7 Bankruptcy Helps You 127

Using Chapter 7 Bankruptcy to Keep Your House 130

Using Chapter 7 Bankruptcy to Delay a Foreclosure Sale
    in Good Faith 134

The Chapter 7 Bankruptcy Process: An Overview 138

Do You Qualify for Chapter 7 Bankruptcy? 140

Will You Need a Lawyer? 143

7 Fighting Foreclosure in Court 145

How to Fight a Foreclosure (And How Long You Can Delay
    the Sale of Your House) 147

When It Might Be Worth Fighting 154

The Statute of Limitations Has Expired...172

When You Can Sue for Money..174

8 If You Decide to Leave Your House 177

Let the Foreclosure Proceed..179

Be Community Minded 182

Be Wary of Leaving the Home Before the Foreclosure Sale.............................182

Sell the House in a Short Sale...184

Offer the Lender a Deed in Lieu of Foreclosure..193

Avoiding Deficiency Judgments 194

Income Tax Liability for Deficiencies 195

9 How Long Can You Stay in Your House for Free?.........199

When You Miss Your First Few Payments...202

After You Receive a Formal Notice of Foreclosure..203

The Redemption Period 206

After the Sale 206

Eviction Lawsuits After Foreclosure 207

10 Resources Beyond the Book...209

HUD-Approved Housing Counselors 210

Real Estate Brokers..211

Mortgage Brokers..212

Lawyers...212

Foreclosure Websites...220

Books..221

Looking Up Foreclosure Statutes..223

Glossary 227

Appendix

State Information 247

Alabama 249	Montana 279
Alaska 251	Nebraska 280
Arizona 252	Nevada 281
Arkansas........................253	New Hampshire 283
California 254	New Jersey....................284
Colorado 256	New Mexico 286
Connecticut...................258	New York 288
Delaware 259	North Carolina...............290
District of Columbia..............260	North Dakota 291
Florida 261	Ohio 292
Georgia 262	Oklahoma 293
Hawaii...........................263	Oregon..........................294
Idaho............................264	Pennsylvania 295
Illinois...........................265	Rhode Island 296
Indiana 266	South Carolina...............297
Iowa.............................267	South Dakota 298
Kansas 268	Tennessee 299
Kentucky........................269	Texas 300
Louisiana 270	Utah 301
Maine............................271	Vermont........................302
Maryland 272	Virginia.........................304
Massachusetts 273	Washington....................305
Michigan 274	West Virginia 306
Minnesota.....................276	Wisconsin......................307
Mississippi 277	Wyoming.......................308
Missouri........................278	

Index 309

Your Foreclosure Companion

No word strikes greater fear in a homeowner's heart than "foreclosure." This book deals with how to think about foreclosure and provides different pathways and options depending on your circumstances, where you live, and what kind of mortgage you have.

If you want to keep your home, your best option is to work something out with your mortgage lender in a way that will satisfy both of you. If, on the other hand, you're ready and willing to leave your property, you can follow the path that will leave you relatively flush rather than destitute.

Many people want to stay in their homes but need to change some aspects of their mortgages: the amount of principal, the interest rate, the monthly payment. Your options largely depend on what entity, like FHA, VA, USDA, Fannie Mae, or Freddie Mac, owns or guarantees your loan.

For example, Fannie Mae and Freddie Mac (the government-supported enterprises that own or back many mortgages in the U.S.) offer the Flex Modification program. Lenders are also free to provide programs for settling mortgage issues. Many offer in-house ("proprietary") modifications, forbearance agreements, or repayment plans. Ch. 4 of this book explains how homeowners can ask for relief under these programs.

For other homeowners, the best strategy is to walk away from the home rather than put money into what could be a hopeless cause. If you take this approach, it might make sense to stay in your home throughout the foreclosure process—the longer you can live in your home without making mortgage payments, the better off you'll be financially. But if you're contemplating walking away, you should be aware of, and take into consideration, the consequences like a possible deficiency judgment.

A short sale or deed in lieu of foreclosure might work better in your circumstances by allowing you to transfer title to the property without going through a foreclosure.

The goal of this book is to help you choose and implement the best strategy for your particular situation.

Changes in the Eighth Edition

In 2008, when the first edition of this book was published, home values were in free fall, and foreclosures were all too common. Now, thirteen years later, foreclosure rates have significantly fallen, but that doesn't mean the economy is flourishing. The coronavirus (COVID-19) pandemic has left millions of people struggling to make their mortgage payments.

Fortunately, federal and state laws and other actions protect homeowners facing foreclosure. This edition discusses new laws and trends, including:

Coronavirus-specific information. People affected by COVID-19 have access to special foreclosure protections, such as mortgage forbearances and foreclosure moratoriums. We've flagged these protections throughout the book, so be sure to look for them. You'll also find the latest developments at www.nolo.com/legal-updates/legal-updates-for-foreclosure. Coronavirus-specific information for a variety of legal areas of interest is found at www.nolo.com/legal-encyclopedia/covid-19.

State foreclosure laws. Since the last edition of this book, some states have changed existing laws. For example, some aspects of foreclosure law changed in several states, including California, Michigan, New Jersey, New York, Oregon, and Virginia.

Better foreclosure avoidance options in some states; fewer in others. The Hardest Hit Fund programs, initially offered in 18 states and the District of Columbia, in some states have closed because their allocated funds ran out. Other states have enhanced their existing Hardest Hit Fund programs or added new state-specific programs to help homeowners affected by the coronavirus crisis.

Help for victims of natural disasters. After a natural disaster, home owners often need help with their mortgage payments. This edition covers the latest foreclosure-avoidance programs for victims of natural disasters, like hurricanes and wildfires.

What You'll Find in This Book

In addition to explaining changes that have occurred in the past several years, this book explains:

- the ins and outs of foreclosure procedures, with state-by-state information
- how to decide whether you should try to keep your house
- how you can get free help with a mortgage modification
- how filing for bankruptcy can help you keep your house, and
- how to avoid foreclosure "rescue" scams.

The book also explains ways to make the most of your situation if your income and mortgage payments preclude keeping your house, such as:

- how long you'll likely be able to stay in your house—and save up money—if the foreclosure goes ahead
- how to do a short sale or deed in lieu of foreclosure if either strategy would be useful in your situation
- how to use bankruptcy to temporarily or permanently stop a foreclosure, and
- how bankruptcy can eliminate debts and tax liabilities typically associated with foreclosure.

For many people who feel overwhelmed with debt and are considering filing for bankruptcy, it makes absolutely no sense to keep putting money into houses they're destined to lose. For others, it's completely sensible to do everything they can to keep ownership. Sometimes the reasons for these decisions are personal; sometimes, they're economic.

In the end, you must make this decision for yourself. This book provides some useful guidance in helping you decide and then helps you succeed in whichever strategy you choose to follow. If it's not practicable for you to keep your house, the book shows you how to derive the greatest possible benefit from the situation.

The book also tries to provide some perspective on home ownership. To sum it up, your house is not your home. Owning the house where you live might feel like the American dream, and losing it might seem like the end of that dream. It's not. If you're eventually forced to give up the house you're living in, painful as it might be, it's a loss that you'll recover from over time, both emotionally and financially.

But in the meantime, you can take steps to restore your financial health and gain control of the situation.

Get Legal Updates and More at Nolo.com

You can find the online companion page to this book at:

www.nolo.com/back-of-book/FIFO.html

You'll find important updates to the law and links to online articles on foreclosure, including many articles on state-specific foreclosure procedures, state mediation programs, and other foreclosure articles tailored to the law in your state and more.

Foreclosure: The Big Picture

What to Expect 7

Your Options: An Overview 8

Reinstate Your Mortgage 9

Arrange a Loss Mitigation Option 10

Redeem the Property Before the Sale 11

File for Chapter 7 Bankruptcy 12

File for Chapter 13 Bankruptcy 12

Take Out a Reverse Mortgage 14

Fight the Foreclosure in Court 15

Give Up Your House 15

How You Can Stay in Your House Payment Free 19

Why Foreclosure Doesn't Have to Be So Bad 20

Don't Get Scammed by a Foreclosure "Rescue" Company 21

Scams That Target Home Equity 21

If You Don't Have Much Equity 23

Mass Joinder Lawsuit Scams 24

Forensic Loan Audit Scams 24

State and Federal Laws Governing Foreclosure Consultants 26

Beware of Property Preservation Companies 26

The Lender Might "Secure" Your Home If Vacant 26

How the Process Works 27

Tips to Keep the Lender From Treating Your Occupied Home
as Vacant 28

Foreclosure doesn't usually come as a big surprise to homeowners. You'll probably know, well before it happens, that you're going to have trouble making your mortgage payments. Maybe you've become unemployed or face unexpected medical bills, or maybe that adjustable-rate mortgage you took out a few years ago is scheduled to reset at a much higher rate, making payments out of reach.

Once you do fall behind, you'll probably have a few months before your lender even starts the foreclosure process, thanks to federal mortgage servicing laws. The fact that foreclosure is a process—sometimes a long one—is good news for you. You don't need to panic. You'll have time to plan and evaluate your options—*if* you act quickly. The more time you have, the better.

If your only problem is a few missed payments, your lender will probably be willing to let you get current over time. If you've missed four or five payments, your lender might not be flexible—but you still might be able to work something out.

Indecisiveness Can Cost You Big Time

If you're likely to lose your house, your failure to immediately face this reality can cost you thousands of dollars. Here's why: Any mortgage payments you make now will do you no good if you end up losing your house in foreclosure. Assume your mortgage payment is $2,000 a month and you scrape together enough money each month to pay your mortgage because you don't want to lose your house. If $2,000 is more than you can afford and you end up in foreclosure, the payments you scraped together will have been for nothing unless you somehow find a way to get current on your mortgage payments or you file and complete a Chapter 13 bankruptcy. On the other hand, if you stopped paying your mortgage six months earlier, you would have $12,000 more for relocation costs and other expenses.

> **⚠ CAUTION**
>
> **Check for updates.** Federal and state foreclosure laws sometimes change. You can find the latest developments at www.nolo.com/legal-updates/ legal-updates-for-foreclosure.

Don't wait for your loan servicer to contact you. As soon as you realize you're going to have trouble making your mortgage payments, you should start working on the problem. This chapter will show you how.

> **⚠ CAUTION**
>
> **Don't panic—and don't get scammed.** Foreclosure rescue scams have sprung up all over the country. Almost without exception, you'll be worse off with these scams than if you let a foreclosure go through. (To find out how scammers work and what to look for, see "Don't Get Scammed by a Foreclosure 'Rescue' Company," below.)

What to Expect

What happens next depends on whether you're trying to stay in your home or are resigned to moving on. (More about that choice later.)

If you want to keep your home, your first move should be to find a HUD-approved housing counselor to help you figure out what options are best for you, whether it be a modification, a refinance, or another mortgage solution. Housing counselors provide foreclosure-avoidance assistance and won't charge you for it. Go to www.consumerfinance.gov and search for "Find a housing counselor" or call 888-995-HOPE and ask for a HUD-approved counselor in your area.

Your HUD-approved housing counselor will help you determine which option is best for you, explain what documents you will need to provide to your mortgage company, and might contact the mortgage company on your behalf.

If a modification or another foreclosure alternative isn't possible, and depending on the procedure your state requires, you'll receive some sort of notice (usually a formal written notice) that foreclosure is coming. Foreclosure procedures differ greatly depending on where you live and the nature of the loan. (Ch. 2 explains these procedures and highlights the variables you'll want to know about when planning your strategy.)

Unless you use one of the remedies explained briefly below (and in detail in later chapters), the foreclosure will end with the sale of the property, typically at a public auction. The foreclosure process is explained in detail in Ch. 2.

Your Options: An Overview

Here's a look at your main alternatives when you think foreclosure is on the horizon. We'll talk about these scenarios in detail later. For now, just try to get an idea of what you're dealing with.

Your Options If You Are Facing Foreclosure

- Reinstate the existing loan by making up the missed payments, plus costs and interest.
- Arrange a loss mitigation option that keeps you in the home (such as a forbearance, repayment plan, or loan modification) using the help of a free HUD-approved housing counselor.
- Redeem the property before the sale, like by refinancing the entire loan.
- Delay the foreclosure sale by filing for Chapter 7 or Chapter 13 bankruptcy.
- Take out a reverse mortgage if you qualify.
- Fight the foreclosure in court and either stop or delay it.
- Give up your house by walking away or with a short sale or deed in lieu of foreclosure.

Foreclosure Moratoriums During the Coronavirus Crisis

The Department of Housing and Urban Development (HUD), the Department of Veterans Affairs (VA), the Department of Agriculture (USDA), and the Federal Housing Finance Agency (FHFA) set foreclosure moratoriums for federally backed mortgage loans, including FHA-insured, VA-guaranteed, USDA loans, and Fannie Mae- and Freddie Mac-backed loans through at least June 30, 2021. Also, many states and localities imposed a foreclosure suspension when the coronavirus pandemic began. While many of these moratoriums have expired, some were still in place at the time of writing. To find out whether any moratoriums are ongoing in your area, talk to a foreclosure lawyer. You can also find the latest developments at www.nolo.com/legal-updates/legal-updates-for-foreclosure.

Reinstate Your Mortgage

If you have enough cash or access to another loan, you can "reinstate" your mortgage loan by making up all the missed payments, including principal and interest, plus fees and costs. Your loan contract and state law will probably give you a deadline to complete a reinstatement (or "cure the default"). (You can check your state's rule in the appendix.)

For example, in a California nonjudicial foreclosure, you have the right to reinstate your loan for three months after the lender records a "notice of default." After that period ends, if you haven't brought the loan current or worked out an alternative, the lender will send you a notice of trustee's sale, telling you that the house will be put up for sale 20 days after the end of the three-month period. California state law provides a further right to reinstate the loan until five business days prior to the foreclosure sale.

Also, many mortgage contracts have a clause giving the borrower the ability to reinstate the loan by a specific deadline. Even if the mortgage contract doesn't provide this right, lenders often prefer to let you reinstate the loan rather than foreclose.

Arrange a Loss Mitigation Option

As mentioned, you should start with a HUD-approved housing counselor. (See Ch. 4 for more on this topic.) With this assistance, you might be able to get one of the following loss mitigation options. ("Loss mitigation" is what the mortgage-servicing industry calls the process where borrowers and their loan servicer work together to avoid a foreclosure.)

- **Forbearance.** In a forbearance agreement, the lender agrees to reduce or suspend your payments for a set amount of time.
- **Repayment plan.** With a repayment plan, the lender temporarily increases your monthly payment by adding part of the overdue amount to your current payments so that you can get caught up on the loan.
- **Loan modification.** In a modification, the lender typically lowers your monthly payment by, say, reducing the interest rate, and brings the loan up to date by adding any past-due amounts to the balance of your debt.

RESOURCE

For updates to the information in this book, visit www.nolo.com/ back-of-book/FIFO.html. That page, which is dedicated to this book, is where we alert readers to significant changes since this edition published.

Forbearances During the Coronavirus Pandemic

Homeowners with a federally backed mortgage loan experiencing a financial hardship due to COVID-19 can get a forbearance that lasts up to 180 days and can be extended up to 180 additional days, longer in some cases. (See Ch. 4 for more information.) At the time of writing, the deadline to request a forbearance in most cases was June 30, 2021. You can find the latest developments at www.nolo.com/legal-updates/legal-updates-for-foreclosure.

Even if your loan isn't federally backed, your servicer might offer you a forbearance or another form of relief, like a waiver of late fees or a loan modification. Also, your state might provide special protections or programs for mortgage borrowers affected by the coronavirus crisis.

Redeem the Property Before the Sale

To "redeem" the property before the sale, you must pay off the total amount of the loan. All states allow borrowers to redeem the property before a foreclosure sale. (Some states also provide foreclosed borrowers with a "redemption period" after a foreclosure sale, during which they can buy back the home. See Ch. 9.)

If you can refinance at a better rate and pay off your old loan, you can start fresh. Unfortunately, in most cases, refinancing is available only if you have equity in your home and an acceptable credit score. But if you have a Fannie Mae or Freddie Mac loan, you might qualify for a refinance even if you owe more than your home is worth under Fannie Mae's High Loan-to-Value Refinance Option or Freddie Mac's Enhanced Relief Refinance. (See Ch. 4 for more information.)

File for Chapter 7 Bankruptcy

If you're current on your mortgage or can get current before you file, Chapter 7 bankruptcy can reduce your total debt load and help prevent foreclosure in the long run. Chapter 7 bankruptcy is quicker than Chapter 13 (see below), taking approximately three to four months to complete. It's also inexpensive if you represent yourself, although if you're worried about losing your home, it's wise to retain a lawyer. Chapter 7 bankruptcy typically will wipe out your unsecured debt— for example, credit card debt, personal loans, medical debts, and most money judgments. Whatever income you were using to pay down those debts can then go toward your mortgage payments.

Even if you've decided to leave your house, bankruptcy can help keep you in your home for a few extra months free of charge while giving you a fresh start by wiping out liabilities arising from your mortgage and the mortgage obligation itself.

Despite these benefits, Chapter 7 bankruptcy might not be appropriate for you. For example, you might have more equity in your house than you can protect (exempt) in your bankruptcy, which means the bankruptcy would trigger an involuntary sale of your home. (Chapter 7 bankruptcy is discussed in Ch. 6 of this book.)

File for Chapter 13 Bankruptcy

In this kind of bankruptcy, you come up with a plan for making your regular monthly mortgage payments and paying off the arrears. If the bankruptcy court approves your plan, you'll have three to five years to make the payments. Also, Chapter 13 bankruptcy can reduce your total debt load, making your mortgage more affordable in terms of your overall budget. In some situations, you can get rid of a second or third mortgage entirely or reduce a first mortgage on a vacation or rental home to the market value of the house. Chapter 13 bankruptcy is discussed in Ch. 5.

Chapter 7 or Chapter 13 Bankruptcy: A Quick Comparison		
	Chapter 7	**Chapter 13**
Who qualifies	Anyone whose household income is below the state median OR who passes a "means test"	Anyone who has enough income to propose a reasonable repayment plan
Effect on foreclosure	Delayed two to three months. Chapter 7 doesn't have a mechanism that will let you catch up on arrearages.	Delayed; possibly avoided. In Chapter 13, you can bring the mortgage current by spreading out arrearages over three to five years.
What happens to your property	The mortgage amount is discharged, but the lien created by the mortgage remains. You must be current and continue making payments to avoid foreclosure and keep the home. Otherwise, the home will go back to the bank.	Your first mortgage will remain intact on your residence; second and third mortgages can be eliminated if they are not secured by the house's value. The mortgage on an investment or vacation home can be reduced to the value of the property, but the entire balance must be paid in the repayment plan.
What happens to your debts	Most debts are wiped out (discharged); some debts, such as child support, student loan debt, and new back taxes, survive.	You repay a percentage of debt over three to five years under a repayment plan. You'll repay nondischargeable debt in full, such as support obligations and tax debt, as well as mortgage and car loan arrearages. If you finish the plan, the balance on most other debt is wiped out.
How long it takes	Three to four months.	Three to five years.
Will you need a lawyer?	Not necessarily, but it's a good idea.	Almost always, with little exception.

Take Out a Reverse Mortgage

A "reverse mortgage" is one way, though not necessarily a good one, to tap into the equity of your home without selling the house. You get money from a lender and generally don't need to pay it back as long as you live in the house. The loan must be repaid if you sell your house, move out, die, or fail to comply with the loan contract.

To qualify for a reverse mortgage (the most popular type is called a "home equity conversion mortgage" or "HECM"), you must have substantial equity and be over age 62. The Department of Housing and Urban Development (HUD) administers the HECM program, and almost all reverse mortgages are currently made under this program. Getting a reverse mortgage can prevent foreclosure. However, a reverse mortgage has many downsides, including taking part or all of your equity, which leaves less value for you to pass on to your heirs at your death or less money if you decide to sell the home, and high fees.

Even though you don't have to make payments on the reverse mortgage, you're responsible for paying the property taxes and insurance, as well as maintaining the property. Since 2015, lenders must complete a financial assessment before making a HECM loan to make sure that the borrower can afford to keep up with the property taxes and insurance payments. If the assessment reveals that the borrower is likely to fall behind in these expenses, the lender must establish a set-aside account. A set-aside is an amount drawn under the HECM that is reserved for payment of these expenses. The account reduces the amount of money the borrower will receive.

Reverse mortgages are discussed further in Ch. 3.

RESOURCE

More information about reverse mortgages. To learn more about reverse mortgages, including their many downsides, go to the AARP website (www.aarp.org) and search for "reverse mortgage."

Fight the Foreclosure in Court

If you can show that the foreclosing party violated federal law, your state's procedural rules for foreclosures, or the terms of your mortgage agreement, you might be able to derail the foreclosure, at least temporarily.

Some courts require foreclosing parties to present documentary evidence of ownership and authority for bringing the foreclosure action before the process can proceed. And because of how mortgages are sold and resold, this evidence is sometimes missing.

Foreclosure defense attorneys have also uncovered instances of lenders violating laws governing the recording, notarization, and assignment of mortgages. In some cases, major mortgage lenders temporarily ceased foreclosure activities pending internal investigations of their foreclosure practices.

Finally, violations of federal fair lending rules and other federal and state laws regarding consumer transactions could also provide a defense against foreclosure. (Fighting foreclosures in court is discussed in Ch. 7.)

> **TIP**
>
> **Extra protections for service members.** If you're on active duty in the military, or have been on active duty within the previous year, and you took out the mortgage loan before your period of military service, you can delay the foreclosure lawsuit—and get other help as well. (See Ch. 4.)

Give Up Your House

For some people, it makes good economic sense to give up the home and move on. If you arrive at this decision, you'll want to choose the method that causes the least financial and emotional upset to you and your family. (Learn more about making this decision in Ch. 3.)

Walk Away

Although this book covers several basic approaches to giving up your home, sometimes the best approach is to stop all further mortgage payments. When you walk away, you will almost certainly lose your house in foreclosure. But while the foreclosure process moves along, which can take months, you don't have to make mortgage payments to anyone but yourself, resulting in sizable savings. You can then put these savings toward getting a new place to live. The subject of "walking away" is discussed throughout this book, most specifically in Ch. 8. Here, we give you a brief overview of the subject.

Strategic Defaults

Walking away from a home when you can afford to pay the mortgage has been labeled a "strategic default," and it was a common tactic during the Great Recession and related foreclosure crisis. The default is "strategic" because the homeowner voluntarily chooses to default after completing a cost–benefit analysis.

Several risks are involved for those who choose this route. If you strategically default, you probably won't be eligible for a Fannie Mae-backed mortgage for seven years from the date of the foreclosure. Fannie Mae has also stated that it will take legal action to recoup the outstanding mortgage debt from borrowers who strategically default on their loans in jurisdictions that allow for deficiency judgments.

Rather than strategically defaulting, you might be able to give up the home through a short sale or deed in lieu of foreclosure. Fannie Mae and Freddie Mac will let some borrowers who are delinquent or current on their payments give up their properties under special deed in lieu of foreclosure programs if the borrowers meet certain criteria. These programs could provide an alternative to strategic default for some borrowers. (For more on this topic, see Ch. 8.)

People walk away for two main reasons. The most common reason is that the mortgage has become unaffordable due to an increased interest rate, the loss of employment, or some other unexpected occurrence. Even after a mortgage modification, circumstances might still render the loan unaffordable.

The second reason for walking away is that your home has turned into a lousy investment. Even if you can afford your mortgage payments, you might be better off walking away if your mortgage is deeply underwater and you bought the house as an investment rather than a place to live. Still, even if your situation isn't improving, a better option might be available to you, such as a short sale or a deed in lieu of foreclosure. You might even get some money to help with your relocation costs if you complete one of these options. (For more on this topic, see Ch. 8.)

Aside from not being able to acquire a new home loan for several years after walking away, taking this tactic can lead to other negative consequences:

- In most states, you can be sued for the difference between the amount your house was sold for at foreclosure and the amount you owed at the time of the foreclosure sale. Your liability for this difference, called a "deficiency," can be discharged in bankruptcy, but if bankruptcy isn't for you, you could be stuck with a large debt.
- The mortgage lender might write off the deficiency as a loss. The amount of the deficiency would then turn into taxable income for you. This tax liability can be avoided in several ways—including declaring insolvency or bankruptcy—but if you don't qualify for one of the exceptions, you can be on the hook for a lot of money. More information about the potential tax liabilities related to foreclosure is provided in Ch. 8.

Arrange a "Short Sale" to Avoid a Foreclosure

You can ask your lender for permission to sell your house for less than the amount you owe on your mortgage loan. This kind of sale is called a "short sale." If you live in a state that allows your lender to sue you for the deficiency (the difference between the amount you owe on the mortgage and the sale price of your home), a short sale can be a good idea, but only if you get your lender to agree in writing to let you off the hook for the deficiency. However, keep in mind that you might face tax consequences if the lender forgives the deficiency.

If you have a second or third mortgage, you'll also need to get those lenders to sign off on the short sale. Getting all lenders to agree to the transaction might be difficult because, by definition, a short sale produces less than is owed on the first mortgage, and the holder of the second or third mortgage stands to get little or nothing from the deal. If you can talk the first mortgage lender into giving some of the proceeds from the sale to the second and third mortgage lender, you'll have a better chance of getting the deal done.

Another pitfall of short sales is that the buyer of your home will probably want you to leave immediately after the sale closes. This requirement won't be a problem if you don't mind leaving, but you'll miss out on the opportunity to save money while living in the house during a foreclosure without making mortgage payments.

Hand Over the House With a Deed in Lieu of Foreclosure

You might be able to get your lender to let you deed the property over so that no foreclosure is necessary; this transaction is called a "deed in lieu of foreclosure." But before you go this route, you'll want to have a written agreement that the lender won't go after you for any deficiency. With a deed in lieu of foreclosure, the deficiency amount is the difference between the total debt and the fair market value of the property. Again, you might face tax consequences if the lender forgives the deficiency.

This remedy won't be available if you have second or third mortgages on your home because those lenders won't get anything out of the deal.

How Will Your Choice Affect Your Credit?

Foreclosures, short sales, and deeds in lieu of foreclosure are all bad for your credit. Only a bankruptcy is worse. If you avoid owing a deficiency with a short sale or deed in lieu, your credit score probably won't fall as much, but overall, these events are pretty similar when it comes to how they affect your credit.

It's virtually impossible to predict how much damage a foreclosure, short sale, or deed in lieu of foreclosure will do to your credit. For one thing, credit scoring systems change over time. For another, credit scoring agencies don't make their formulas public, and your score will vary based on your prior and future credit practices and those of others with whom you are compared.

But it also depends, in large part, on your credit before you lose your home. Most people who resort to foreclosure, short sale, or a deed in lieu of foreclosure have already fallen far behind on mortgage payments. According to experts, late payments cause a huge dip in your credit score, which means a subsequent foreclosure won't matter as much because your credit is already seriously damaged. If you're one of the rare homeowners who hasn't missed a payment before doing a short sale or deed in lieu of foreclosure, those events will cause more damage to your credit.

For more information on the subject of consumer credit and how to rebuild it, see *Credit Repair: Make a Plan, Improve Your Credit, Avoid Scams* by Amy Loftsgordon and Cara O'Neill (Nolo).

How You Can Stay in Your House Payment Free

If early on, you decide that you don't want to keep the house and will ultimately be moving on, you'll be able to skip payments for several months before the foreclosure process finally begins. If you apply for a modification once the foreclosure starts, the proceedings are put on hold pending an assessment by the mortgage servicer regarding whether you qualify for a payment reduction or some other loss mitigation option (see Ch. 4). During this time, you don't have to make any payments.

After the foreclosure sale, the chances are good that you can keep living in the house for at least a little while longer free of charge. You might be able to live in the home during the redemption period if state law provides one. (See the information for your state in the appendix.) And, in some states, you can stay in your house until the new owner gives you a formal written notice demanding that you leave and a court orders you out after you receive notice and a hearing is held. Though, generally, it's best to vacate your home after you get the notice demanding that you leave and avoid a formal eviction.

Having payment-free shelter for many months—before the foreclosure action is brought, during the foreclosure, and perhaps after the sale—gives you a golden opportunity to save some money. And those savings can make it easier to find a new place to live. (See Ch. 9 for more on how to come out of foreclosure with some cash in your pocket.)

Why Foreclosure Doesn't Have to Be So Bad

Home ownership can be overrated. People often assume that owning a home is superior to renting one, especially if you have a family.

However, home ownership isn't an automatic key to happiness. (We go into this in more detail in Ch. 3.) For now, just try to be open to the possibility that renting rather than owning isn't always a bad way to go and that your particular dream doesn't have to include home ownership. And, even if you go through a foreclosure, you'll likely be able to buy another home eventually if you decide you want one.

> TIP
> **Getting a new mortgage loan after foreclosure.** To be eligible for another mortgage loan following a significant derogatory credit event, such as a foreclosure, short sale, or deed in lieu of foreclosure, Fannie Mae and Freddie Mac, for example, require a waiting period and reestablished credit. In general,

the waiting period is seven years after a foreclosure. But if you've gone through a job layoff, divorce, or have incurred significant medical bills, and you can document the event's impact on your finances, the waiting period is typically three years. For other kinds of loans, the waiting period before you can get a new mortgage loan generally ranges between two and eight years following a foreclosure.

Don't Get Scammed by a Foreclosure "Rescue" Company

A large "foreclosure rescue" industry, much of which is a scam, has mushroomed in past years. If you're going through a foreclosure, you might receive an offer of help from a foreclosure rescue company. These scammer companies go through public records and contact homeowners who've received foreclosure notices.

The con artists who run these businesses will tell you that they have resources unavailable to HUD-approved housing counselors and that they care about you and will find a way for you to save your property from foreclosure. But unlike HUD-approved housing counselors, these scammers aren't really trying to keep you in your home; they're trying to make money. If you have equity in your house, they go after it. And if you've only got money in the bank, they'll go after that, instead.

Scams That Target Home Equity

If you have significant equity in your home, you're a prime target for the mortgage rescue scams aimed at getting ownership of your house away from you.

One common trick sounds especially good because the mortgage gets quickly reinstated, at least temporarily.

What you'll hear: "We'll buy your house right now—just temporarily, of course. We'll make the mortgage payments. You can stay right where you are, lease the house from us, and buy the house back when the loan is paid off."

How to Protect Yourself

- Never rely on an oral promise, such as, "Don't worry; you'll get the deed back in no time." Get everything in writing.
- Never sign an agreement unless you understand every word and phrase in it, even if you've had help from a HUD-approved housing counseling agency.
- Never sign anything that has blank lines or spaces. Representations and information you had no knowledge of can be inserted and appear to be part of the signed agreement.
- Never transfer ownership of your property to the "rescuer" or a proposed third-party lender.
- Never accept a loan that you can't afford or that must be paid back quickly at a high interest rate as a condition of staying in your house.
- Better yet, don't deal with a foreclosure rescue company at all.

What really happens: The scammer takes out a new loan on the property, using up all the equity. To make things worse, you'll probably discover that the lease includes a rental price you can't afford and virtually no chance you'll ever be able to get the home back. The scammer then might move to evict you for failing to pay the rent. Eviction comes quickly because you have only the status of a tenant under the lease or rental agreement that was supposed to be temporary. By contrast, if the house had gone through foreclosure, you would have been able to stay there for months payment-free as the foreclosure process wore on.

Another scam involves wresting ownership away from the homeowner without the homeowner's knowledge.

What you'll hear: "We'll work out a deal with the lender for you to keep the home. We'll handle everything—just send your mortgage payments to us, and we'll pass them on to the lender."

What really happens: The papers you sign actually transfer ownership to the company. This scam can easily be accomplished because people expect legal documents to be full of gibberish they don't understand or don't notice that the documents they sign have blank lines that can be filled in later with terms they never agreed to. In this transaction, you'll likely be completely unaware that you've signed over ownership of your home to the scammer. Like a leaseback scam, the company then strips the equity from the property or sells the property to someone else, leaving you without equity or a foreclosure alternative.

If You Don't Have Much Equity

If you have little or no equity in your home, you probably won't be approached by anyone who wants title; what would be the point? Instead, for a large up-front fee—often in the thousands of dollars—the scammer offers to help you fight your foreclosure by finding affordable loans or by negotiating with your lender for a mortgage modification, an interest rate freeze, or an arrangement in which your missed payments get added to the end of your loan. Not only will you not get results, but these people will probably disappear once your money is in their hands.

> **EXAMPLE:** Flora and Theo are in foreclosure. They wake up one morning to find a flyer on their doorstep advertising the Compassionate Care Foreclosure Rescue Service, which seems tailor-made for their difficulties. The flyer asks, "Is your home about to be sold at a foreclosure sale? Do you want help negotiating a loan modification with your mortgage servicing company? Want to refinance your mortgage at a low interest rate? We can help!"
>
> They call the number on the flyer and are referred to a "foreclosure rescue specialist," Nick, who tells them in a soothing voice that Compassionate Care has helped "thousands of people just like you" work out their mortgage difficulties and stay in their homes. After Flora and Theo give him information about their plight, Nick tells them that he can negotiate a loan modification with the servicer on their behalf and get an extension of the foreclosure sale date. The fee: $3,500—up front.

Flora and Theo borrow the $3,500 from Flora's son and send a cashier's check to Nick at a post office box, along with a signed power of attorney form that Nick says he needs so he can negotiate with the servicer. A few days, later Nick tells them that he has gotten the foreclosure sale postponed. Two weeks later, though, the home is sold at a foreclosure auction. Flora and Theo get a call from someone they've never heard of telling them that he bought their home at the foreclosure sale and wants to make arrangements for them to move out. Flora and Theo call Nick in a panic. The number has been disconnected. Flora and Theo have lost their home—and paid $3,500 for the privilege.

Mass Joinder Lawsuit Scams

In a "mass joinder" scam, a group claiming to be a law firm (often it's not a law firm at all or they use unqualified attorneys) sends out unsolicited mailings inviting distressed homeowners to participate in a lawsuit. The mailing informs you that you can join together with other homeowners to sue your lender and force it into providing loan modifications or stopping foreclosure. You then call the number listed on the mailing and talk to a sales representative who provides false information or makes misleading claims about the success of such a suit. To join in the mass joinder lawsuit, you must pay up-front legal fees that can range from $5,000 to over $10,000. Typically, once the scammers have taken your money, they either do nothing and disappear with the funds or file untenable lawsuits that end in dismissal.

Forensic Loan Audit Scams

In a forensic loan audit scam, you pay a company an up-front fee of several hundred dollars for a so-called forensic loan auditor to review your mortgage loan documents to determine if your lender complied with mortgage lending laws. Companies offering this type of service often claim that the audits find lender violations 90% of the time. They further claim that if a forensic loan audit finds violations of the law, you can use the results to stop a foreclosure, force the lender to give you a loan modification or rescind (cancel) your loan.

But forensic loan audits aren't effective in accomplishing any of these things. First of all, the "audit" is typically completed by a processor who simply plugs information from your loan origination documentation into loan compliance software, which then supposedly identifies violations and compiles them into an automated report. Secondly, often only minor violations are found. Even if the audit does find fraud, predatory lending, or other significant violations of state or federal law, you would need to file a lawsuit against the lender either as an answer to the lender's judicial foreclosure complaint or as your own lawsuit in a nonjudicial foreclosure to stop a foreclosure. Sending a copy of the audit report to the lender or telling it that you had a forensic loan audit done will have no effect on your foreclosure.

Profile of a Scammer: What to Look For

The people who prey upon homeowners in foreclosure use many tactics to gain your trust. Be wary of anyone who:

- contacts you by phone, text, email, or mail or knocks (anyone offering legitimate foreclosure help won't seek you out; you must go to them)
- provides little or no information about the foreclosure process
- claims government affiliation
- uses "affinity marketing"—Spanish speakers marketing to Spanish speakers, Christians to Christians, senior citizens to senior citizens, and so on
- offers "testimonials" from other customers
- claims the process will be quick and easy (dealing with foreclosure is never quick and easy) and uses messages such as "Stop foreclosure with just one phone call" or "I'd like to $ buy $ your house" or "Do you need instant debt relief and CASH?" or
- tells you to cease all contact with the mortgage lender.

State and Federal Laws Governing Foreclosure Consultants

If a company approaches you using the above tactics, it very well might be breaking the law. Many states have laws governing the activity of foreclosure consultants. In addition, in 2010, the Federal Trade Commission (FTC) promulgated rules regulating "mortgage assistance relief services" (MARS) in an effort to protect homeowners from foreclosure consultant scams. Among other things, the MARS rule, now known as Regulation O, requires MARS providers to make certain disclosures about their services, prohibits advance fees, and bans certain misleading advertising claims. The FTC and the Consumer Financial Protection Bureau (CFPB) enforce the MARS regulation. To lodge a complaint with the FTC about a MARS company (in English or Spanish), call 877-FTC-HELP (877-382-4357), or go to www.ftc.gov. You can also submit a complaint with the CFPB at www.consumerfinance.gov.

To learn more about the MARS regulation, go to www.ftc.gov and search for "Mortgage Assistance Relief Services Rule" and follow the link.

Beware of Property Preservation Companies

Mortgage servicers hire property preservation companies to secure homes when homeowners move out before the foreclosures are complete. Over the years, many homeowners have reported property preservation companies illegally changing locks, removing belongings, or taking other actions while the homeowners were still living in their homes.

The Lender Might "Secure" Your Home If Vacant

While you have the right to occupy the home during foreclosure, if you abandon (move out of) the place during the process, most mortgages give the lender the right to do whatever is reasonable or appropriate to protect its interest in the property. For example, the lender could do the following things to secure a vacant property:

- enter the property to make repairs
- change the locks or padlock the entrance
- replace or board up doors and windows
- remove debris or trash
- have utilities turned on or off, and
- eliminate building or other code violations or dangerous conditions.

Generally, the task of securing the home falls on the mortgage servicer on behalf of the lender, which typically farms out these services (called "field services") to property management firms, which are called "field service companies" or "property preservation companies." Property preservations companies are hired to inspect, clean, and secure abandoned homes. Unfortunately, however, these contractors can get it wrong and clear out homes where people are still living. They might prematurely change your locks, remove your belongings, or take other actions even though you're still living in your house.

How the Process Works

When you fall behind in your home mortgage payments or go into foreclosure, the servicer will usually hire someone to do a drive-by inspection to figure out if the home is occupied or vacant. If the inspector determines that the home is vacant (sometimes mistakenly), the servicer might take steps to secure and maintain the home, such as making sure that trash is picked up and that the home is protected against the weather. In too many instances though, property preservation companies have been known to let themselves into currently occupied homes, causing damage and illegally taking the homeowners' personal property.

Tips to Keep the Lender From Treating Your Occupied Home as Vacant

If you're in foreclosure, you want to make sure your home and your belongings are protected. Here are several steps you can take to ensure that your mortgage lender or servicer (or the field services company that it hires) doesn't treat your occupied home as vacant.

Call your lender/servicer when you're late in payments. If you're behind in your payments, call the mortgage lender or servicer (the company you make your payments to) and let it know you still live in the property. (To figure out who your loan servicer is, look at your monthly mortgage payment coupon.) All loan servicers keep communication logs that note each time you call and include information about the conversation. While the communication logs are not especially detailed, if later on a dispute arises about the property's occupancy, at the very least there should be a note in the servicer's records that you said you are still living there. When you call, you can also ask about loss mitigation options.

Inform your loan servicer in writing that you're still living in the property. You can also send a letter or email to the lender or servicer informing it in writing that you're still occupying the property. If you write a letter, send it by certified mail, return receipt requested, so you can prove that you sent it and that the lender or servicer received it.

If the field service company leaves a notice, call it too. A field service company might post a notice informing you that it has deemed your property vacant before locking you out. If so, be sure to call the company and let it know that you're still living in the home. It's also a good idea to send a letter via certified mail, return receipt requested, to prove that you've notified the company of your occupancy.

Even if you take all of these precautions, a property preservation company might still lock you out or illegally take your belongings. If this happens, consult with an attorney to figure out your next steps.

Foreclosure Nuts and Bolts

How Much Time and Notice You'll Have Before a Foreclosure Sale 33

In or Out of Court? 37

    Do You Have a Mortgage or a Deed of Trust? 38

    Judicial Foreclosures 39

    Nonjudicial Foreclosures 43

Deficiency Judgments: Will You Still Owe Money After
    the Foreclosure? 49

Taxes 50

    Income Taxes 50

    Capital Gains Tax 50

This chapter provides a general picture of how foreclosures work in your state. You might feel like skipping this information and getting on with deciding what to *do*—get caught up on the loan, fight the foreclosure, or walk away with the help of a short sale or the bankruptcy court. But you can't make smart decisions without some knowledge of how a foreclosure proceeds.

At the very least, you need to know what's coming if foreclosure is imminent. Here are the big issues:

- **How much time you'll have before your house is sold.** If you know that your house can be sold at auction in just 30 days after you first get official notice of the foreclosure, you'll need to act differently than if you can count on three or four months in which to work out an arrangement with the lender or try other strategies. Fortunately, even in short-notice states, you can pretty much count on learning about the intended sale in time to use one of the strategies explained in later chapters.

- **Whether your foreclosure will go through court.** In a little fewer than half the states, foreclosures are judicial, meaning they go through court; in the others, your house can be sold without a judge's approval in what is called a "power of sale" (nonjudicial) foreclosure. If you know that you won't lose your house unless a judge gives an official go-ahead, your strategy will likely be different than if your foreclosure will be proceeding without judicial oversight. Court foreclosures usually take longer than nonjudicial ones and it's easier to raise the common defenses to foreclosure when you automatically get face time with a judge.

- **Whether you'll be liable for a "deficiency judgment" if the foreclosure goes through.** If the house sells for less than you owe, in many states, the lender can sue you for at least some of the difference. Homestead laws (state laws that protect your home equity from creditors) don't help you because mortgage debt has priority over any homestead rights your state's law provides. One reason many people file for bankruptcy when faced with foreclosure is that bankruptcy eliminates liability for deficiencies.

Understanding Foreclosure Terminology

Here are a few terms you'll want to know. Check out the glossary to learn even more definitions. As with any system, understanding the terms is half the battle.

Promissory note. A "promissory note" is a written promise by one party (a borrower) to pay a specific amount of money (called "principal") to another party (such as a home loan lender), which often includes a specified amount of interest on the unpaid principal amount and penalties for failure to pay according to its terms. Homebuyers usually think of the mortgage or deed of trust as the contract they're signing with the lender to borrow money to purchase a house, but it's actually the promissory note that contains the promise to repay the amount borrowed. (The mortgage or deed of trust pledges the home as security for the loan.) A promissory note is basically an IOU that contains the promise to repay the loan, as well as the terms for repayment.

Mortgages and deeds of trust. When you got a loan to buy your house, you agreed that the home would secure the loan; if you default on your payments, the owner of the loan can foreclose— that is, sell the house to repay the debt. Security agreements such as these are filed (recorded) in the local land records office. In some states, this security agreement is termed a "mortgage," while in others, it's called a "deed of trust" or something similar. With a few exceptions, mortgages are typically foreclosed in court, while deeds of trust are foreclosed without going through court.

In this book, except when it makes a difference, we use the term "mortgage" to refer to either an actual mortgage or a deed of trust.

First, second, and third mortgages. The first loan you took out to buy your home is called the "first mortgage." If you also borrowed a lesser amount for the down payment, or if you later took out a loan against your equity, this later loan is called a "second mortgage." And finally, if you took out a third loan or arranged a line of credit to be secured by your home, you have a "third mortgage."

Understanding Foreclosure Terminology (continued)

Assignments and endorsements. An "assignment" is the document that is the legal record of the transfer of the mortgage or deed of trust from one bank (or holder) to another. Assignments are typically recorded in the county land records. When the loan changes hands, the promissory note is "endorsed" (signed over) to the new owner of the loan. In some cases, the note is endorsed in blank, which makes it a bearer instrument under Article 3 of the Uniform Commercial Code. Any party that possesses the note has the legal authority to enforce it. Assignments and endorsements prove which bank owns the debt and has the right to start a foreclosure.

Lenders, investors, and mortgage servicers. Chances are, the bank or other lender you got your mortgage from (the mortgage originator) quickly sold the mortgage to another entity, called an "investor," which in turn resold it, and so on. You're supposed to get notice of these transactions, but the notifications aren't written in plain English, so you might not know who really owns your mortgage or who's entitled to foreclose if you default. In this book, we use the term "lender" to refer to the investor unless the distinction is important.

Whether you know who your lender or investor is, you've probably been dealing with a company termed a "mortgage servicer." The servicer could be the bank that made the loan or some other entity. Servicers purchase and sell servicer rights independent of the loan. The servicer receives your payments and passes them on to whoever is entitled to receive them— perhaps an overseas bank or a trustee for a mortgage trust.

If you default on your payments but want to keep your house, your mortgage servicer will represent the lender in the loss mitigation (workout) process. If you aren't able to work out an alternative, the servicer will begin the foreclosure proceeding.

In the past, servicers were almost always banks. Now, servicing rights are often sold to nonbank servicers.

TIP
Read the law. This book explains various federal mortgage servicing laws and the laws of each state are summarized in the appendix. Nonetheless, you might be curious to find out for yourself what the statutes actually say, word for word. Reading the law will give you a better understanding than the summaries in the appendix. So if you have access to a law library or the Internet and some patience, use the citations on your state's page to look up the law for yourself. (Ch. 10 provides help on finding your state's laws online.)

How Much Time and Notice You'll Have Before a Foreclosure Sale

Under federal mortgage servicing laws, in most cases, the servicer can't officially start a foreclosure (that is, make the first notice or filing required by state law) until you're more than 120 days delinquent on payments. This rule applies to mortgage loans secured by the borrower's principal residence. So, in a judicial foreclosure, the servicer can't file a court document, such as a complaint, petition, order to docket, or notice of hearing, until after you're more than 120 days behind. If the foreclosure is nonjudicial, the lender can't begin the foreclosure by recording or publishing the first notice until after you're 120 days delinquent on the loan. (If state foreclosure law doesn't require a court filing or a document to be recorded or published, the first notice is the earliest document that establishes, sets, or schedules a date for the foreclosure sale.)

The 120-day rule doesn't apply in the following situations:

- You violated a due-on-sale clause. Most loan contracts contain a "due-on-sale" provision that allows the lender to accelerate the full loan balance if you transfer the property to a new owner. When triggered, you have to repay the loan's entire balance; otherwise, a foreclosure will begin. Federal law restricts the enforcement of a due-on-sale clause in some circumstances.

- When the servicer is joining the foreclosure action of a superior or subordinate lienholder. (Superior lienholders are sometimes called "senior lienholders." Subordinate lienholders are also sometimes called "junior lienholders.")

The 120-day time frame is supposed to give you time to work out a way to avoid foreclosure. Many people facing foreclosure are like the proverbial deer in the headlights: stunned and unable to react quickly. Don't be one of them. Use the time before the foreclosure starts to plan a strategy advantageous to you.

The 120-Day Rule Applies to Breaches Other Than Nonpayment

The 120-day foreclosure restriction also applies to a nonmonetary breach of the mortgage agreement, such as if you:

- fail to pay property taxes when they aren't escrowed
- commit waste (cause damage that lowers the value of the home), or
- fail to occupy the home if the mortgage requires it.

In this type of situation, when the borrower commits a nonpayment-related breach, the servicer can "accelerate" the loan (call the full amount due) if the mortgage contract allows it. If the borrower doesn't pay the accelerated amount on its due date, the delinquency begins. Assuming the property is the borrower's principal residence, the servicer can't foreclose until the account is more than 120 days delinquent.

The servicer is allowed to send you other early notices during this time, such as those that provide information about housing counseling, preforeclosure mediation, or other helpful information. For example, in most situations, the servicer will send a letter informing you that you're late in your payments, that your loan is in default, and how to cure the default. The exact type and timing of the notice will depend on your mortgage documents and state law. Many home mortgages and deeds of trust contain a clause that requires the lender to send a notice, typically called a "breach letter" (see below), informing you that you get, say, 30 days to cure the default. And all states require that you get at least some form of notice before your house is sold at a foreclosure sale. See your state's page in the appendix for information on what kind of notice you can expect to receive.

Depending on your state and your circumstances, the foreclosure will be either judicial or nonjudicial. If it's a judicial foreclosure (one that goes through court), you'll get some time, typically between 20 and 30 days, to respond to the court complaint that starts the foreclosure lawsuit. In some states, when it approves the foreclosure, the court orders the lender to publish a "notice of sale," which gives you even more time before you have to move. Because a court is involved throughout a judicial foreclosure, it often takes longer than a nonjudicial foreclosure.

Early Intervention Requirements

Under a 2014 federal law, the servicer must attempt to make contact with you to a discuss workout option (called "loss mitigation") no later than 36 days after the loan becomes delinquent and again within 36 days after each subsequent delinquency, even if the servicer previously contacted you. The servicer must also send you a written notice that describes any options not later than the 45th day of the delinquency and again no later than 45 days after each payment due date for as long as you remain delinquent on the loan. The servicer does not, however, have to provide the written notice more than once during any 180-day period. (Federal law provides a few exceptions to some of these requirements, like if you've filed bankruptcy or asked the servicer not to contact you pursuant to the Fair Debt Collection Practices Act, and the servicer is subject to this law.) Also, the mortgage servicer is required to assign personnel to help you by the time you fall 45 days delinquent. The personnel must be available by phone and able to advise you about loss mitigation options, how to apply for a mortgage workout, the status of any loss mitigation application, and applicable deadlines. (See Ch. 4 for further information.)

You also get some presale notice for nonjudicial foreclosures. Some states require as few as 30 days (Georgia, for example) or as much as several months. In some states, including California, you get two notices: one giving you a period of time to make up the missed payments (cure the default) and a second one (a notice of sale) giving you the date of sale in the event you haven't caught up on the payments.

In most states, in addition to mailing you a notice by certified or first-class mail, the foreclosing entity must publish a notice in the "legal notices" section of a local newspaper of general circulation. Publishing notice is an admittedly weird concept that assumes you read the legal notices section. Sometimes posting a notice on the property is required as well.

> ⓘ **CAUTION**
>
> **Scammers read the legal notices.** Once a formal notice of foreclosure is published, recorded at the local land records office, or filed in court, it's public knowledge that the homeowner is in financial trouble. Con artists might try to prey upon you, knowing that you're under stress. Don't fall for a foreclosure "rescue" scam. (How to spot risky deals and outright crooks is discussed in Ch. 1.)

It is also a common requirement that the foreclosing party post notices on the courthouse door and in other public places. In fact, in Mississippi, this posting might be the only notice you get, along with publication.

If you or a family member is on active military duty, you have extra protections, including the right that a judge evaluate the merits of the foreclosure even if you're living in a state where nonjudicial foreclosures are the norm (so long as you took out the mortgage before your period of military service began). (The federal Servicemembers Civil Relief Act is discussed in Ch. 4.)

In or Out of Court?

Again, foreclosures take one of two major paths: judicial (in court) or nonjudicial (out of court). Subject to a few exceptions, if your home loan is secured by a mortgage, chances are you'll go through a judicial foreclosure. (Some mortgages contain a "power of sale" clause that allows the lender to foreclose nonjudicially.) If your loan is secured by a deed of trust, you'll probably face a nonjudicial foreclosure. The real estate industry in a particular state—and the laws that industry's lobbyists have pushed through that state's legislature—pretty much determine whether mortgages or deeds of trust are used there.

A judicial foreclosure often takes a lot longer than a nonjudicial one. This kind of foreclosure also gives you a ready-made opportunity to oppose the foreclosure and assures that your home won't be lost to foreclosure unless a judge signs off on it. Judicial oversight is an important protection against illegal tactics by the foreclosing party.

Foreclosure by Possession

In Massachusetts, New Hampshire, and Rhode Island, an arcane procedure called "foreclosure by possession" lets the lender take possession of a house by "peaceful entry." Because of legal uncertainties regarding title and what constitutes peaceful entry, these laws are not used very often, if ever. If you live in one of these states, you should ask a HUD-approved housing counselor (see Ch. 4) or an attorney whether this method of foreclosure is used in your area.

Do You Have a Mortgage or a Deed of Trust?

As you'll see, it isn't always clear what the foreclosure process will be. Even in a state that typically requires foreclosures to go through court, nonjudicial foreclosure might be permitted if the loan is secured by a deed of trust rather than by a mortgage and if allowed by state law. On the other hand, even if your home loan is secured by a deed of trust, your lender might decide to foreclose judicially if a court needs to resolve some matter associated with the loan, such as issues with the property's title, or to obtain a deficiency judgment. For example, in Alaska, the lender can't get a deficiency judgment after a nonjudicial foreclosure, but a deficiency judgment is allowed if the foreclosure goes through the courts.

Not sure which document was used to secure your home loan? You can find out by:

- reviewing your original paperwork (that pile of documents you got when you closed escrow on your house)
- calling your mortgage servicer (the company to whom you make your payments)
- visiting your local land records office and pulling up the recorded document (under your name or address) on the public-access computer, or
- checking your local county clerk and recorder's website. Sometimes, an online search tool is available that you can use to find out which documents have been recorded (such as a mortgage or deed of trust) on your property.

In some states, the borrower has a right to request a judicial foreclosure even if a deed of trust authorizes a nonjudicial foreclosure. See your state's page in the appendix for more information on whether you've got this option.

Before Foreclosure Starts, You'll Likely Get a Breach Letter

Many mortgages and deeds of trust require the lender or servicer to send you a notice, commonly called a "breach letter," that your loan is in default before accelerating the loan and proceeding with a foreclosure. (The mortgage or deed of trust's "acceleration clause" permits the lender to demand that the entire balance of the loan be repaid in the event of a default.)

Typically, the breach letter will provide the following information:

- the reason for the default (for instance, failing to make a payment)
- the action required to cure the default (such as paying the missed payment)
- the date that you must cure the default (usually at least 30 days from the notice date), and
- the consequences of failing to cure the default.

If you don't cure in a timely manner, foreclosure proceedings can begin. In most instances, the servicer will send this letter when you're about 90 days behind in payments.

Judicial Foreclosures

If you live in one of the states listed in the table below, the foreclosure will probably take place in court.

In judicial foreclosures, your lender gets the process started by filing a foreclosure lawsuit in the local court. You'll receive official notice of the lawsuit when a sheriff or process server personally serves you with (or posts on your door, leaves a copy at your home with a person of suitable age and discretion, and mails you, in some cases):

- a summons explaining your right to file a written response to the lawsuit and telling you how long you have to do so, and
- a copy of the document (called a "petition" or "complaint") that requests the foreclosure and sets out the reasons the judge should issue a foreclosure order.

States Where Judicial Foreclosure Is Customary

Connecticut	Kansas	North Dakota
Delaware	Kentucky	Ohio
District of Columbia	Louisiana	Oklahoma
Florida	(executory proceeding)	Pennsylvania
Hawaii	Maine	South Carolina
Illinois	New Jersey	South Dakota
Indiana	New Mexico	Vermont
Iowa	New York	Wisconsin

You can contest the foreclosure or let it proceed. If you don't respond, the lender will most likely get a default judgment authorizing the sale of the home. (A "default judgment" means that you automatically lose the case because you didn't respond to the suit.) If you do respond by filing an answer with the court, the foreclosing party can't get a default judgment. Instead, it will likely file a motion of summary judgment. You must respond to the motion or else the lender will win.

Even if you respond, the court might grant summary judgment in favor of the foreclosing party if no dispute exists regarding the important facts of the case and the law isn't on your side. But if you have a valid defense and the court doesn't grant summary judgment, the case will proceed to trial. After you and the lender present your evidence and arguments the judge will either:

- order the foreclosure to go ahead and in many states, set the sale date, or
- dismiss the case, sending the lender back to the drawing board. (In two states, Connecticut and Vermont, a judge who approves the foreclosure can order ownership transferred to the foreclosing lender then and there. This kind of transfer happens in a "strict foreclosure.")

At the foreclosure sale, the property often goes to the lender, or subsequent loan owner, when no one else bids on the property. The property is then known as "Real Estate Owned" (REO).

Judicial foreclosures are seldomly permanently derailed, but they can be significantly delayed. If you have grounds to fight the foreclosure, either because the foreclosing party can't prove its case or because you offer proof that casts doubt on the foreclosure's legality, such as evidence that the party seeking to foreclose doesn't own the loan, it can take many months before the case is resolved one way or the other.

Eventually, if the foreclosure is legally appropriate, the judge authorizes your house to be sold at auction or, in the strict foreclosure states, transferred directly to the lender.

Here's how a typical judicial foreclosure might proceed:

Peter and Maddie bought their house several years ago at the price of $400,000. They made a 10% down payment and borrowed the other $360,000. Maddie lost her $80,000-a-year job and now earns $20 an hour. Peter previously quit his job to be a stay-at-home dad. Now, they can't afford their payments. They live in Ohio, where foreclosures are judicial.

Under federal law, in most cases, a foreclosure can't begin until the borrowers are over 120 days delinquent. So, once they're 90 days delinquent on payments, the lender sends them a written notice—a breach letter—that foreclosure proceedings won't start for 30 days and that Peter and Maddie can avoid a foreclosure if they make up the missed payments plus costs and interest. Peter and Maddie decide to let the foreclosure happen, given that they won't be able to make the payments (even if modified downward). They let the 30 days expire without paying the amount needed to cure the default.

Two weeks later, Peter and Maddie are served with a copy of a summons and foreclosure complaint that the lender has filed in the local court. They have 28 days to respond. (In other states, the amount of time might be different, though it is usually between 20 and 30 days.) They visit a lawyer, who tells them they might be able to put off the foreclosure sale by filing a response contesting the allegations in the complaint. Unfortunately, the lawyer wants too much money. Peter and Maddie could do some research into possible defenses and represent themselves, but they decide they really can't afford the house any longer and will have to move anyway. They let the 28 days go by without responding.

The court issues a default judgment that authorizes the property's sale. After the judgment, the property is appraised because, under their state's laws, the home can't be sold for less than two-thirds of its appraised value at the foreclosure sale. Then, a notice of the date, time, and place of sale is published for three consecutive weeks in a newspaper of general circulation in the county where the property is located. The lender files the notice of sale with the court at least seven days prior to the sale and sends a copy to Peter and Maddie, and to the other parties that have appeared in the case. Then, on the specified date, the property is put up for sale at auction. The lender makes a credit bid, which is the highest and only bid on the home. With a credit bid, the lender bids the debt that the borrower owes. Basically, the lender gets a credit in this amount.

The entire process, from the time Peter and Maddie first missed a payment until the auction, takes about ten months. Had Peter and Maddie contested the foreclosure, the process might have dragged on for many more months.

After the auction, the court must confirm the sale and the new owner gets title to the property. In Peter and Maddie's case, confirmation happens within 30 days after the sale. If they haven't left the property by this time, the new owner (the lender) will take steps to evict them from the home.

The lender asks the court for a writ of possession, which orders the sheriff to remove Peter and Maddie from the property. The lender doesn't have to file a separate lawsuit to evict them. But in some states, the new property owner has to file a lawsuit to evict foreclosed homeowners. At this point, a representative from the sheriff's office will notify Peter and Maddie of the date they must vacate the premises.

Nonjudicial Foreclosures

If you live in one of the states listed below, the foreclosure will probably be nonjudicial. A court usually won't be involved in the procedure, except in a few states, where a court has to sign off on foreclosures. The foreclosure could be judicial, though, for various other reasons (for example, because of a title issue). Also, see your state's page in the appendix for information about your possible right to choose a judicial foreclosure.

Generally, a deed of trust authorizes the entity named as "trustee" (a third party that administers the foreclosure) in the deed of trust to foreclose on the property if you ever default. The deed of trust typically contains a power of sale clause, which allows the foreclosure to proceed outside of court.

Your state's law sets out the specifics of the foreclosure procedure, including how much notice you get, how the property will be sold (usually at a public auction), and what rights (if any) you have to reinstate the loan before the foreclosure date or recover title to the property after it's sold.

Depending on what state law requires, you might get:

- a notice of default that gives you time to reinstate your loan by making up all the back payments, followed by a notice of sale
- a combined notice of default and sale stating that the property will be sold on a certain date unless you make up the missed payments
- only one notice—a notice of sale announcing that the property will be sold on a specific date unless you pay off the loan, or
- in a couple of states, notice only by publication and posting. (See your state's page in the appendix to get information about the process where you live.)

If you don't find a way to stop the foreclosure, the home will be sold at auction once the lender completes all steps that state law requires. As with judicial foreclosures, the property often goes to the lender when no one else bids on the property.

Here's how a typical nonjudicial foreclosure might proceed:

When Jason and Emilia bought their home for $600,000, it seemed like a great deal—but now it's worth only about $550,000, less than they owe on their loan. Jason and Emilia live in California, where nonjudicial foreclosures are typical. Like most California homebuyers, they signed a promissory note and a deed of trust.

States Where Nonjudicial Foreclosure Is Customary	
Alabama	Nevada
Alaska	New Hampshire
Arizona	New Mexico (allowed)
Arkansas	North Carolina
California	Oklahoma (homeowner can request
Colorado	judicial foreclosure)
District of Columbia (sometimes)	Oregon
Georgia	Rhode Island
Idaho	South Dakota (homeowner can
Maryland	request judicial foreclosure)
Massachusetts	Tennessee
Michigan	Texas
Minnesota	Utah
Mississippi	Virginia
Missouri	Washington
Montana	West Virginia
Nebraska	Wyoming

CAUTION

Time might be short. You have to be alert when a foreclosure looms in a nonjudicial state. You might get little notice of the foreclosure sale, and once it happens, you could be permanently out of luck.

The deed of trust states that the "trustee" (again, the third party that handles nonjudicial foreclosures in California and some other states) can sell the property at a public auction if Jason and Emilia default on their monthly payments or breach the terms of the deed of trust in some other way. However, the terms of the deed of trust and California law require the lender to first give them some time to get current on the debt—called "reinstating" the loan—by making up the missed payments plus costs and interest. (See Ch. 1.)

After they miss four payments, Jason and Emilia receive (by mail) a 30-day notice—a breach letter—notifying them that if they don't catch up on all of the payments, a foreclosure will be initiated. Also, as California law requires, the loan servicer contacts Jason and Emilia to discuss working out an alternative to foreclosure, like a loan modification. The servicer suggests that Jason and Emilia send in a loss mitigation (foreclosure alternative) application to find out if they qualify for any other options. But Jason and Emilia decide to let the home go because they have no equity in the house and can't afford the payments. They let the 30 days given in the breach letter expire without reinstating and don't submit an application to their loan servicer for an alternative to foreclosure. After Jason and Emilia are more than 120 days behind on payments, they receive (by certified mail) a notice of default. It gives them three months to cure the default by making up the missed payments, plus interest and costs. (See your state's page in the appendix to find out whether you'll receive a notice of default or similar notice and, if so, how much time it gives you to cure the default.) Jason and Emilia don't have the cash to make up the payments. After the three months pass, they get a notice of sale, telling them that that the property will be sold at an auction on the courthouse steps at a specific time. In California, the sale has to be least 20 days after the end of the three-month cure period.

At the auction, the lender buys the home using a credit bid when no one else makes a bid. Because the lender doesn't take immediate action to have Jason and Emilia evicted, they continue living there payment-free for another month. The lender then tries to negotiate a move-out date with Jason and Emilia, but that doesn't work. So the lender follows the California eviction laws for taking possession from former homeowners and serves Jason and Emilia with a three-day notice to quit.

Although Jason and Emilia are legally entitled to stay until the lender goes to court and gets an eviction order, they decide to move out to avoid having the eviction case on their credit record. An eviction is a matter of public record and could hurt Jason and Emilia's ability to rent or lease a new place to live after the foreclosure. Even so, Jason and Emilia have remained in their home for about nine months without making a payment. They managed to save most of the money they would have paid for shelter during that period, which will make it easier for them to move out and find a new place to live. (See Ch. 9 for more on coming out of a foreclosure with some serious cash in your pocket.)

Dos and Don'ts When You're in Foreclosure

Going through a foreclosure can be nerve-wracking. The stress of potentially losing your home can drive you to make mistakes, either by doing the wrong thing or failing to act at all. Because your actions are vitally important if you want to keep your home—or at least get through the process with as little anxiety as possible—it's essential that you learn the dos and don'ts when facing a foreclosure.

Do:

- **Contact your mortgage servicer.** As soon as you think you're going to have trouble making your monthly payment—or shortly after you fall behind—call your servicer. You might be able to work out a forbearance agreement or a repayment plan. (See Ch. 4.)

Dos and Don'ts When You're in Foreclosure (continued)

- **Contact a HUD-approved housing counselor for assistance.** If you want to apply for a foreclosure alternative—like a loan modification, short sale, or deed in lieu of foreclosure—a HUD-approved housing counselor can tell you more about these options, evaluate your financial situation, and help you deal with your servicer. (See Ch. 4.)

- **Find out more about how foreclosure works.** Learn each step in the process, as well as the state laws that protect you during foreclosure, so you understand your rights and aren't caught off guard at any point. (To learn the procedures and laws where you live, check your state's page in the appendix.) Also, find out about key federal foreclosure laws. (See Ch. 4.)

- **Make a record of all your communications with your servicer.** Keep track of when you call, who you spoke to, and what you talked about. You might need this information later on to help you fight the foreclosure. Also, keep a folder with all correspondence from the lender, servicer, court, or foreclosure trustee. This way, you'll have a good idea about the status of your case, as well as information you might need to defend against the foreclosure.

- **Participate in foreclosure mediation if your state, county, or city, offers it.** Foreclosure mediation brings the borrower and lender (or its representative) to the table, along with a neutral mediator, with the goal of working out a way to resolve the delinquency. (See Ch. 4.) Homeowners who participate in mediation are more likely to avoid foreclosure than those who don't.

- **Find out if your state has a Hardest Hit Fund or another kind of homeowner-assistance program.** Hardest Hit Fund and other state-specific programs offer financial assistance to homeowners. For instance, you might qualify for money to get caught up on the loan or pay future mortgage payments. (See Ch. 4 for more information.)

- **Avoid foreclosure rescue scams.** Be wary of letters and phone calls from for-profit companies, especially companies offering to help you get a loan modification. While these companies' letters look official and their sales pitch might sound good, companies that offer to stop the foreclosure for a fee are often scammers. (See Ch. 1 to learn about foreclosure rescue scams to avoid.)

Dos and Don'ts When You're in Foreclosure (continued)

Don't:

- **Ignore phone calls or letters from your servicer.** Calls and letters from your servicer will likely explain any options you have to avoid a foreclosure and how to apply for those options.
- **Ignore notices from the court or a foreclosure trustee.** Correspondence from the court or a trustee will contain foreclosure information, including important dates—like the sale date—and details about your rights during the foreclosure.
- **Assume the servicer is always correct.** Servicers are known for making mistakes that violate the law when processing foreclosures. Again, you should understand the specifics of both federal and state foreclosure laws and procedures. If the servicer messes up, you might have a defense to the foreclosure.
- **Wait until the foreclosure is almost over to try to save your home.** You'll have more options if you address the problem early on. The longer you wait and the further you fall behind in payments, the fewer options you'll have.
- **Pay up-front fees or fees for help that you can get for free.** If a foreclosure rescue company asks for a hefty up-front fee from you, beware. Many states have laws prohibiting companies from collecting money before performing foreclosure services, as well as other restrictions on foreclosure rescue activities. You also shouldn't pay a fee to a private company for housing counseling. HUD-approved housing counselors will help you without charge.
- **Make your mortgage payments to anyone other than your mortgage servicer.** Foreclosure rescue companies sometimes say you should pay them instead of your servicer, which is always bad idea. The company might take your money, fail to stop the foreclosure (or not even try), and then you'll be even further behind on your payments.
- **Move out early.** If you abandon the home, you'll miss out on the chance to stay there for free during the foreclosure. Also, to qualify for financial and loss mitigation assistance, homeowners usually have to be living in their home. Another thing to keep in mind is that you're still responsible for the property until the foreclosure ends, even if you aren't living there. You don't want to become the victim of a zombie foreclosure after moving out early. (See Ch. 9.)

Deficiency Judgments: Will You Still Owe Money After the Foreclosure?

When deciding whether to fight a foreclosure, take steps to avoid it, or just walk away, you'll want to know whether you'll be liable for any deficiency resulting from the foreclosure sale. The "deficiency" is usually measured as the difference between the foreclosure sale price and the amount of your debt. The deficiency could be many thousands of dollars.

> **EXAMPLE:** Jonas owes $350,000 on a house he bought for $400,000. The property is now worth $300,000, according to a recent appraisal. He's no longer able to earn overtime at his job and falls behind on his payments. The lender threatens foreclosure, and Jonas doesn't qualify for a loan modification or other loss mitigation option. Not wanting to fight the foreclosure or file for bankruptcy, Jonas sends the keys to the lender and walks away.
>
> The lender forecloses nonjudicially on the property and at the auction makes a credit bid of $300,000. No one else bids on the house, so the property goes to the lender. In Jonas's state, the lender can then sue for the deficiency—in this case, $50,000. Unless Jonas files for bankruptcy to wipe out this debt, the lender (or perhaps a collection firm) will probably sue to get a deficiency judgment, then use that judgment to go after his paycheck and bank account.

You might not have to worry about a deficiency judgment. Some states prohibit lenders from suing for deficiencies under specific circumstances. Loans that fit in this category are called "non-recourse" loans because the lender has no recourse if you default.

With nonjudicial foreclosures, the lender can't recover a deficiency without bringing a separate lawsuit and getting a money judgment. In a judicial foreclosure, though, most states allow the lender to seek a deficiency judgment as part of the underlying foreclosure lawsuit; a few states require a separate lawsuit.

Many states limit the deficiency amount to the difference between the loan and the property's fair market value. For instance, if the loan is for $400,000, the fair market value is $350,000, and the property is sold for $300,000 at a foreclosure sale, the deficiency judgment is limited to $50,000 even though the lender technically lost $100,000— the difference between the loan amount and the sales price. Fair market value typically is determined by a fairly complex statutory appraisal process set out in state statutes.

You can wipe out a deficiency judgment by filing for Chapter 7 or Chapter 13 bankruptcy. Check the appendix to find your state's rules on deficiency judgments.

Taxes

Unsurprisingly, how you deal with foreclosures can have tax consequences.

Income Taxes

Essentially, if a foreclosure, short sale, or deed in lieu of foreclosure results in a deficiency, and the lender later cancels or forgives the debt, the forgiven amount is generally considered your taxable income unless you qualify for an exception or exclusion. (This issue is discussed in more detail in Ch. 8.)

Capital Gains Tax

If your adjusted tax basis on your house is less than the sale price of the house, you might incur a capital gains tax. For example, if you bought your home for $200,000 and it sells for $300,000, you have a $100,000 capital gain, minus the cost of any improvements you added to the property. This gain will be taxed at the capital gains tax rate, subject to your one-time exclusion ($250,000 for one person, $500,000 for a married couple). Check with a tax expert to see whether you'll face a capital gains issue at the sale or foreclosure of your house. If you will, consult a bankruptcy lawyer for advice on how filing for bankruptcy might help.

Can You Keep Your House? Should You?

The Emotional Part of Foreclosure 52

    Dealing With Fear...52

    Grieving for Your Loss..53

    Your House Is Not Your Home...55

    You Are Not Your House..55

    Renting Has Advantages..55

The Economics of Foreclosure: What You Need to Know 56

    Do You Have Equity in Your House?.. 56

    Can You Keep Making Your Monthly Payments? 58

    Could You Reduce Your Debt Load?...61

When It Makes Sense to Keep Your House...62

    You Have at Least Some Equity in Your House 62

    You Can Afford Future Monthly Loan Payments...................................62

    You Have Equity and Can Get a Reverse Mortgage.............................62

When It Makes Sense to Give Up Your House 65

f a foreclosure is imminent because you've missed some payments, or you think you will soon, it's time to face what's probably the toughest question of the whole process: whether you should try to keep your house.

Of course, you must take a good look at whether it's financially feasible to try to retain the property. But this decision isn't always a simple matter of finances and cash flow. You'll need to sort through some emotional factors, too. Would the loss of your residence be so upsetting that you would do anything to keep it, or might you be better off letting go and moving on? Could you accept it as an economic setback rather than a personal failing?

This chapter will help you figure these things out. Then you can move forward, either to take steps to keep your house or to start planning how to give it up in the most emotionally and economically advantageous way. The next chapters discuss how to take these next steps after you decide what direction you want to go in.

The Emotional Part of Foreclosure

It's important to acknowledge that the prospect of losing your house can be a psychological blow as well as a financial and practical one. You can't avoid these emotional realities, but facing them can help you approach the situation calmly and rationally.

Dealing With Fear

If you're like many homeowners, the thought of foreclosure triggers fears of ending up on the street. It doesn't happen like that.

Foreclosure is an orderly process. You'll get notice before the process starts and before the house is eventually sold, if it comes to that (see Ch. 2). You might also have the right to live in the home during the redemption period, if state law provides one, after the sale. (See Ch. 9 for a more detailed explanation of how this works.)

Even when the property ends up in the hands of a new owner at the foreclosure sale, in many states, the new owner will have to give you a formal written notice to leave. Typically, you'll have from three to 30 days. And if you don't leave at the end of that period, the new owner will have to go to court and get an eviction order, though you might decide that moving out earlier is in your best interest. In other words, you'll almost certainly have enough time to make new housing arrangements.

Were You Nesting or Investing When You Bought Your House?

Much of this chapter—and the book, for that matter—assumes that you have an emotional attachment to your house. But maybe you don't, or at least not much of one. Maybe you bought your house primarily as a way to build some wealth. Some of the people we've worked with lived in rental apartments and rented out the houses they owned. Others, while living in their houses, were ready to move on, if necessary, in the same way any other small business owner would move on when the economics of the business dictate.

If you bought your house primarily as an investment, your decision-making process should be based on the economics of your situation. If you owe more than your home is worth, get out the best way you can. If you're close to gaining equity in the property, decide whether to hang in there and hope things get better. If you're living in your house but aren't particularly attached to it, stay as long as legally possible without making a payment. (See Ch. 9.)

Grieving for Your Loss

You might not have thought of it in these terms, but you're likely to go through a grieving process when faced with the loss of your house. It's something like what you might experience if you were contemplating the loss of your marriage or career.

In her seminal book, *On Death and Dying*, psychiatrist Elisabeth Kübler-Ross identified five stages that patients commonly experience when given a terminal prognosis. To a lesser extent, people facing the possibility of foreclosure often go through similar stages, which are:

- denial (This isn't happening to me!)
- anger (Why is this happening to me?)
- bargaining (I promise I'll make every mortgage payment on time from now on!)
- depression (I don't *care* anymore.)
- acceptance (I'm ready to make lemonade out of lemons.)

Denial. People commonly ignore the first warning signs of impending foreclosure—the missed payment, the call from the lender, even the formal notice that is the prelude to a foreclosure sale. Envelopes are unopened, notices go unread, and phone messages are quickly deleted. Homeowners know something bad is happening but cling to the hope that something—anything—will come along to bail them out or that they can ride out the current situation.

Anger. When it finally dawns on them that they might actually lose their house, they become angry—with themselves, their spouse, the lender, or any number of people.

Bargaining. Anger gives way to negotiation. They tell themselves that if somehow they can avoid losing their home, they will make all their mortgage payments on time, hew to a strict budget, and even get a second job, if necessary.

Depression. As the foreclosure sale draws nearer, the reality of the possible loss of their home sets in and they could become physically ill and unable to deal with the daily grind.

Acceptance. The state of depression turns into a state of acceptance that the foreclosure is coming and must be dealt with—which typically results in:

- a search for new housing
- a plan to fight the foreclosure
- a visit to a bankruptcy attorney, or
- a resolve to remain in the home as long as possible, payment free.

Your House Is Not Your Home

You'll likely have an easier time dealing with foreclosure if you understand (and remind yourself regularly) that your house and your home are not necessarily the same thing. A "home" is where you and your loved ones live. It's about your neighbors, your memories, and shelter from the storm. Your home is where you sit down to a family meal, entertain friends, and get in touch with your creative side by arranging furniture, hanging art and family portraits, or changing the paint color. A home is where you can relax after work or return after a trip.

In essence, "home" is a concept you can take with you whether you buy another house or end up renting. Sure, you would probably rather stay where you are, but the fact that you might have to move should be seen for what it is: a temporary interruption in your life from which you can recover. In fact, finding a new place to live can lead you to new opportunities, new friends and neighbors, new community activities, and a different perspective on life.

You Are Not Your House

In the same way your house is not your home, you are not your house. It's deeply ingrained in our culture that the size and location of the house we live in indicates our value as human beings. For example, given the opportunity, most of us would prefer to live in a large house with a stunning view. It's not because we need a large house—average household size has gone down just as average house size has gone up. But for most of us, a large fancy house provides status and self-esteem.

Renting Has Advantages

Renting has definite advantages. It offers freedom from the economic burdens and stress every homeowner feels when faced with the need to pay for rodent control, new paint, roof or furnace repairs, an expensive city assessment for road improvements, increasing property taxes, broken water pipes, and a variety of other problems that homeowners are naturally heir to. It can be a real luxury to be able to call the landlord when a big-ticket maintenance problem—for example the water heater—rears its ugly head.

If you need to relocate, get away from neighbors, or travel over long periods of time, renting gives you flexibility that you lack with home ownership. And if you want to stay put, a long-term lease is a good hedge against having to move before you're ready.

If you're putting an inordinate amount of money into your mortgage payment, you quite likely are making sacrifices in other important areas of your life, such as your family's health, your children's education, charitable contributions, or visits to faraway relatives, to name but a few common expenses. Living in poverty-like conditions just to remain in your house doesn't make a whole lot of sense.

The Economics of Foreclosure: What You Need to Know

Apart from the emotional considerations that surface whenever a foreclosure is threatened, you just can't ignore certain economic factors. Before you can decide whether to try to keep your house, you need to answer a few questions about your financial situation—which has no doubt changed since you bought the property.

Do You Have Equity in Your House?

To a large degree, your options depend on whether you have equity in your home. When you bought your house, presumably it was worth more than the amount you borrowed to buy it. If your property is still worth at least as much as you owe on it, it might make sense to oppose the foreclosure (see Chs. 5, 6, and 7) or sell it and get out from under the loan.

Estimates of real estate values are traditionally based on the amounts that similar houses in the neighborhood have recently sold for. To find out that information, you can use www.zillow.com or similar websites (search for "home value calculators"). Local real estate brokers and agents can also give you an estimate by looking at similar sales in your neighborhood.

If other foreclosures are going on in your community, a house similar to yours might have sold for far less than you could get for your house if you could afford to be patient. Also, buyers will pay substantially more for a well-kept home than for one that has been trashed, as many foreclosed homes are.

Take the best estimate you can come up with and use the simple worksheet below to help you determine what, if any, equity you have in your house.

Homeowners' Equity Worksheet

1. Market value of your home $ _____

2. Costs of sale (if unsure, put 10% of market value) $ _____

3. Amount owed on all mortgages $ _____

4. Amount of all other liens on the property $ _____

5. Total of Lines 2, 3, and 4 $ _____

6. Your equity (Line 1 minus Line 5) $ _____

Where the Housing Market Stands Today

At the time of this writing, foreclosure filings in the U.S. were down 80% from the previous year. But this figure is misleading because foreclosure moratoriums covered most of the mortgages in the United States—around 70%—until at least June 30, 2021. About 2.7 million households didn't make their mortgage payment in January 2021, mainly because the homeowners were on forbearance plans. Those forbearance plans and moratoriums will eventually end. A report from the Consumer Financial Protection Bureau found that once these protections expire in the months ahead, more than 11 million families, close to 10% of U.S. households, will be at risk of eviction and foreclosure. At that time, the foreclosure rate in the U.S. could very well go up. You can find the latest developments on the current state of foreclosures, foreclosure laws, moratoriums, and more at www.nolo.com/legal-updates/legal-updates-for-foreclosure.

Can You Keep Making Your Monthly Payments?

It's not worth putting time and effort, not to mention emotional energy, into trying to hang on to your house if you really, truly can't afford it. It's not uncommon for people to pay upwards of 50% of their gross (not take-home) income toward their overall mortgage debt. That leaves little or nothing left for food, utilities, transportation, out-of-pocket medical costs, and the like. Quite simply, this economic position is untenable.

Here's how to think about whether you can afford your current loan.

Use the Standard Ratios

For decades, the conventional wisdom was that you shouldn't pay more than 25% of your gross income for housing. Slowly that figure crept up as lenders relaxed their rules to underwrite ever-increasing numbers of mortgage loans. Over time, this percentage has settled in at 31%. Under this thinking, if you're paying more than 31% of your gross income on your first mortgage, you're at serious risk of default. So, for example, if you pay $3,100 a month on your first mortgage, including taxes and insurance, your annual gross income should be in the neighborhood of $120,000. If your income is $75,000 a year, your first mortgage payment, including taxes and insurance, shouldn't exceed about $1,938 a month.

In terms of deciding whether your home is affordable as a factual matter, sometimes the 31% figure can be thrown out the window. If, for example, you have a child with special needs or two kids in college, your mortgage payment might not be affordable even if it's below the 31% threshold. And if you have few other expenses (for example, you live simply, don't own a car, and grow some of your own food), you might be able to afford a mortgage payment that's a higher percentage of your income.

How Much of Your Income Should Go to Your Mortgage?		
	Maximum Mortgage Payment	
Annual Gross Income	25% of monthly income	31% of monthly income
$50,000	$1,042	$1,292
$75,000	$1,562	$1,938
$100,000	$2,083	$2,583
$125,000	$2,604	$3,229

Use an Online Calculator

The Internet offers many calculators that purport to tell you how much house you can afford. Do an online search for "home affordability calculators." The calculators will tell you how much you can borrow, according to the general opinion of the housing finance industry. They're very easy to use, but keep in mind they make some assumptions that might not quite work for you.

Do a Budget

You can take a no-nonsense look at your income and expenses and see whether your budget has room for your current or projected mortgage payments. If the numbers don't add up the first time around, see what expenses you can trim.

Don't know where to start? As you might guess, lots of websites offer budgeting software and spreadsheets. Or just search for "online budget planning" to come up with a list.

RESOURCE

Get budgeting help. For more information about how to create a budget and control your spending, get *Solve Your Money Troubles: Strategies to Get Out of Debt and Stay That Way,* by Cara O'Neill and Amy Loftsgordon (Nolo).

Ask a Budget-Counseling Agency

Everyone who files for bankruptcy must, by law, take a budgeting class in order to receive a discharge of their debts. To meet this demand, hundreds of companies, for-profit and nonprofit alike, have set up shop to deliver debtor education classes. These organizations can also help you with budgeting, even if you're not planning to file for bankruptcy.

The courses are taught online or by telephone and mail. The fee varies for this service, though $20 to $30 is common.

For a list of agencies that the Department of Justice has approved for bankruptcy purposes—although you don't have to file for bankruptcy to use them—go to www.justice.gov/ust and search for "Credit Counseling & Debtor Education Information." Follow the link and then look for a link to a "List of Approved Credit Counseling Agencies." Because budgeting is pretty much the same everywhere, and because you don't need to show up in person, you can use a service even if it's far from where you live.

HUD-approved housing counselors can also provide budgeting help to people trying to save their homes from foreclosure. (See Ch. 4.)

Could You Reduce Your Debt Load?

If you don't have enough cash each month to keep making your existing mortgage payments, you might be able to make them affordable. You'll need to either get the payment amount reduced or get your hands on more cash.

Here are the main ways to go about this (all of which are discussed elsewhere in the book):

- **Modify your mortgage.** Your modification options often depend on what entity, like FHA, VA, USDA, Fannie Mae, or Freddie Mac, owns or guarantees your loan. For example, Fannie Mae and Freddie Mac offer the Flex Modification program. If you have an FHA-insured loan, you're entitled to a special loss mitigation process that might help you qualify for a modification. Also, almost all lenders offer proprietary (in-house) modifications to borrowers who are struggling to make mortgage payments. (You can get details in Ch. 4.)
- **File for Chapter 13 bankruptcy** and come up with a repayment plan that will let you reduce the amount of your monthly payments on your other debts and get rid of them altogether in three to five years.
- **File for Chapter 7 bankruptcy** to get rid of your unsecured debts, such as those from credit cards, medical services, or signature (personal, unsecured) loans, so you'll have a greater share of your income to devote to your mortgage.

When It Makes Sense to Keep Your House

Your answers to the questions discussed above, about your equity and your budget, will largely determine whether you should try to keep your house.

You Have at Least Some Equity in Your House

If you have equity in your house and are facing foreclosure because of missed payments or a rapid increase in your mortgage interest rate, it might make sense to hold on to the house if for no other reason than to protect your equity. Needless to say, the more equity you have, the stronger this reasoning.

You Can Afford Future Monthly Loan Payments

If you have some equity in your house and think you can afford future monthly mortgage payments, it's probably worth it to try to keep your property.

If you don't think you can afford your monthly payments, see "Could You Reduce Your Debt Load?" above, for ideas on how to free up more of your income or change the payments themselves.

You Have Equity and Can Get a Reverse Mortgage

If you're 62 or older, you might benefit from taking out a reverse mortgage. Before you get a reverse mortgage, though, learn how they work, and consider both the upsides and, especially, the downsides. With a reverse mortgage, a homeowner can tap into the equity in the home to provide cash. A reverse mortgage is different from a traditional forward mortgage in that it doesn't require the borrower to make monthly payments to the lender to repay the loan.

Instead, loan proceeds are paid out to the borrower according to a plan, which typically consists of a lump sum, monthly payment, or line of credit (or a combination of monthly payments and a line of credit). The most widely available reverse mortgage is the Federal Housing Administration (FHA) Home Equity Conversion Mortgage (HECM). These federally-insured loans are available through an FHA-approved lender.

In the past, many reverse mortgage borrowers immediately took out the full amount of the loan in a lump sum, leaving them with less money in later years to pay for taxes, insurance, and home maintenance costs. A large number of defaults and foreclosures resulted and caused the Department of Housing and Urban Development (HUD), which oversees the FHA, to change its reverse mortgage policies. HECM rules now limit the amount you can take out in a lump sum or during the first year to 60% of the total amount (called the "principal limit"). If you have mandatory obligations, such as an existing mortgage, the initial disbursement is limited to the amount needed to pay off the mandatory obligations plus 10% of the principal limit. The goal of this change is to encourage people to access their home equity slowly and steadily over the years, rather than all at once. It also allows borrowers to keep some equity in their homes.

In addition, as of late April 2015, a lender must complete a financial assessment and credit analysis when making a reverse mortgage loan to ensure that homeowners can afford the future taxes and insurance payments. If a lender determines that a homeowner might not be able to keep up with these payments, the lender must also establish a set-aside account. The set-aside is an amount drawn under the HECM that is then reserved to pay property taxes and insurance.

If the lender doesn't require a set-aside account, you can pay the taxes and insurance with a voluntary set-aside or, in some cases, by having the lender withhold sufficient amounts from the monthly disbursements, or by charging funds to the line of credit. You could also choose to pay the taxes and insurance on your own.

The HECM becomes due and payable when:

- **The home is no longer the borrower's principal place of residence.** The borrower might still own the property but live somewhere else most of the time. So, if you move out and let your kids live in the home or rent the property out, the lender can call the loan due.
- **The borrower moves out due to a physical or mental illness and is gone for more than 12 consecutive months.** If your health declines and you have to move into a care facility, like a nursing home, the lender can call the loan due after you've been out of the property for more than 12 months.
- **The borrower sells the home or transfers title (ownership) to someone else.** If you sell or transfer title to the property (or transfer your beneficial interest in a trust owning all or part of the property) and no other borrower retains title to the home or retains a leasehold that meets certain conditions, the lender may call the loan due.
- **The borrower dies, and the property is not the principal residence of at least one surviving borrower.** However, a nonborrowing spouse might be able to remain in the home if specific eligibility requirements are met.
- **The borrower breaches the loan agreement.** For example, if you don't pay the property taxes or homeowners' insurance (assuming you don't have a set-aside account as described earlier), fail to keep the property in reasonable shape, or breach any of the other mortgage requirements, the lender can foreclose.

Reverse mortgages are heavily advertised on television by aging actors who describe these loans as "government-insured," implying that this is a big plus. In reality, this claim doesn't mean much. It simply means:

- If the lender can't collect the full amount of the loan from the sale of the home or foreclosure, the government will pay the lender the difference. You won't be liable for the deficiency.
- If the lender stops making payments it owes you, the government will make those payments to you.

Because reverse mortgages are premised on stable real estate values, you're unlikely to qualify for one unless you have a lot of equity in your house—at least enough to convince the lender that it'll recoup its investment. A reverse mortgage also comes with high fees and uses up part or all of your equity, leaving less value for you to pass on to your heirs at your death or less money if you decide to sell the home.

You're required to receive counseling before you get a HECM reverse mortgage. Counseling agencies usually charge a fee for their services. Unfortunately, because counselors are sometimes paid out of the loan proceeds, they have a financial interest in encouraging you to get a loan, even if it's not in your best interest. HECM counselors have reported that it typically takes at least two hours to explain the costs and consequences of these mortgages. Reverse mortgages can be risky and aren't a good idea for everybody. Even after a long counseling session, many borrowers still don't fully understand all of the terms and requirements. The bottom line is that reverse mortgages are complex and don't always work out well for the borrower. If you're considering one, it's a good idea to speak with a C.P.A., a financial planner, or an elder law attorney first.

When It Makes Sense to Give Up Your House

It's not an easy decision, but if you're behind on house payments and find yourself owing more on your mortgage loan than your home is worth, it doesn't make sense from an economic perspective to try to keep the house—unless you can get your mortgage payment reduced with a modification or work something else out with your lender. (Many lenders do want to keep you in your house; see Ch. 4.)

Keep in mind, though, that even if you wouldn't lose any equity by walking away from your mortgage, you could end up liable for some or all of your mortgage debt or home equity loan debt if you don't file for bankruptcy. And you could be taxed on any amount of the mortgage debt the lender forgives (although you might be able to avoid this tax liability). (See Ch. 8.)

If you decide that the smartest course is to give up the house, how you choose to proceed can make a very big difference to your financial future.

Your options, all of which are discussed later in the book, include:

- a short sale—that is, getting the lender's permission to sell the house for less than you owe
- a deed in lieu of foreclosure (getting your lender to accept the deed in exchange for an agreement to call off the foreclosure)
- letting the foreclosure happen, staying in your house payment-free for months until you get a notice to leave, and building up your cash reserves, or
- filing for Chapter 13 or Chapter 7 bankruptcy to eliminate foreclosure-related liabilities and delay the foreclosure sale for at least several months, thereby extending the time you can remain in the house payment-free.

Although for many it's painful to give up a house, try to keep in mind that doing so might make things much easier for you and your family in the long run. You'll probably be able to stay in the house for months without making any more mortgage payments—giving you time to save some money, which will make moving easier.

Working Out a Way to Avoid Foreclosure

Do You Have Enough Time to Work Out an Alternative
  to Foreclosure? 69

Using a HUD-Approved Housing Counselor 76

Basic Loss Mitigation Options..81

  Repayment Plan: Keeping Current and Catching Up 82

  Forbearance: Getting a Break From Payments 82

  Modification: Lowering Your Payments...85

Loss Mitigation Options for Government-Backed Mortgages.......................90

  Fannie Mae and Freddie Mac Loans..90

  FHA-Insured Loans 93

  VA-Insured Loans...96

  Rural Housing Service (RHS) Loans...97

Foreclosure Avoidance Mediation Programs...97

Hardest Hit Fund and Other Statewide Mortgage-Relief Programs..............98

Special Protections for Servicemembers on Active Duty...............................101

  Judicial Foreclosure Is Required..101

  A Court Can Adjust Your Mortgage 102

  Protections Against Default Judgments..103

  Interest Rates Must Be Reduced...104

  More State Protections 105

Mortgage Relief for Borrowers After a Natural Disaster 105

  Federal Housing Administration (FHA) Loans...106

  Veterans Affairs (VA) Loans...106

  Fannie Mae and Freddie Mac Loans..106

  Relief for Borrowers With Any Type of Loan...107

When you're at risk of defaulting on your mortgage or have already fallen behind on payments, you might have a number of options for keeping your house.

Refinance your mortgage. Usually, refinancing is available only if you have equity in your home. However, if you have a Fannie Mae or Freddie Mac loan, you might qualify for a refinance even if you're underwater on your loan. Fannie's "High Loan-to-Value Refinance Option" and Freddie's "Enhanced Relief Refinance" are discussed later in this chapter.

Get a repayment plan or forbearance agreement. With a repayment plan, you arrange to make up missed payments over time and stay current on your ongoing payments. Under a forbearance agreement, the lender agrees to reduce or suspend your mortgage payments for a period. These options are usually available if you aren't too far behind in your payments.

Lower your monthly mortgage payment with a modification. You would do well to use a HUD-approved housing counselor to help you if you want to try to get your mortgage payments reduced through a modification. The counselor can explain your options, work with your lender, and do a lot for your peace of mind. (See "Using a HUD-Approved Housing Counselor," below.)

File for bankruptcy. If you can't work out an agreement that will let you stay in your house under certain conditions—and you don't have the ability to reinstate your mortgage (see Ch. 1)—your next step is to explore filing for Chapter 13 or Chapter 7 bankruptcy. Chapter 13 can give you time to make up your missed payments and might lower your other secured debt payments (your car note or a short- term home equity loan, for example). Chapter 7 bankruptcy can quickly do away with credit card and other unsecured debt and free up income to use toward your mortgage payments, thereby allowing you to keep your home.

Challenge the foreclosure in court. Finally, you might be able to successfully challenge the foreclosure in court because of irregularities in the paperwork or the procedures. You will likely take this route only if you can't work out a way to avoid a foreclosure with the lender.

This chapter concentrates on the various ways you can change the terms of your mortgage or the amount of your monthly payment as a strategy to keep your home. Later chapters cover filing for bankruptcy and fighting foreclosure in court.

How Bankruptcy Can Help

Filing for bankruptcy can be a good way either to save your house or at least to stay in it payment-free for longer than you would otherwise.

It's important to understand that Chapter 7 bankruptcy will keep you in your home long-term only if you file while you' are still current on your mortgage. It will help you by wiping out (discharging) other debts, freeing up your income to make your house payments. Chapter 13 bankruptcy, however, can keep you in your home long-term even if you' are behind on your payments. (See Chs. 5 and 6.)

Do You Have Enough Time to Work Out an Alternative to Foreclosure?

It can take a while to work things out with your lender (typically through its representative, a mortgage servicing company). If you're not sure how much time you've got left before your house is sold in foreclosure, find the page for your state in the appendix and see how much notice you're entitled to. Also, remember that, in most cases, federal law gives you 120 days before foreclosure can start so that you can begin exploring options. Your failure to keep track of time constraints can sink your attempt to keep your house.

During the Great Recession and related mortgage crisis it was common for homeowners to negotiate with their servicers right up to the moment of the scheduled foreclosure sale. Then, when the negotiations fell through—as they frequently did—there wasn't enough time to stop the sale from going through.

Because of this practice, which is called "dual tracking"—that is, proceeding with foreclosure while simultaneously working with the homeowner on a loan modification or another form of loss mitigation— many homeowners who were sure that a modification was forthcoming were shocked to ultimately lose their homes to foreclosure. Now, federal and various state laws are in place to prevent dual tracking and provide other protections to people trying to save their homes.

In particular, the Dodd-Frank Wall Street Reform and Consumer Protection Act of 2010 imposed new requirements on servicers and gave the Consumer Financial Protection Bureau (CFPB) the authority to both implement the new requirements, as well as adopt new rules. On January 10, 2014, the CFPB's final mortgage servicing rules under the Real Estate Settlement Procedures Act (RESPA), also known as Regulation X, and the Truth in Lending Act (TILA) known as Regulation Z, went into effect. These laws establish national mortgage servicing standards and impose various requirements on most lenders and servicers.

Many of the laws are designed to ensure that homeowners get a fair shot at getting a mortgage modification or other foreclosure relief. (See 12 C.F.R. § 1024.30 and following.) They generally apply to mortgage loans secured by a property that's the borrower's principal residence, subject to some exceptions.

The servicer can't start a foreclosure for 120 days. As discussed in Ch. 2, a servicer can't make the "first notice or filing" under state law unless the loan is more than 120 days delinquent. So, in a judicial foreclosure, the foreclosing party can't file a court document, such as a complaint, petition, order to docket, or notice of hearing, until after you're 120 days behind. If the foreclosure is nonjudicial, the servicer can't begin the foreclosure by recording or publishing the first notice until after the 120th day of the delinquency. If state foreclosure law doesn't require a document to be recorded, published, or filed with the court, the first notice is the earliest document that establishes, sets, or schedules a date for the foreclosure sale. This 120-day time period is supposed to give you time to work out a way to avoid foreclosure.

Even if you're more than 120 days delinquent, if you submit a complete loss mitigation application before the servicer makes the first notice or filing required to initiate a foreclosure process, it may not start the foreclosure process unless:

- the servicer informs you that you're not eligible for any loss mitigation option, and the time for an appeal is over
- you reject the loss mitigation option that the servicer offers to you, or

- you accept a loss mitigation option but fail to comply with the terms of the deal, such as not making payments during a trial modification.

The two exceptions to this law are: The servicer can proceed with a foreclosure during the 120-day time period if it is joining the foreclosure action of a subordinate lienholder or if the foreclosure is because you violated a due-on-sale clause. (A "due-on-sale clause" is a provision in a mortgage or deed of trust that allows the lender to demand immediate payment of the balance of the mortgage if you sell or transfer the home's ownership.)

Servicers must provide homeowners with assistance. Federal law requires the servicer to work with you if you're having trouble making your mortgage payments. If you fall behind in payments, the servicer must attempt to contact you to discuss the situation no later than 36 days after the delinquency and again within 36 days after each subsequent delinquency. No later than 45 days after you miss a payment, the servicer must inform you in writing about loss mitigation options that might be available. The servicer must do so again no later than 45 days after each missed payment for as long as you remain delinquent. The servicer does not, however, have to provide the written notice more than once during any 180-day period. Some exceptions apply, like if you've filed bankruptcy or asked the servicer not to contact you pursuant to the Fair Debt Collection Practices Act and the servicer is subject to this law.

Single point of contact. Federal law also requires the servicer to assign personnel to help you by the time you fall 45 days delinquent. This requirement is technically called the "continuity of contact" rule, but is often referred to as the "single point of contact" requirement. Personnel must be accessible to you by phone and able to advise you about the status of your loss mitigation application and applicable timelines.

Because of this rule, lenders now have lower loan-to-employee ratios and provide improved service when it comes to loss mitigation. (In the past, servicers were overwhelmed with loss mitigation requests and didn't have enough staff to keep up with all of the requests for help.)

Loss mitigation applications. If you submit a loss mitigation application 45 days or more before a foreclosure sale, the servicer must acknowledge it within five days, excluding weekends and holidays, after receiving the application. The servicer must also tell you whether it needs more information and, if so, what information it needs.

Generally, the servicer is required to evaluate the application for all loss mitigation options within 30 days after receiving it. A servicer generally doesn't have to review more than one loss mitigation application from you. But if you catch up on payments after submitting a complete loss mitigation application, you're eligible for reevaluation. This benefit should prove useful if, after a modification, you fall behind again due to a hardship, such as a job loss or the death of your spouse.

Payment-Deferral Option After a Coronavirus Forbearance

A CFPB interim final rule allows servicers to get out of complying with some of the mortgage servicing requirements discussed in this section if they offer payment deferrals to borrowers who finish coronavirus-related forbearances. (See "Forbearances During the Coronavirus Pandemic," below). If you accept the servicer's payment-deferral offer, you pay the forborne payments when:

- you sell the house
- you refinance the current mortgage
- the mortgage insurance on an FHA-insured loan terminates, or
- the loan matures.

You won't have to pay the overdue amounts in an immediate lump sum or through a repayment plan. This kind of payment-deferral plan isn't limited to just federally backed mortgage loans; all borrowers with coronavirus-related forbearances are potentially covered.

Under the CFPB rule, the servicer can provide you with this kind of payment deferral based upon an evaluation of an incomplete loss mitigation application. If the servicer offers a deferral based on an incomplete application, it doesn't have to try to get additional information from you to complete your application or evaluate you for any other loss mitigation possibilities. It also doesn't have to provide an incomplete acknowledgment notice. But be aware that most foreclosure protections under federal law kick in after you submit a *complete* loss mitigation application.

Restrictions on foreclosure when you request help. If you submit a complete loss mitigation application more than 37 days before a foreclosure sale, the servicer may not move for a foreclosure judgment or order of sale, or conduct a foreclosure sale, until it evaluates the application and:

- informs you that you're not eligible for any loss mitigation option and the time to appeal is over if you're eligible to appeal (the servicer must give you the reasons if it denies you a trial or permanent loan modification option)
- you reject all loss mitigation offers, or
- you fail to comply with the terms of a loss mitigation option such as a trial modification.

You can appeal a loan modification denial so long as the complete loss mitigation application was received 90 or more days prior to a scheduled foreclosure sale.

If you submit your application 37 days or fewer before a foreclosure sale, the servicer must review the application in accordance with any requirements established by the owner or assignee of your mortgage loan.

Your time frame to accept or reject an offer. If you submit a complete loss mitigation application 90 days or more before a foreclosure sale, the servicer must give you at least 14 days to accept or reject an offer of a loss mitigation option. If a complete loss mitigation application is received less than 90 days before a foreclosure sale, but more than 37 days before a foreclosure sale, the servicer must give you at least seven days to accept or reject a loss mitigation offer.

Additional laws. Since the laws went into effect in 2014, the Consumer Financial Protection Bureau has finalized additional rules and made changes to some of the existing laws including:

- Servicers must communicate with, and provide protections to, family members who inherit a home upon the death of the borrower. These "successors in interest" must receive the same protections under mortgage servicing rules as the original borrower.

- Servicers must give additional information to borrowers who are in bankruptcy, including providing periodic statements and an early intervention notice letting the borrower know about loss mitigation options.
- Servicers must notify the borrower when a loss mitigation application is complete.

More information about the rules can be found at www.consumer finance.gov. (Run a search for "mortgage servicing rules" and follow the links.)

Also, some states, like California, Colorado, Nevada, and Minnesota, have passed laws that restrict dual tracking and provide other protections to homeowners facing foreclosure. Talk to an attorney to find out what foreclosure protection laws your state has in place and how these laws might be able to help you.

Despite these laws, homeowners and consumer advocates have found that servicers often don't comply and continue to conduct foreclosure sales before properly reviewing modification requests. You should be aware of when a foreclosure sale might happen and know the date before which you should take other steps to prevent the foreclosure sale—such as filing for bankruptcy or suing to stop the foreclosure in nonjudicial foreclosure states.

The lessons are obvious: Get started as soon as you can, and be assertive if you don't get a timely response.

If a foreclosure sale is imminent—two weeks should have the alarm bells ringing—consult a lawyer immediately. You might want to file bankruptcy to halt the sale. Bankruptcy is the only sure way to stop an impending sale. (See Chs. 5 and 6 for more on bankruptcy.)

CAUTION

Avoid foreclosure rescue scams. Companies that offer to rescue you from foreclosure on the eve of a foreclosure sale are all too often scammers. (See "Don't Get Scammed by a Foreclosure 'Rescue' Company," in Ch. 1.)

Why Lenders Sometimes Delay Foreclosing

Just because a lender can foreclose doesn't mean it will. Lenders delay foreclosing for a number of reasons.

Delay can be due to abrupt policy changes by major banks, whether they are servicers, investors, or lenders. For example, when word leaks out about an irregular practice engaged in by one lender, both that lender and other lenders will announce a moratorium on foreclosures until they investigate the matter further.

Take, for example, the "robosigning" scandal in 2010, which was uncovered in a deposition in a Chapter 13 bankruptcy. In the deposition, a bank official admitted to signing thousands of documents every week, falsely stating under oath that he had personal knowledge of the information in those documents. It turned out that this practice, known as robosigning, was used by a broad spectrum of mortgage servicers and entities seeking foreclosures in judicial foreclosure states. Once word of the robosigning scandal spread, virtually all the major servicers and lenders announced temporary holds on foreclosures, at least in judicial foreclosure states where signed affidavits typically are required. This delay lasted for several months.

Delay is also frequently caused by changes in federal or state law or federal regulations that require banks to take additional steps before initiating foreclosure. Lenders and servicers often back off from foreclosing until they're confident they have appropriate procedures in place to comply with the latest requirements.

RESOURCE

Looking for a lawyer? Asking for a referral to an attorney from someone you trust can be a good way to find legal help. Also, two sites that are part of the Nolo family, Lawyers.com and Avvo.com, provide excellent and free lawyer directories. These directories allow you to search by location and area of law, and list detailed information about and reviews of lawyers.

Whether you're just starting your lawyer search or researching particular attorneys, visit www.lawyers.com/find-a-lawyer and www.avvo.com/find-a-lawyer.

Foreclosure Moratoriums During the Coronavirus Crisis

The Department of Housing and Urban Development (HUD), the Department of Veterans Affairs (VA), the Department of Agriculture (USDA), and the Federal Housing Finance Agency (FHFA) set foreclosure moratoriums for federally backed mortgage loans, including FHA-insured, VA-guaranteed, USDA loans, and Fannie Mae- and Freddie Mac-backed loans through at least June 30, 2021.

Also, many states and localities imposed a foreclosure suspension when the coronavirus pandemic began. Many of these moratoriums have expired, but some are still in place. To find out whether any moratoriums are ongoing in your area, talk to a foreclosure lawyer. You can also find the latest developments at www.nolo.com/legal-updates/legal-updates-for-foreclosure.

Using a HUD-Approved Housing Counselor

As a general rule, the sooner you talk to a HUD-approved housing counselor, the better. These counselors work for free (they're paid through government grants and, in some cases, grants from major mortgage lenders who really do want to avoid foreclosures if at all possible) and are well trained in the various foreclosure-prevention programs and techniques of negotiation. You can have no better advocate if you're trying to avoid a foreclosure or get a mortgage modification.

When you call a HUD-approved counselor, you will be scheduled for an interview (by phone or in person) that will probably take between 60 and 90 minutes. The counselor will want to review your income, your debts, your property, your mortgage, the value of your home, and the type of arrangement you think you can live with. You can expect your housing counselor to:

- review your financial situation and spending habits
- help you set up a budget and determine the maximum amount you can pay toward your mortgage payments

- explore why you fell behind in payments and document these reasons so you can include them in a hardship letter or affidavit
- tell you about available options
- help you figure out the best solution for your circumstances, and
- propose a recommendation for your next steps.

Finding a HUD-Approved Counselor

The federal Department of Housing and Urban Development (HUD) has a list of approved counselors. You can find a counselor at www.hud.gov (search for "Talk to a Housing Counselor") or by calling 800-569-4287.

You can also find a counselor by visiting the Homeownership Preservation Foundation at https://995hope.org or by calling 888-995-4673.

For general information about HUD-approved housing counselors, visit the Making Home Affordable website at www.makinghome affordable.gov. (While the programs under the Making Home Affordable initiative are no longer available, the website still offers useful information for homeowners who need mortgage help.)

TIP

Know your options if you don't use a HUD counselor. If you decide to handle the loss mitigation process on your own, first get a good understanding of the different types of options available, such as loan modifications, repayment plans, forbearance agreements, short sales, and deeds in lieu of foreclosure. (Loan modifications, repayment plans, and forbearance agreements are discussed later in this chapter, while short sales and deeds in lieu of foreclosure are covered in Ch. 8.)

Once you call your servicer or your HUD-approved housing counselor contacts the servicer on your behalf, the servicer will, in most cases, send you a loss mitigation package of forms, along with some information about your options. Your counselor can help you fill out these forms and contact the servicer for you during the loss mitigation process.

The servicer will have some discretion to make deals, but will have to contact the lender for anything out of the ordinary. For example, say you're three months behind on your mortgage because you were laid off, but you're now back at work and can make up the missed payments over six months in addition to meeting your current obligation. Most mortgage servicers have authority to sign off on this kind of short-term repayment arrangement. But if you need considerably longer to make up the missed payments, the servicer might have to get permission from the lender.

If Your Case Is Easy to Resolve

You've missed only two or three payments because of a temporary economic setback through no fault of your own, and you can show that you'll be able to make your payments in the future.

The counselor will call your mortgage servicer's dedicated loss mitigation hotline and probably get a resolution on the spot. Typically, you'll get a repayment agreement (see below) that lets you make up the missed payments over a period of three, six, or nine months, depending on your situation, along with paying your regular mortgage payment. You probably won't get a longer repayment plan because borrowers tend to have trouble making bigger than usual payments for an extended period. Alternatively, you might qualify for a forbearance agreement (see below), in which the lender gives you permission to make reduced mortgage payments—or no payments at all—for a while. You might qualify for a forbearance agreement if you're currently having trouble making the payments, but you can convince the servicer that you'll be able to afford them in the near future.

It's hard to generalize about how long it will take to get an agreement but these types of cases are usually resolved pretty quickly. Sometimes, one phone call is all it takes.

Information to Gather Before You Call

- Information about your first mortgage loan (have your monthly mortgage statement handy).
- Recent bank statements.
- Recent pay stubs and other income documentation.
- Utility bill showing your name and address.
- Benefit statements from Social Security, disability, unemployment, retirement, or public assistance.
- Your last two tax returns.
- If you're self-employed, an up-to-date profit and loss statement.
- Monthly household expenses.
- Information about any second mortgage or home equity line of credit on the home.
- Account balances and monthly payments due on all of your credit cards, student loans, car loans, and so on.
- Information about your savings and other assets.

If You Need Serious Help to Keep the House

You've missed four or five payments and are on the verge of foreclosure. If you're going to be able to make future payments, you need some type of modification, and you need a way to deal with the missed payments.

You'll work with the counselor to prepare and submit a loss mitigation application to the servicer. If the application is approved, the lender will modify your mortgage loan, which will make it possible to stay in your house.

In the past, servicers were unable to keep up with loss mitigation requests, and those who needed a modification to avoid a foreclosure were often disappointed when their request was denied, or the house was sold while the application sat in limbo. Now, mainly due to changes in the law, like the "continuity of contact" rule discussed earlier in this chapter, servicers generally try to work with those who are facing financial difficulties to keep them in their home if at all possible. They've increased their personnel and streamlined the process to stay current in responding to loan modification applications.

Can a HUD-Approved Housing Counselor Always Help You?

Housing counselors can do a lot, but they're limited by servicer and lender policies known as "loss mitigation guidelines." Under the guidelines, you might not qualify for a mortgage workout no matter what you or the counselor does. The days of actually negotiating a loan modification are long gone. Now, the loss mitigation process is ruled strictly by numbers and whether you meet specific eligibility criteria.

Still, even if you think you won't qualify for a modification, it doesn't hurt to talk to a counselor and submit a loss mitigation request to the servicer—either before the foreclosure officially starts or even if the foreclosure has already begun. Under federal and some state laws, the servicer can't start or continue with a foreclosure while your application is pending, and you might get a more affordable mortgage payment for the future. Or you might be eligible for another loss mitigation option that you hadn't previously considered.

If the Only Way to Avoid Foreclosure Is to Sell or File for Bankruptcy

If the foreclosure has already started, you're unlikely to have enough income to stay current on your payments (even if they're reduced, and even if you could reduce your overall debt load by filing for Chapter 7 bankruptcy).

Your counselor will probably tell you that a satisfactory modification isn't going to happen. The counselor will likely suggest unloading your house in a short sale or offering a deed in lieu of foreclosure to the lender.

Some counselors might suggest that you consult a lawyer about the possibility of filing for bankruptcy. Many, however, avoid talking about bankruptcy because the lenders (or in many cases, their funders) don't like it. Keep in mind that foreclosures aren't always a bad thing, and bankruptcy is sometimes the most appropriate response. For example, a short sale might be marginally better for your credit record in the future, but you most likely would have to leave your house much sooner than you would if you let the foreclosure continue. You would give up the opportunity to save money by staying in your house for months— perhaps many months—without making payments. Finally, in a short sale you might be liable for the deficiency or, if your lender forgives you for the deficiency, the income tax on that forgiven debt, whereas bankruptcy would help you avoid these liabilities. Keep in mind that a counselor who attempts to convince you to do a short sale or talk you out of bankruptcy could be passing on the lenders' and servicers' views and might not best serve your economic interests.

If you still want to keep your home, even if your counselor tells you a loss mitigation option isn't possible, it's time to think about bankruptcy. Filing for Chapter 13 bankruptcy might allow you to keep your house. (See Ch. 5.) At this stage, filing for Chapter 7 bankruptcy won't keep you in your house in the long run, but it can help you stay there payment-free for an extra couple of months. (See Ch. 6.)

Basic Loss Mitigation Options

Some loss mitigation options—like a repayment plan, forbearance agreement, or loan modification—permit the borrower to keep the home. Other alternatives, like a short sale or deed in lieu of foreclosure, allow the borrower to give up the property without going through a foreclosure. Here are the basic options if you want to keep your home. (See Ch. 8 to learn about various alternatives if you decide to leave your house.)

Repayment Plan: Keeping Current and Catching Up

With a repayment plan, you arrange to make up missed payments over time and stay current on your ongoing payments. This approach is usually the most feasible and easiest to get from your servicer. For it to work, your income will have to be able to cover both current and makeup payments.

For example, if you're three months behind on your monthly payments of $1,500 a month (a total of $4,500 behind), you might qualify for plan in which you pay $750 extra each month over the next six months, or $2,250 a month for six months. At the end of the repayment period, you resume making your regular monthly payments of $1,500 a month.

The longer it will take you to catch up, the likelier it is that your servicer will have to get permission from the lender. If the lender will have to sign off on your proposed plan, and you're running up against your foreclosure sale date, you should definitely ask—in writing—for an extension that the servicer thinks will be sufficient to either work out an arrangement or give you time to fight the foreclosure. Some servicers will tell you right up front whether a proposed plan will work or is off the table. Other servicers will string you along. You'll just have to make sure that you aren't forgoing other possible solutions (such as bankruptcy, a court action challenging the foreclosure, a statutory reinstatement, or redemption of the mortgage), just because the servicer tells you a solution is in the pipeline.

Forbearance: Getting a Break From Payments

Under a forbearance agreement, the servicer (or lender) agrees to reduce or suspend your mortgage payments for a specific amount of time. In exchange, you promise to start making your full payment at the end of the forbearance period, plus an extra amount to pay down the missed payments. Alternatively, you might be able to pay the skipped amounts:

- in a lump sum

- in a payment deferral program (the lender defers repayment of the entire forbearance amount, usually until you sell the home, refinance the property, or pay off the loan), or
- through a loan modification (see below) in which the lender adds the unpaid amounts to the loan balance.

Forbearance is most common in situations when someone can't make any payments now but will likely be able to make them in the future.

In forbearance, unlike a repayment plan, the lender agrees in advance for you to miss or reduce payments for a while. Forbearance for three to six months is typical, though a longer period might be possible, depending on the lender's guidelines and your situation.

RESOURCE

For updates to the information in this book, visit www.nolo.com/ back-of-book/FIFO.html. That page, which is dedicated to this book, is where we alert readers to significant changes since this edition published.

Don't Forget: Statutory Reinstatement or Redemption

Many states give you, by law, the right to reinstate your mortgage (make it current) or redeem the loan (pay off the entire loan). (See Ch. 1.) Your state's page in the appendix lists the time limits for the exercise of these procedures if they're available in your state. Typically, you must complete them before the foreclosure sale date, although some states give you some time after the sale date to redeem the property and reclaim the home by paying off the debt in full, plus interest and costs.

If you think either of these options might work for you, pay attention to the deadlines. If your funds aren't delivered on time, the foreclosure sale will proceed, or you might miss your opportunity to redeem. So, you could lose your home if a courier delay happens or due to a bank processing error. If you can, hand-deliver your funds in-person to the proper contact or arrange a wire transfer well before the deadline. Or, if you mail in your funds, send the check via an overnight courier so you can track it.

Forbearances During the Coronavirus Pandemic

Under the Coronavirus Aid, Relief, and Economic Security (CARES) Act, homeowners with a federally backed mortgage loan experiencing a financial hardship due to COVID-19 can get a forbearance that lasts up to 180 days and can be extended up to 180 additional days, longer in some cases.

A "federally backed mortgage loan" includes any loan that's secured by a first or subordinate lien on residential real property, including individual units of condominiums and cooperatives, designed principally for the occupancy of one to four families. The property must also be:

- insured by the Federal Housing Administration (FHA)
- insured under section 255 of the National Housing Act
- guaranteed under section 184 or 184A of the Housing and Community Development Act of 1992
- guaranteed or insured by the Department of Veterans Affairs (VA)
- guaranteed, insured, or made by the Department of Agriculture (USDA), or
- purchased or securitized by Fannie Mae or Freddie Mac.

If you want a forbearance and have one of these types of loans, contact your loan servicer and explain that you've suffered a financial hardship due to the COVID-19 emergency. The servicer isn't allowed to ask for any documentation to support your request.

At the time of writing, the different federal agencies were taking various approaches to deadlines for requesting forbearances. For FHA-insured, VA-guaranteed, and USDA loans, the deadline was June 30, 2021. The Federal Housing Finance Agency, which regulates Fannie Mae and Freddie Mac, hadn't issued guidance giving a deadline to request an initial forbearance. So it's unclear exactly how long borrowers get to request forbearances for Fannie Mae- and Freddie Mac-backed mortgage loans. You can find the latest developments at www.nolo.com/legal-updates/legal-updates-for-foreclosure.

It's important to note that forbearance isn't the same as forgiveness; you'll still owe the skipped amounts after the forbearance period ends. You might be able to pay the forbearance amounts in one of several ways discussed above: a lump sum payment, a repayment plan, a payment-deferral

> ### Forbearances During the Coronavirus Pandemic (continued)
>
> program (you pay when you sell the home, refinance the property, or pay off the loan), or with a loan modification that adds the unpaid amount to the loan balance. Your options will depend on the entity that guarantees or owns your loan. FHA, VA, USDA, Fannie Mae, or Freddie Mac have issued official guidance stating that a lump-sum payment to bring the loan current isn't required at the end of a COVID-19 forbearance unless the borrower can afford it.
>
> Even if your loan isn't federally backed, your servicer might offer you a forbearance or another form of relief, like a waiver of late fees or a loan modification. Also, your state might provide special protections or programs for mortgage borrowers affected by the coronavirus crisis.

Modification: Lowering Your Payments

Many homeowners can't come close to making their current payments now or in the future. Some of the many reasons you might need a modification include:

- Your income stream was disrupted by a layoff or injury, and a new job at the same pay isn't available.
- Your interest rate reset higher (currently not a big problem due to continued low short-term interest rates engineered by the Federal Reserve).
- Something happened in your life requiring you to change your budget—for instance, a medical emergency or a divorce.

If you can't afford your mortgage payment now and won't be able to anytime soon, a modification is the best approach to remaining in your house. Unlike repayment plans and forbearance, modifications are designed to lower your monthly payments over the long term. Your modification options generally depend on what entity, like FHA, VA, USDA, Fannie Mae, or Freddie Mac, owns or guarantees your loan (see below). For example, Fannie Mae and Freddie Mac offer the

Flex Modification program. If you have an FHA-insured loan, you're entitled to a special loss mitigation process that might help you qualify for a modification. Also, almost all lenders offer proprietary (in-house) modifications to borrowers struggling to make their monthly mortgage payments and who meet eligibility criteria for assistance.

To be eligible for a mortgage modification, along with meeting other investor-specific guidelines, you'll generally need to show that:

- the home is your primary residence
- you've gone through a financial hardship, like you had to take a lower-paying job or you went through a divorce and experienced a loss of household income, and
- that you have enough steady income to make regular payments under a modification.

To apply for a modification, you or your housing counselor will need to contact your servicer's loss mitigation department, sometimes called a "home retention" department, and ask for a loss mitigation application. You can find contact information on your monthly mortgage statement or the servicer's webpage. You'll need to submit the application to your servicer and likely include:

- a completed questionnaire that includes your personal information, mortgage information, property information, and so forth
- recent pay stubs or a profit and loss statement if self-employed
- bank statements
- tax returns
- an income and expense financial worksheet, and
- a hardship statement or affidavit.

Depending on the situation, you might also have to provide additional documentation or answer questions from the servicer. In most cases, you'll have to complete a trial period plan, often for around three months, to demonstrate you can afford the new amount before the loan is permanently modified.

Tips for Completing Your Modification Application

Here are some suggestions for completing your application:

- Apply as soon as possible. It's best to submit your application once you know you'll have trouble making your payments or shortly after you fall behind. If you take several weeks or months to put your paperwork together, you'll have less time to work out a foreclosure alternative.
- Fill out all of the paperwork (don't forget to sign the application) and attach any and all documentation that the servicer requests. For example, if the servicer requests copies of your two most recent pay stubs, you must actually send your latest pay stubs. Do not send two random pay stubs that you just happened to have handy.
- When sending items such as copies of your bank statements, be sure to send copies of all statement pages—even if they're blank. Send all of the forms and supporting documentation together, so it's less likely that any items will get misplaced.
- If you mail the application to the servicer, send it by some method you can track (FedEx, UPS, etc.).
- Write your name and complete loan number at the top of each page.
- Don't send illegible documents. When you send your paperwork to the servicer, be sure that all pages are readable. Otherwise, the servicer might deem them unacceptable and deny your application. The servicer won't put in a lot of effort to decipher words or numbers that are potentially unclear. It's in your best interest to make it easy for the servicer to read the documents.
- Don't pay for modification assistance. Loan modification companies charge $1,000 or more for services that you can get for free from a HUD-approved housing counselor. If you decide to pay for help, use a qualified attorney—not one affiliated with a modification company. Hiring an attorney might be a good idea if your servicer

Tips for Completing Your Modification Application (continued)

isn't following the laws that govern the process. An attorney can help you enforce your rights, review the conditions of any modification that the lender offers, make sure the servicer doesn't include any illegal charges in the total balance (like improper fees or advances), and verify that the modification is in your best interest.

• After you apply, be sure to keep all correspondence received from the servicer, such as a confirmation letter that the servicer received your complete application or a letter telling you that certain items are missing. This information could be useful if you want to challenge a foreclosure by showing the servicer didn't comply with servicing laws.

• Be sure to learn about laws that protect you in the process. Servicers sometimes make mistakes when processing borrowers' modification applications. Find out about the federal and state laws that protect you in the loss mitigation process so you can enforce your rights.

Some of the ways your servicer might modify a mortgage to reduce your payments are by:

• Reducing your mortgage's interest rate to the current market rate if it's lower than what you're supposed to be paying now.

• Converting the loan from a variable rate to a fixed rate, which could bring the payment down if the interest has already reset and will prevent a jump in payments if a reset looms in the future.

• Extending the loan's repayment period—for instance, from 30 years to 40—which will bring down the monthly payment but delay for many years the time when you can begin to build equity.

• Forbearing some of the principal balance. "Forbearing" the principal sets aside a portion of the total debt before calculating the borrower's monthly payment. The borrower typically has to pay the set-aside portion in a balloon payment when refinancing or selling the home, or when the loan matures.

- Capitalizing the overdue amounts and reamortize the loan. This process involves adding the amount of the missed payments to the principal balance and, usually, issuing a new interest rate for a new period. Reamortization can result in an increased payment (for example, if the interest rate stays the same or increases) or a reduced one (for example, if the interest rate is reduced and the loan period is increased).

Before signing off on new mortgage terms, ask yourself whether you'd be better off keeping your house or giving it up. If you can get a lower payment, you might be more inclined to keep it. But the decision might depend on the size of the reduction and whether you truly can afford the modified payment. It might make more sense to use the foreclosure process as a way to save some money. If you decide to let the foreclosure go through, the modification process is likely to lengthen the time you can stay in the home because the servicer must suspend foreclosure proceedings during the processing period.

The Impact of a Loan Modification on Your Credit

The impact of a loan modification on your credit mainly depends on how the lender reports the modification. According to FICO, the largest and most ubiquitous credit scoring company, if your lender reports the modification as "paid as agreed," the modification will not affect your FICO score. But if the lender reports the modification as "paying under a partial payment agreement" or something else indicating you're not paying as agreed, this kind of reporting will probably negatively impact your credit score—although it depends on your overall credit profile. And any impact on your credit will certainly not be as bad as a short sale, deed in lieu of foreclosure, or foreclosure. Once you start making timely payments under the modification, your credit should improve. And keep in mind that as the negative information ages, its impact on your credit will fade.

Loss Mitigation Options for Government-Backed Mortgages

Special loss mitigation options, for both keeping or giving up your home, are available to you if your mortgage is:

- owned or guaranteed by the Federal National Mortgage Association (Fannie Mae) or the Federal Home Loan Mortgage Association (Freddie Mac)
- insured by the Federal Housing Administration (FHA), which operates under regulations and guidelines issued by the federal Department of Housing and Urban Development (HUD)
- guaranteed by the Veterans Administration (VA), or
- financed by a direct or guaranteed loan from the Rural Housing Service (RHS).

Your mortgage servicer can give you more information about the special options available for your particular type of mortgage, including those discussed below, and even distribute any explanatory materials produced by the governmental entity for its customers.

Fannie Mae and Freddie Mac Loans

Fannie Mae and Freddie Mac offer the Flex Modification program, among other types of modification options, to borrowers having trouble making their mortgage payments. Eligible borrowers can expect to receive a 20% payment reduction through a mortgage modification.

With a Flex Modification, the servicer lowers the borrower's payment by:

- capitalizing the overdue amounts
- adjusting the interest rate
- extending the term of the loan, or
- forbearing some of the principal balance.

Both Fannie Mae and Freddie Mac require their servicers to review all borrowers for a Flex Modification after the borrower is 90 days behind in payments. So, your servicer might offer you this type of modification, even if you don't apply for it. But you can also apply, as long as a foreclosure sale hasn't happened yet.

How to Find Out Who Owns or Backs Your Mortgage Loan

- The easiest way to determine if any of these entities own or back your loan is to call the servicer and ask.
- You can also send a qualified written request to your servicer asking who owns or guarantees the loan.
- If your loan is in the Mortgage Electronic Registration System (MERS) (see Ch. 7), you might be able to find out who owns or backs your loan by calling MERS at 888-679-6377 or running a check on the MERS website at www.mersinc.org/homeowners/mers-servicerid.
- Check the Fannie Mae lookup tool (www.knowyouroptions.com/loanlookup) and Freddie Mac loan-lookup tool (https://loanlookup.freddiemac.com) online to find out if Fannie Mae or Freddie Mac owns your loan. Many loans are sold to these government-sponsored enterprises.
- You could look for an FHA case number on your mortgage contract. Sometimes, though, loans lose their FHA-insured status. Call your servicer or HUD's National Servicing Center at 877-622-8525 if you have questions about your loan's status. You can also check your billing statement to see if you pay a mortgage insurance premium (MIP). MIP is what FHA calls its mortgage insurance. If you're paying MIP, then you have an FHA-insured loan.
- VA-guaranteed loans contain specific language in the note and mortgage that identifies it as a VA loan. Also, fees paid to the VA will be shown in the closing documents.
- Borrowers with mortgages directly extended by the USDA's Rural Housing Service (RHS) should be aware that they have this kind of loan. But homeowners with privately serviced RHS-guaranteed loans might not know about their loan's status. To find out if you have an RHS-guaranteed loan, ask the servicer or check your closing documents from when you took out the loan. To learn more, go to the USDA Rural Development website at www.rd.usda.gov/about-rd/agencies/rural-housing-service.

To be eligible for a Flex Modification, Fannie Mae or Freddie Mac must own your loan. To find out if either Fannie Mae or Freddie Mac owns your loan, call your servicer or use the Fannie Mae and Freddie Mac online loan lookup tools (see "How to Find Out Who Owns or Backs Your Mortgage Loan," above). Also, you, your home, and your mortgage loan have to meet specific criteria, like:

- the loan must be a conventional first mortgage
- you must have a stable income that will support a monthly payment, and
- you must have taken out your mortgage at least 12 months before being evaluated for a Flex Modification.

The requirements to get this type of modification are rather extensive and complicated. Call your servicer to find out if you qualify and to learn how to apply.

Also, Consider Refinancing Your Mortgage

Generally, refinancing is available only if you have equity in your home and you have an acceptable credit score. But Fannie Mae offers the "High Loan-to-Value Refinance Option," and Freddie Mac offers an "Enhanced Relief Refinance" for borrowers with high loan-to-value (LTV) ratios. So, you might qualify even if you're underwater on the loan (you owe more than your home is worth).

To be eligible, you must have an existing Fannie Mae or Freddie Mac loan and meet other criteria, like having no more than one 30-day delinquency in the past 12 months. To find out if you have a Fannie Mae or Freddie Mac loan, use their online lookup tools. To learn more about eligibility criteria, call your servicer or go to Fannie Mae's High LTV Refinance Option website at https://singlefamily.fanniemae.com/originating-underwriting/mortgage-products/high-ltv-refinance-option or Freddie Mac's Enhanced Relief Refinance Mortgage website at https://sf.freddiemac.com/working-with-us/origination-underwriting/mortgage-products/enhanced-relief-refinance-mortgage.

If you're not underwater on your loan, you could be eligible to complete a traditional refinance.

Before the servicer finalizes the modification, you'll have to successfully complete a trial period plan that normally lasts three or four months. If you make all of the trial payments, you'll get a permanent loan modification that likely waives previous late charges, penalties, and other fees.

Fannie Mae and Freddie Mac also have other home-retention options, including repayment plans, forbearances, payment deferrals, and disaster relief. (If you decide to give up the property, see Ch. 8. Fannie Mae and Freddie Mac also offer short sales and deeds in lieu of foreclosure.)

To contact Fannie Mae, call 800-2Fannie (800-232-6643). To contact Freddie Mac, call 800-FREDDIE (800-373-3343) and ask to speak to someone about loss mitigation.

FHA-Insured Loans

The FHA, part of HUD, offers protections and options to homeowners who have FHA-insured loans and are facing foreclosure. Under HUD policy, the loan servicer must review a borrower who has an FHA-insured loan and is behind in payments, or about to fall behind, for loss mitigation alternatives using what's called a "waterfall" process.

In this process, the servicer usually, subject to a few exceptions, has to evaluate the borrower to determine which, if any, of the below options is appropriate to avoid a foreclosure. The servicer must evaluate the borrower for these loss mitigation alternatives in the following specific order, and once a borrower is deemed eligible for a particular option, the evaluation stops:

- forbearance (informal, formal, or a special forbearance)
- repayment plan
- loan modification
- partial claim
- loan modification plus partial claim
- preforeclosure sale (short sale), or
- deed in lieu of foreclosure.

Informal and Formal Forbearances

Under a forbearance plan, the borrower makes reduced payments, or doesn't make any payments, for a specific amount of time.

- **Informal forbearance.** An "informal forbearance plan" is an oral agreement between the servicer and borrower. The servicer (on the lender's behalf) agrees to let the borrower make reduced payments or to stop making payments for a period of three months or less.
- **Formal forbearance.** A "formal forbearance plan" is a written agreement that allows the borrower to make reduced payments or to stop making payments for a period greater than three months, but not more than six months unless otherwise authorized by HUD.
- **FHA special forbearance for unemployed homeowners.** HUD's Special Forbearance-Unemployment option is for borrowers who've become unemployed and can't continue to make their monthly mortgage payments.

Repayment Plan

The servicer will also evaluate whether the borrower has enough income and a sufficiently reasonable payment for a repayment plan.

Loan Modification

Under HUD guidelines, a modification might:

- lower the interest rate
- capitalize the delinquent principal, interest, or escrow amounts
- extend the time the borrower has to repay the mortgage, or
- reamortize the balance due.

While the federal Home Affordable Modification Program (HAMP) and its associated programs expired at the end of 2016, FHA still calls its main loan modification program "FHA-HAMP."

COVID-19 Loss Mitigation Options for FHA-Insured Mortgages

FHA offers an expanded list of home retention alternatives to help homeowners bring their mortgage current at the end of a COVID-19 forbearance. The servicer must include these options in the waterfall process.

First, the servicer must review the borrower for a COVID-19 National Emergency Standalone Partial Claim. Generally, a partial claim (see below) is an interest-free loan from HUD to get caught up on the overdue payments. The loan doesn't have to be repaid until the first mortgage is paid off. A COVID-19 National Emergency Standalone Partial Claim takes all overdue mortgage amounts and puts them in a separate, junior lien of up to 30% of the mortgage's unpaid principal balance. This junior lien is repayable when the mortgage ends, which, for most borrowers, is when they sell or refinance their home.

If the homeowner doesn't qualify for the COVID-19 National Emergency Standalone Partial Claim, the servicer must consider these additional alternatives in the following order at or before the end of the borrower's forbearance period:

- **The COVID-19 Owner-Occupant Loan Modification.** This type of loan modification alters the interest rate and term of the existing mortgage. It's for homeowners who don't qualify for the COVID-19 National Emergency Standalone Partial Claim.
- **The COVID-19 Combination Partial Claim and Loan Modification.** With this option, the homeowner gets a partial claim up to 30% of the unpaid principal balance, and any remaining amounts are dealt with in a loan modification. This option is available to homeowners who aren't eligible for just a partial claim or modification alone.
- **The COVID-19 FHA-HAMP Combination Loan Modification and Partial Claim.** This option reduces the amount of documentation needed to obtain a modification and partial claim. It's available to those homeowners who aren't eligible for any other home retention solution under the waterfall. (As noted above, while the federal Home Affordable Modification Program or "HAMP" and its associated programs expired at the end of 2016, FHA still calls its main loan modification program "FHA-HAMP.")

These options are available to homeowners whose mortgages were current or less than 30 days past due as of March 1, 2020.

Partial Claim

A partial claim is an interest-free loan from HUD to get caught up on the overdue payments. The loan doesn't have to be repaid until the first mortgage is paid off, like when you sell the property. Partial claims are sometimes completed along with a loan modification.

Preforeclosure Sale (Short Sale)

A preforeclosure sale (short sale, see Ch. 8) is when the borrower sells the home for less than the amount owed on the mortgage loan. After an FHA preforeclosure sale, the lender can't get a deficiency judgment.

Deed in Lieu of Foreclosure

With a deed in lieu of foreclosure (see Ch. 8), the borrower voluntarily offers the home's deed to HUD in exchange for a release from all obligations under the mortgage. Following an FHA deed in lieu of foreclosure, the lender can't get a deficiency judgment.

If you have an FHA-insured loan, call your servicer to get details about loss mitigation options or the waterfall process. Or, you can call HUD's National Servicing Center at 877-622-8525.

VA-Insured Loans

The main loss mitigation options for borrowers with VA-guaranteed loans are:

- repayment plans
- special forbearance
- modifications
- assumptions (you sell or transfer the property to someone else, and that person takes over the mortgage payments)
- refunding (the VA buys the loan and takes on servicing responsibilities)
- compromise sales (short sales), and
- deeds in lieu of foreclosure.

Borrowers with VA-insured loans should contact their mortgage servicer (the party primarily responsible for helping you avoid foreclosure). If the servicer isn't helpful, a loan technician in one of the various VA Regional Loan Centers can intervene to ensure the servicer explored all options to avoid foreclosure. To learn more, call 877-827-3702 or go to www.benefits.va.gov and click on "Home Loans" and then "Mortgage Servicing Assistance." This website also has a link that will take you to the contact information for the Regional Loan Centers.

Rural Housing Service (RHS) Loans

If your mortgage is a RHA direct or guaranteed loan, you can call the Centralized Servicing Center (CSC) toll-free phone number at 800-414-1226 or go to http://rdhomeloans.usda.gov/fcls.html to learn about loss mitigation options.

Foreclosure Avoidance Mediation Programs

Many states have mediation programs to assist borrowers in finding ways to avoid foreclosure. Some states, such as Oregon and Connecticut, have instituted statewide foreclosure avoidance mediation programs, while in other states, specific counties or municipalities have implemented such programs. The programs vary, but most force the lender to discuss loss mitigation options with you before it can complete the foreclosure. If you participate, you might have a better chance of achieving a foreclosure alternative. Or, by participating, you might be able to delay the foreclosure.

Mediation, sometimes called a "conciliation conference," consists of a meeting between you, your lender, and an impartial third party (the mediator). At the meeting, the parties discuss your financial situation and try to work out a way for you to keep the home or give up the property without going through a foreclosure. Generally, the foreclosure is postponed while the mediation talks are ongoing and, by working together, the parties are sometimes able to reach an agreement to avoid foreclosure by way of a:

- loan modification
- repayment agreement
- forbearance agreement
- short sale, or
- deed in lieu of foreclosure.

Visit the "Foreclosure" area on Nolo.com, for articles on state foreclosure mediation programs. Or check *Home Foreclosures*, by Geoff Walsh, et al. (National Consumer Law Center), for more information on state foreclosure avoidance mediation programs.

Hardest Hit Fund and Other Statewide Mortgage-Relief Programs

In February 2010, the U.S. Department of the Treasury created the Hardest Hit Fund to provide targeted aid to homeowners in those states most affected by the housing market crash. As part of this program, billions in aid money was allocated to the 18 states, plus the District of Columbia, that experienced the most extreme home price declines, as well as high unemployment rates.

Hardest Hit Fund states are Alabama, Arizona, California, Florida, Georgia, Illinois, Indiana, Kentucky, Michigan, Mississippi, Nevada, New Jersey, North Carolina, Ohio, Oregon, Rhode Island, South Carolina, Tennessee, and Washington, D.C. These states (and D.C.) each developed their own programs, administered by that state's housing finance agency, to distribute the funds and assist distressed homeowners in avoiding foreclosure. While all state Hardest Hit Fund programs were scheduled to close by the end of 2020, some have remained open or reopened to help homeowners affected by the coronavirus pandemic.

The available assistance programs vary from state to state, but could include:

- mortgage payment assistance for unemployed or underemployed homeowners
- principal reductions to help homeowners obtain more affordable mortgages
- bringing a delinquent mortgage current with a one-time payment
- eliminating homeowners' second lien loans, and
- helping struggling homeowners transition into more affordable residences after moving out of their homes.

To qualify for assistance, you'll have to submit an application and meet certain criteria. Eligibility requirements vary from state to state; however, they usually include the following:

- You must be a resident of the state in which you apply for assistance.
- You must occupy the property.
- Your total annual income must be less than the amount designated by the state program.
- You must have limited financial resources.
- You must have suffered a hardship, such as unemployment, underemployment, divorce, the death of a spouse, or medical hardship.
- The unpaid principal balance on your mortgage cannot exceed a particular amount.

In many state programs, the homeowner will receive a 0% interest loan (paid directly to the servicer) that is forgiven over a specified period (generally 20% over five years). If you stop occupying the property as your principal residence before the end of the forgiveness period, you'll have to repay the remaining balance.

COVID-19 Homeowner Assistance Fund

The American Rescue Plan Act of 2021, which President Joe Biden signed into law on March 11, 2021, included approximately $10 billion for a Homeowner Assistance Fund. This fund will provide money to the states to establish foreclosure-avoidance and other homeowner-relief programs.

The Homeowner Assistance Fund follows the success of the Hardest Hit Fund and expands that model by providing federal aid to potentially all states to help homeowners stay in their homes. Though states have to apply for funds, and the amount each state gets is based on the average number of unemployed individuals in the state measured over a period of not fewer than three months and not more than 12 months, as well as the total number of mortgagors with mortgage payments that are more than 30 days past due or mortgages in foreclosure.

The state programs, once established, will provide homeowners experiencing a financial hardship due to COVID-19 after January 21, 2020, money to pay for qualified expenses related to mortgages and housing, including:

- mortgage payments
- mortgage reinstatements or other housing-related costs connected to periods of forbearance, delinquency, or default
- principal reductions
- interest rate reductions
- utilities (including electric, gas, home energy, water, and Internet service)
- homeowners' insurance, flood insurance, and mortgage insurance
- homeowners' association dues, condominium owners' association fees, or other common charges, and
- other expenses necessary to promote housing stability for homeowners.

The states have until September 30, 2025, to distribute the money allocated to them from this fund. To find out about homeowner-relief programs in your area, contact your state's housing finance agency. However, homeowners won't be able to get assistance until the states determine eligibility criteria and set up programs to distribute the funds. You can find the latest developments at www.nolo.com/legal-updates/legal-updates-for-foreclosure.

> **CAUTION**
>
> **Beware of scammer copycat websites posing as Hardest Hit Fund application sites.** The Hardest Hit Fund programs never charge a fee for their services. You don't need to pay to apply for assistance.

To find out if the program in your state is still open and what kind of programs are offered, go to https://home.treasury. gov and search for "Hardest Hit Fund." Click on "Hardest Hit Fund (HHF)" and then "Current Program Documents" to find links to each state's program. To get program information from a HUD-approved housing counselor, call 888-995-HOPE (4673).

In addition, some states have started their own programs to provide financial assistance to borrowers affected by COVID-19. To find out if your state has such a program, search online using terms like "emergency mortgage assistance during COVID-19" and the name of your state.

Special Protections for Servicemembers on Active Duty

If you're on active military duty, especially if you took out a mortgage before you went on active duty, you are entitled to a raft of protections against foreclosure. The federal law that provides these benefits is called the Servicemembers Civil Relief Act (SCRA). (50 U.S.C. § 3911 and following.)

Judicial Foreclosure Is Required

Probably the most important protection for families facing a nonjudicial foreclosure (see Ch. 2) is that, if you took out the mortgage before military service, the SCRA requires a court order before your house can be sold in foreclosure. If the lender forecloses without a court order while you're on active duty or within one year thereafter, the sale is invalid (unless you sign a waiver). (50 U.S.C. § 3953.)

Washington Court Says Statute of Limitations for SCRA Claims Is Four Years

In the case of *McGreevey v. PHH Mortgage Corporation*, 897 F.3d 1037 (9th Cir. 2018), the U.S. Court of Appeals for the Ninth Circuit held that a Marine who lost his home to foreclosure waited too long to sue the lender for violating the SCRA. The court said that the federal catchall statute of limitations of four years (28 U.S.C. § 1658(a)) applies to lawsuits claiming foreclosure violations under this federal law. As a result, Jacob McGreevy— a former U.S. Marine challenging a foreclosure that happened in 2010—lost his case because he acted too late. McGreevey was, however, awarded $125,000 under a separate settlement.

Usually, when a federal law like the SCRA doesn't include a limitations period, courts apply the closest state limitations period. Servicemembers can avoid similar statute of limitations issues by making their SCRA claims immediately.

Also, courts tend to interpret the SCRA liberally in favor of military servicemembers. Because judicial foreclosures are much more expensive and typically take much longer than nonjudicial foreclosures, you might have a better chance of working something out with the lender.

You can delay (the legal term is "stay") a foreclosure procedure for a period of time, not less than 90 days, so long as you meet certain criteria and if you request it from the court in writing. (50 U.S.C. § 3932.) A HUD-approved foreclosure counselor (or military legal services if you are deployed out of the country) can help you with a letter to the court.

A Court Can Adjust Your Mortgage

During a foreclosure, the court might provide "equitable" relief as appropriate if your ability to pay or meet the other mortgage obligations is materially affected by your military service. (50 U.S.C. § 3953.) So if you took out the mortgage before going on active duty, the court may reform the mortgage by, for example:

- reducing the mortgage payments, or
- suspending payments altogether during the time you're on active duty.

The court may make an adjustment on its own or in response to your request.

In addition, even if a foreclosure hasn't yet started, you can make an application to a court for mortgage relief, such as a payment reduction or an expanded repayment period if you're behind. Again, you must have taken out the mortgage before going on active duty, and you must apply for the relief during your military service or within 180 days after that. You'll eventually have to repay all of the principal and interest payments that you skipped. (50 U.S.C. § 4021.)

Protections Against Default Judgments

A "default judgment" happens if you fail to respond to a lawsuit, like a judicial foreclosure. The judge then rules against you in your absence. The SCRA generally protects servicemembers against default judgments.

A court can, however, enter a foreclosure judgment against an absent servicemember, but only under certain circumstances. The lender must inform the court if the defendant is in military service. If so, and neither the servicemember—nor an attorney on his or her behalf—appears in the action, the court can't enter a judgment until after the court appoints an attorney to represent the servicemember. If the appointed attorney can't locate the servicemember, the attorney's actions in the case don't waive any defenses the servicemember might have or bind the servicemember. (50 U.S.C. § 3931.)

If for some reason a court does enter a default judgment without complying with these requirements, you can ask the court reopen the judgment if it is entered while you're on active duty or within

60 days after your active duty ends. You must take action to reopen the judgment within 90 days after your release from active duty. To get the judgment reopened, you'll have to show that:

- your military service materially affected your ability in making a defense to the action, and
- you have a meritorious or legal defense to the foreclosure or some part of it. (50 U.S.C. § 3931.)

Interest Rates Must Be Reduced

The interest rate on a mortgage incurred before you entered active duty must be reduced to 6% while you're on active duty and one year thereafter. (50 U.S.C. § 3937.) (The interest rate is also limited to 6% for all other types of obligations, such as car loans and credit cards, while you're on active duty.) Past payments of interest over 6% while you were on active duty must be forgiven (refunded), and the mortgage payment must be reduced to reflect the lower interest rate while it is in force.

To get the interest rate reduction, you must notify the creditor in writing of your duty status and include a copy of the military orders requiring active duty status. You must send this notice no later than 180 days after your active duty status ends. It can be retroactive to the day your active duty started. Keep in mind that you might not get the reduction if a court determines that you can afford the higher rate.

> **EXAMPLE:** Susan is a National Guard member. She and her husband sign a mortgage to buy a house at a subprime interest rate of 9%. Their payments are $1,900 a month. Six months later, Susan is called to active duty and deployed overseas. Her husband continues paying the mortgage at the required rate while Susan serves abroad for 15 months. When she returns home and is released from active duty, she learns that she was entitled to have the mortgage payments reduced while she was on active duty.

> She promptly sends a notice to the lender of her entitlement to the 6% interest rate, with a copy of her deployment orders, and demands that retroactive adjustments be made. She receives a check for $6,000. That's 15 months times $400, the amount her payment would have been lowered had the interest rate reduction been made when she went on active duty.

Lenders can't report negative information to a credit reporting agency just because you asked for or received benefits under the SCRA. Nor can a creditor deny you credit, revoke existing credit, or change the terms on an existing account because you asserted your rights under the SCRA. (50 U.S.C. § 3919.)

More State Protections

In addition to the federal law, many states have their own statutes that provide additional protections for service members. Your state's page in the appendix lists the citations for your state's law.

Mortgage Relief for Borrowers After a Natural Disaster

In the wake of a natural disaster—like a hurricane or wildfire—you might qualify for special foreclosure protections, like a moratorium (a suspension of the foreclosure) or a temporary or permanent reduction in your monthly payment amount. Generally, you can qualify for a moratorium, or other help, if you have an FHA, Fannie Mae, Freddie Mac, or VA loan and you meet specific criteria. If your loan isn't one of these types, you might qualify for financial relief from the Federal Emergency Management Agency (FEMA). Also, lenders and servicers sometimes offer relief options, like forbearances or modifications, to affected homeowners.

Here are a few types of foreclosure relief generally available if you're a victim of a natural disaster.

Federal Housing Administration (FHA) Loans

The U.S. Department of Housing and Urban Development (HUD) often provides a 90-day moratorium on foreclosures of FHA-insured home mortgages following natural disasters, so long as the property was directly affected by the disaster and you don't have other resources, like insurance settlements, to help you catch up. FHA tends to extend moratoriums to 180 days if the disaster affects a large area or is especially severe.

FHA also offers other options, like loan modifications and forbearances, to borrowers who've gone through a disaster and are struggling to make their mortgage payments.

If you have an FHA loan and want to find out if you qualify for any of these protections or options, call your loan servicer.

Veterans Affairs (VA) Loans

During times of natural disasters, the VA encourages loan holders and servicers to:

- establish a 90-day moratorium on initiating new foreclosures, and
- help individuals affected by a natural disaster by offering forbearance or modification of veterans' loans.

Fannie Mae and Freddie Mac Loans

Fannie Mae and Freddie Mac generally implement a 90-day foreclosure sale suspension immediately following a natural disaster if the property is within a federally designated disaster area. They also usually offer modification programs and other forms of assistance to homeowners who've gone through a natural disaster.

To find out if Fannie Mae owns your loan, go www.knowyour options.com/loanlookup. To find out if Freddie Mac owns your loan, go to https://loanlookup.freddiemac.com. For more information on disaster relief, go to Fannie Mae's Disaster Relief website at www. knowyouroptions.com/get-help-overview/disaster-recovery-help-for-homeowners and Freddie Mac's Disaster Relief website at https://sf.freddiemac.com/general/disaster-relief.

Relief for Borrowers With Any Type of Loan

Mortgage lenders and servicers might also provide relief from foreclosure by offering flexible loss mitigation options to borrowers following a natural disaster. Possible relief options include:

- loan modification
- forbearance (a temporary suspension or reduction in payments)
- a waiver of late payments, and
- suspending delinquency reporting to credit bureaus.

Additionally, FEMA typically offers financial assistance so that individuals and families whose property has been damaged or destroyed as a result of a federally declared disaster can make their mortgage payments or repair the home. Go to www.fema.gov for more information.

The U.S. Small Business Administration (SBA) offers low-interest loans for homeowners, renters, and personal property owners to help in recovering from a disaster. If you qualify, you can use the loan proceeds to fix your damaged home or repair or replace your personal belongings after a natural disaster. To learn more, go to www.sba.gov/funding-programs/disaster-assistance.

How Chapter 13 Bankruptcy
Can Delay or Stop Foreclosure

Using Chapter 13 to Keep Your House..111

    Repay Your Mortgage Arrears Over Time...112

    Make Your Mortgage More Affordable by Eliminating Other Debts.......113

    Ask the Court to Reduce ("Cram Down") Certain Secured Debts........... 114

    Contest the Foreclosure.. 115

    Wipe Out a Second or Third Mortgage... 116

An Overview of the Chapter 13 Bankruptcy Process.. 118

Coming Up With a Repayment Plan.. 118

    The Creditors' Meeting... 119

    The Confirmation Hearing.. 120

    Completing the Plan.. 121

    Relief Under Chapter 13 After a Chapter 7 Discharge.................................... 122

Will You Need a Lawyer?.. 123

Chapter 13 bankruptcy can help you save your house if you experience financial difficulties and fall behind on your mortgage. How? It gives you time to make up your missed payments, can make your mortgage more affordable in the long term by reducing your overall debt load, and, in some cases, let you eliminate a second mortgage. In some courts, it also gives you a friendly forum for negotiating a mortgage workout. And even if you decide to give up your house, Chapter 13 can help you delay your move-out date.

You get these crucial benefits by proposing a way to make up your missed payments through a Chapter 13 debt repayment plan while meeting other bankruptcy law requirements. You'll need to show that you earn enough income to meet your regular and necessary living expenses (including your mortgage and payments toward any arrearage). You'll also need to demonstrate you can pay off "priority" debts, such as back taxes and child support. Any money remaining would go toward repaying unsecured debt like credit card bills and court judgments. Chapter 13 plan requirements are explained in more detail below.

Sticking to a repayment plan for three to five years isn't easy, but if you can, you'll be well rewarded. Upon completion, any balance remaining on qualified unsecured debts will be wiped out—and you won't lose your house. Most people leave Chapter 13 owing nothing more than a mortgage payment and student loans if they have them.

Chapter 13 bankruptcy stops foreclosure the minute you file. Your filing triggers the federal bankruptcy court to issue what's known as an automatic stay. This court order (an injunction, technically) prohibits mortgage lenders and many other creditors from attempting to collect a debt you owe without court permission. Once the bankruptcy judge approves your repayment plan, you will be safe from foreclosure as long as you keep making the required plan payments and mortgage loan payments.

RESOURCE

More information on Chapter 13 bankruptcy. This chapter gives only an overview, to help you determine whether Chapter 13 bankruptcy might help you save your house—or at least keep you living in it longer. To learn more about this powerful remedy, see:

- the bankruptcy and foreclosure areas of Nolo.com
- *The New Bankruptcy: Will It Work for You?* by Cara O'Neill, which explains Chapters 7 and 13, and
- *Chapter 13 Bankruptcy: Keep Your Property & Repay Debts Over Time,* by Cara O'Neill, is a detailed guide to Chapter 13 bankruptcy.

Using Chapter 13 to Keep Your House

Chapter 13 bankruptcy allows you to bring your loan current in small affordable steps. Once you have a plan in place, the court orders the lender to go along with it. The court protects your property from foreclosure as long as you pay your regular monthly mortgage payments and mortgage arrears as agreed.

If you stick to your Chapter 13 repayment plan, you can:

- spread out missed mortgage payments (your mortgage arrears) over the life of the repayment plan, three to five years (this essentially forces your lender to accept a mortgage reinstatement plan)
- pay a fraction (or sometimes, nothing) of qualifying unsecured debts, freeing up money for your mortgage
- ask the court to reduce ("cram down") certain secured debts to the value of the collateral (for example, you might be able to reduce your $20,000 car note to the actual value of the car and lower your monthly payments)
- get rid of (strip off) liens on your home created by second and third mortgages, as long as they are wholly unsecured by your home (that is, if you sold your home, you wouldn't get enough to pay back any portion of the junior lien)

- remove a judgment lien if it would otherwise mean you'd lose part of your exemption on the property
- postpone the collection of delinquent student loans, and
- resume your regular monthly mortgage payments.

TIP

You can get a loan modification during your Chapter 13 case. If you file for Chapter 13 bankruptcy, you can still apply for a loan modification. Many homeowners have gotten loan modifications from their lenders during their Chapter 13 bankruptcy cases, and some courts have started initiating loan modification programs. Check with your local bankruptcy court or bankruptcy lawyer.

Repay Your Mortgage Arrears Over Time

If the only reason you are filing Chapter 13 is to bring your mortgage current and you could get a similar deal from the servicer, you'll be better off not filing for bankruptcy. Not only will it be easier on your credit score, but you will avoid paying hefty fees to the bankruptcy trustee. On the other hand, if your mortgage servicer refuses to work with you, then Chapter 13 might be the best way to save your home.

> **EXAMPLE:** Francisco owes $3,600 in missed mortgage payments after being laid off from work. He receives a notice of default that gives him a month to pay up or lose his house. His mortgage servicer refuses to work with him because of a previous notice of default and because the lender doesn't think he's a good credit risk.
>
> Fortunately, Francisco is working again. If he files for Chapter 13 bankruptcy and reduces payments on unsecured debt (like credit cards), he'll be able to afford regular mortgage payments and also make up the arrears over three years. Francisco files for Chapter 13 and proposes to pay down the arrears at the rate of $110 a month: $100 for the debt plus $10 a month for the trustee's fee.

You will be able to keep your house through Chapter 13 only if you have enough income to stay current on your mortgage and pay off the arrearage over the life of your plan. And you must propose a plan showing that you can make plan payments and stay current on your other monthly expenses, such as utilities, transportation, car payment, insurance, and the like. The requirement that makes Chapter 13 too expensive for some would-be filers, however, is this—you must pay some debt types in full through the plan. For example, if you owe recent back taxes, the court won't approve your repayment plan unless it shows that you can pay off the entire balance while your plan is in effect. You'll have to pay off support arrearages, too.

There's one final requirement that can be hard to meet if you own a lot of property. You must be able to pay your unsecured creditors at least as much as they would have received in a Chapter 7 bankruptcy. For instance, suppose that you would lose a $15,000 boat because you couldn't protect it with a bankruptcy exemption. In Chapter 13, you'd keep the boat, but you'd have to pay at least that amount to your unsecured creditors. As a result, if you have a significant amount of nonexempt (unprotected) property equity, the required monthly payment might be too high to afford. (See the discussion of Chapter 7 bankruptcy in Ch. 6.)

Finally, Chapter 13 isn't free. Your plan must pay the trustee roughly 10% of the payment amounts made to creditors through the repayment plan. This fee covers the operating costs of the Chapter 13 bankruptcy program.

Make Your Mortgage More Affordable by Eliminating Other Debts

It's not uncommon for people of moderate means to have credit card debt exceeding $15,000. If you are looking to save your house, and Chapter 13 bankruptcy might get the job done, the chances are excellent that you'll also reduce your debt load, if not eliminate it. Chapter 13 gives you three to five years to work out your mortgage problems and deal with your unsecured debt (debt not secured by collateral, such as credit card balances, medical bills, and personal loans) once and for all.

To eliminate credit card and other qualifying unsecured debt in Chapter 13 bankruptcy, you must commit your disposable income for a three- to five-year period. Any unsecured debt that remains at the end of your plan is discharged (canceled) unless it is one of the types of debt that survives bankruptcy, such as ongoing child support payments or a student loan balance.

If you think that many factors go into a Chapter 13 plan payment, you're right. But there's a quick way to get a rough estimate of what you'd pay in Chapter 13 bankruptcy. After paying your mortgage and monthly living expenses, you'd pay the greater of:

- your remaining disposable income
- the amount your creditors would have received in a Chapter 7 case (the value of the nonexempt property you would lose), or
- the total of your secured arrearages (such as overdue mortgage and auto payments), recent tax debt, and support arrearages.

You'll spread that amount over either three or five years. If you'd qualify for a Chapter 7 case but are filing for Chapter 13 to catch up on a mortgage, the period is three years; otherwise, it's five. Even though some people qualify for a three-year plan, most people opt to pay a lower monthly payment over five years.

Ask the Court to Reduce ("Cram Down") Certain Secured Debts

Chapter 13 bankruptcy judges can reduce (cram down) certain secured debts to the market value of the collateral that secures the debt. They can also reduce interest rates to the going rate in bankruptcy cases (roughly points above the prime rate). If you can get the judge to reduce your payments on a secured debt, you will have more money to pay toward your mortgage—and a better shot at proposing a confirmable Chapter 13 plan that the court will approve.

> **EXAMPLE:** Angelica bought a new car for $38,000, taking a seven-year note for $38,000 (including the principal and interest), with monthly payments of $475. Three years later, when Angelica files for Chapter 13 bankruptcy, she still owes $24,000, even though the car's market value has fallen to $14,000.
>
> As part of her Chapter 13 plan, Angelica asks that the court cram down the note to $14,000 and reduce the interest to the going rate in bankruptcy cases. The court approves the cramdown, cutting Angelica's monthly car payment in half.

A cramdown is usually available only for:

- cars bought at least 910 days before you file for bankruptcy
- other personal property items (furniture, jewelry, computers) bought at least one year before filing
- rental or vacation homes (but not your primary residence), and
- loans on mobile homes that your state classifies as personal property (not real estate).

The catch is that you must repay the entire cramdown amount in your plan. As a result, most people can't use it to reduce the balance owed on real estate.

Contest the Foreclosure

You might be able to fight a foreclosure in your state's courts whether or not you file for bankruptcy. But if you file for Chapter 13 bankruptcy, you can ask the bankruptcy court to decide whether the proposed foreclosure facts are erroneous.

For example, suppose you contest the foreclosure because your mortgage servicer failed to credit some payments. A bankruptcy court decision in your favor might eliminate the basis for the foreclosure. Depending on your jurisdiction, your bankruptcy court might be more sympathetic to a foreclosure challenge than the state court would be. (See Ch. 7 for more on the grounds for contesting a foreclosure.)

The ability to stop a foreclosure action in Chapter 13 is powerful, and some people try to use it to defraud creditors. For instance, filing a questionable case to stop a foreclosure and refiling as soon as the bankruptcy court dismisses it can land you in big trouble. It can take a while for the court to spot a bad-faith filer. But when it finally does, not only will the judge ban the debtor from further filings (temporarily or permanently), but refer the case to the U.S. Attorney for a perjury prosecution if there are any significant misstatements in the paperwork.

Wipe Out a Second or Third Mortgage

If you're like many homeowners, your home is encumbered with a first mortgage, a second mortgage (often used for the down payment in an 80–20 financing arrangement), and even a third mortgage (maybe in the form of a home equity line of credit). Most likely, the holder of the first mortgage brought the foreclosure. But if you have fallen behind on your first mortgage, you are probably behind on your second and third mortgages as well. Would it help you keep your house if you no longer had to pay the second or third mortgage? You likely know the answer: Reducing your overall mortgage debt load could help if you have enough income to meet your first mortgage obligation.

One of Chapter 13 bankruptcy's great features is the ability to strip off mortgages that aren't secured by your home equity. Let's say that the first mortgage is $300,000, the second mortgage is $75,000, and you owe $50,000 on a home equity line of credit. Presumably, the value of your home when you took on these debts was at least equal to the total value of the mortgages, or $425,000. But if the house is now worth less than $300,000, the house no longer secures the second and third mortgages. If you sold the house, there would be nothing left for the second or third mortgage holders.

If your second and third mortgages were considered secured debts, you would have to stay current on them in your Chapter 13 plan. However, when the judge agrees to strip them off, they are reclassified as dischargeable unsecured debts. You repay only a portion of them—just like your other unsecured debts. And, as explained earlier, it's the amount of your disposable income, not the debt amount, that determines how much of your total unsecured debt you must repay. You'll pay the same amount regardless of whether the mortgages are in the unsecured debt group—so it's better to include them if you can.

> **EXAMPLE:** Sean files for Chapter 13 bankruptcy and proposes a three-year plan to make up his missed mortgage payments. He also owes $60,000 in credit card debt and has disposable income of $300 a month. His house's value is $250,000. He owes $275,000 on his first mortgage, $30,000 on the second, and $15,000 on a home equity loan.
>
> He owes more on the first mortgage than what the house is worth, leaving no equity to secure the second mortgage or home equity loan. If he can prove this to the bankruptcy judge, he will be able to classify these two formerly secured debts as unsecured, giving him a total of $105,000 unsecured debt. Because all he has is $300 per month in disposable income, his plan would repay a little more than 10% of his unsecured debt. The remaining 90% would be discharged at the plan's completion—including the remaining balances of his formerly secured second and third mortgage debt.

If the court allows you to strip off junior liens, you won't have to make up payments missed on the junior mortgages, which will reduce the required total monthly payment considerably. Finally, once the lien has been completely removed from your property, the former lender won't have any right to collect payment or to recover your property—even if your home value increases.

An Overview of the Chapter 13 Bankruptcy Process

When you file for Chapter 13 bankruptcy, your court papers must disclose all of your income and assets (real estate and personal property), your debts and expenses, and several years of financial transactions. You'll also need to have filed income tax returns for the previous four years.

But before you can even file for bankruptcy, you must complete some basic credit counseling. And you'll have to take a class in financial management after you file but before you get your Chapter 13 discharge.

Coming Up With a Repayment Plan

The heart of a Chapter 13 bankruptcy is your repayment plan. It shows how much income you have to repay your debts, how long the plan will last, and the amount of debts you propose to repay.

There is no set percentage of your debt that you must repay. It all depends on how much disposable income you have available for this purpose. (Disposable income is the amount that remains after subtracting allowable expenses.) Keep in mind that courts will consider any income you receive from roommates, domestic partners, and other members of your household if they are chipping in to help you save your home.

A Chapter 13 repayment plan lasts several years: three if your income is below the median income for your state and five if it is over. (See Ch. 6 for how to determine whether your household income is above or below your state's median.)

Your plan must show that your income (plus proceeds from any property you plan to sell) will let you do all of the following:

- stay current on all your contractual obligations, such as a mortgage and car note unless you plan to give the house or car back to the lender voluntarily
- pay off any arrears you owe on these contractual obligations
- meet your regular monthly expenses

- pay off certain priority debts, such as back taxes and child support or alimony, in full over the life of your plan (if the delinquent family support was assigned to a third party for collection, you don't have to pay it in full during the plan; the remaining balance won't be discharged though)
- devote all of your disposable income to repayment of a percentage of your unsecured debt, such as credit card and personal loan debt, and
- pay your unsecured creditors at least as much as they would have gotten had you filed for Chapter 7 bankruptcy—that is, the value of your assets that would be sold in a Chapter 7 bankruptcy to pay your creditors (see Ch. 6), and pay the bankruptcy trustee (the official who collects the money you pay under your plan and distributes it to your creditors) a fee of about 10% of all payments you make under the plan.

Not everyone can propose a plan that the court will approve. For example, a plan must provide for paying most types of priority debts in full. So if you owe $50,000 in back taxes, and your disposable income would pay only $25,000 of the taxes over the life of your plan, the judge will refuse to confirm the plan. Many of these roadblocks to plan confirmation, however, can be overcome. Be sure to talk to a bankruptcy attorney for help qualifying for Chapter 13.

RESOURCE

More information on repayment plans. See Nolo.com for more on the requirements for Chapter 13 bankruptcy plans.

The Creditors' Meeting

About a month after you file for Chapter 13 bankruptcy, you are required to attend a creditors' meeting conducted by the trustee assigned to your case by the court. At this meeting, the trustee might go over your proposed plan and explain how it should be changed. If you disagree, the trustee will file a plan objection with the court.

TIP

Know when your first Chapter 13 payment will be due. It's common to think that you won't need to make a payment until after the court approves your plan, but that's not how it works. Not only will you be required to make your first payment soon after filing your case (within the first month), but if you fall behind, your matter will likely get dismissed. To avoid this pitfall, find out your payment due date before you file and, of course, budget accordingly. If your plan isn't confirmed, the trustee will return your payments, with a few exceptions. For instance, the trustee will likely pay your car payment if doing so is part of the plan.

The Confirmation Hearing

About a month after the creditors' meeting, your case will be set for a confirmation hearing in the bankruptcy court. At the confirmation hearing, the bankruptcy judge will decide whether or not to approve your proposed plan. Before the hearing, the trustee and your creditors can file an objection to your repayment plan with the court. If the objection raises a valid point, you might want to continue the hearing date, correct the problem, and file an amended plan. If you disagree with the objection, you can file a response stating your reasons. Ultimately, the court will review all of the submitted documents, listen to any argument presented at the hearing, and then do one of the following: confirm (approve) your plan; give you a chance to fix an issue; order your case to be dismissed; or allow you convert your case to Chapter 7 bankruptcy.

The Typical Chapter 13 Timeline	
Day 1	Papers filed to start the bankruptcy
Day 14	Repayment plan must be filed
Day 31	First plan payment must be made (check with your court— it could be sooner)
Day 46	Creditors' meeting held
Day 76	Confirmation hearing held
Day 106	Second confirmation hearing held, if necessary

Completing the Plan

It's tough to complete a Chapter 13 repayment plan. Not only is a person who files for Chapter 13 bankruptcy in a fragile economic condition, but all discretionary income goes into the plan. All it takes is a layoff, medical emergency, divorce, or simply fatigue at living within a strict budget to cause someone to fall behind on plan payments.

If your income does drop significantly during your Chapter 13 bankruptcy, you might be able to modify your plan or get a hardship discharge. More likely, however, you will be given a choice to convert your case to a Chapter 7 bankruptcy or have it dismissed entirely. Most people faced with this choice opt to convert to Chapter 7 bankruptcy and discharge what's left of their debts. But you might choose to let the court dismiss your Chapter 13 case instead if you have nonexempt property you would be forced to part with in Chapter 7 bankruptcy (for example, your family grand piano which the trustee could sell for $5,000).

Just because you might not complete your Chapter 13 bankruptcy doesn't mean you shouldn't start it. If and when you do default, you might be in a better situation to keep your house or at least sell it for a profit.

Suppose you do complete your plan and meet the other Chapter 13 requirements (such as giving the trustee an annual financial report and keeping current on your taxes and any child support obligations). In that case, you will receive a bankruptcy discharge. It usually cancels whatever nonpriority unsecured debt balance (but not student loans) remains.

There are a few exceptions to a Chapter 13 discharge, the most common of which are:

- debts you didn't list in your bankruptcy papers
- civil judgments arising from willful or malicious acts
- debts for death or personal injuries arising from drunk driving
- back child support or alimony not paid off as part of your plan
- taxes first due less than three years before your bankruptcy filing date, for which a return was filed less than two years before your bankruptcy filing date, and which were assessed within 240 days of your bankruptcy filing date (other conditions might apply)

- debts arising from your fraudulent acts (if proven by the creditor in bankruptcy court), and
- court-imposed fines and restitution.

Relief Under Chapter 13 After a Chapter 7 Discharge

The bankruptcy code prohibits you from receiving a Chapter 13 discharge if your case is filed within four years of the filing of a prior Chapter 7 case (in which a discharge was granted). However, most courts have decided you are entitled to file a Chapter 13 bankruptcy any time after a Chapter 7, even if you won't qualify for a discharge of your debt.

Why would you want to file a Chapter 13 bankruptcy if you can't discharge debt under it? Simply, many Chapter 7 debtors are left with liens and debts that survive the Chapter 7 bankruptcy, and Chapter 13 provides a structured way to deal with them. Because, by definition, your Chapter 7 bankruptcy has discharged all (or most) of your debt, you don't need the Chapter 13 discharge. For instance, some homeowners who file Chapter 7 are left with second mortgage liens on their home—because liens aren't discharged in Chapter 7 bankruptcy. Chapter 13 would provide a way to pay off the lien over the life of the plan, or in some instances, get rid of it altogether. However, some courts will not allow lien stripping in a Chapter 13 bankruptcy if you are not eligible for a discharge. Check with a local bankruptcy attorney to determine the rule in your jurisdiction.

Another reason: Suppose you come out of Chapter 7 owing a lot of back child support (which is not discharged in Chapter 7). You can file a Chapter 13 and propose a repayment plan that would be considerably more affordable than what you are being offered by the child support enforcement agency. Again, you wouldn't be discharging the child support but rather obtaining protection from the court against unreasonable repayment demands, garnishments, and the like.

Why You Need a Lawyer in a Chapter 13 Case

- Chapter 13 bankruptcy can require negotiating with creditors and the bankruptcy trustee to reach agreement on an acceptable repayment plan.
- Chapter 13 bankruptcy requires at least one appearance in court before the bankruptcy judge (the confirmation hearing) and often several more.
- Chapter 13 cases can have many variables, such as valuation of property, reducing liens to the value of the collateral, creating a plan that doesn't discriminate among debtors, and often, requests for plan modifications or hardship discharges.
- An experienced lawyer can help you understand the specifics of your case, including the types of debts you have and the amount or percentage you must repay.
- Local rules, court procedures, and how judges interpret the law vary by jurisdiction and court. A knowledgeable local bankruptcy attorney will know what's standard in your area.

Will You Need a Lawyer?

It's hard to handle your own Chapter 13 bankruptcy; you most likely will need an attorney to represent you, especially if you are trying to save your house. An involuntary dismissal (a greater possibility if you are representing yourself) would significantly set back your plans to keep your house. However, you do have the right to represent yourself, and you might have to if you can't afford to pay the attorneys' fees. (See Ch. 10 for information on finding, choosing, and working with a lawyer and other helpful resources.)

An Attorney Might Be More Affordable Than You Think

If you currently are not paying anything on your mortgage but could afford to pay at least some of it, it might only take you a couple of months to save enough money to pay a lawyer to represent you in Chapter 13 bankruptcy. Most attorneys will take a down payment—sometimes even as low as $100—and allow you to pay the remaining attorney fees through your repayment plan.

RELATED TOPIC

How to find a good attorney. Ch. 10 provides tips on how to choose a lawyer.

How Chapter 7 Bankruptcy Can Delay or Stop Foreclosure

How Chapter 7 Bankruptcy Helps You 127

   What Happens to Property in Chapter 7 Bankruptcy? 128

   What Happens to Debts in Chapter 7 Bankruptcy? 129

Using Chapter 7 Bankruptcy to Keep Your House 130

   Staying Current on Payments 130

   Protecting Equity 131

   You Can't Eliminate Payments on a Second or Third Mortgage 133

Using Chapter 7 Bankruptcy to Delay a Foreclosure Sale
in Good Faith 134

   How Much Time You'll Get 135

   Timing Your Filing 136

   Keeping Money Saved Before Filing for Bankruptcy 136

The Chapter 7 Bankruptcy Process: An Overview 138

Do You Qualify for Chapter 7 Bankruptcy? 140

   Means Test: The Six-Month Gross Income Test 140

   Means Test: Deducting Expenses 142

   The Actual Income and Expenses Test 142

Will You Need a Lawyer? 143

Chapter 7 bankruptcy will delay a foreclosure rather than block it permanently. If you're behind on payments and want to keep your house, you'll have to file for Chapter 13 bankruptcy because Chapter 7 doesn't have a mechanism that will allow you to catch up (see Ch. 5). But even if you'll have to give up your house, Chapter 7 bankruptcy can still be very valuable when you're facing foreclosure, depending on your situation. It can help you stay in the home for two to three months and wipe out any deficiency balance if the home sells for less than you owe. And filing for Chapter 7 before the foreclosure can help you avoid tax liability in some cases.

If you want to keep your house and are current on your house payment, you can get other debt canceled, freeing up money that may make it easier to pay your mortgage.

It's important to understand that unlike Chapter 13, a Chapter 7 bankruptcy will not wipe out (discharge) a second or third mortgage. If you keep your house, you'll have to pay all of the debt associated with the home, even if its value is less than what you owe on the first mortgage. Even though the debt gets wiped out, the lender's lien does not. So if you don't stay current on your payment, the lender will use its lien rights to foreclose on the property.

If you decide to give up your house, you might be able to:

- delay foreclosure proceedings for two to four months, and
- get all or most of your debts permanently canceled so you have a fresh start after foreclosure.

Bankruptcy is a great way to deal with various debts. Simply put, with a few exceptions, qualifying debts all go away. Credit card debts, medical bills, and most money judgments arising from lawsuits over breach of contract or negligence are all dischargeable. So if you are up to your neck in these types of bills, bankruptcy is something to consider seriously. Whether discharging debt will free up income you can use to pay your mortgage, or whether you are headed toward foreclosure and want to get a fresh start, Chapter 7 bankruptcy might be the right chapter for you.

Of course, Chapter 7 bankruptcy is not for everyone. You must qualify to file, and if you have good credit, it will take a hit. However, most people filing for bankruptcy already have bad credit, so filing for bankruptcy won't make a huge difference. Interestingly enough, with a bit of work, there's a good chance that your score will recover reasonably quickly after bankruptcy.

CAUTION
If you're interested in modifying your mortgage, see a HUD-approved counselor or bankruptcy lawyer before you file for bankruptcy. If you want to modify your mortgage principal or payments or refinance your current mortgage either in or out of the government programs described in Ch. 4, talk to a HUD-approved housing counselor before filing bankruptcy. A lawyer can also advise you about the modification process in bankruptcy.

How Chapter 7 Bankruptcy Helps You

Whether or not you plan to give up your house, you can buy some time just by filing for bankruptcy. As soon as you do, foreclosure proceedings must stop—at least for a while. When you file for bankruptcy, the federal bankruptcy court automatically issues a court order called a stay. It bars creditors, including mortgage lenders, from taking any measures to collect a debt you owe unless the creditor seeks permission from the bankruptcy court to proceed, and the court grants permission after notice and a hearing.

The automatic stay immediately stops foreclosures as well as most other creditor actions. Suppose your home will go to auction on December 5 at 10 a.m., and you file for bankruptcy at 9:59 a.m. that day. If you notify the lender of the filing, the sale is "stayed" and has no effect even if it goes ahead after you file. But if you file at 10:01 a.m., just one minute after the sale, the sale would go through.

In most cases, it takes about four months to complete a Chapter 7 bankruptcy case. After the court grants a Chapter 7 discharge, the party seeking to foreclose on your home is free to continue with the foreclosure and take the next step under your state's foreclosure laws.

Keep in mind that there is no guarantee the foreclosure will remain stayed during the entire bankruptcy. A foreclosing lender can file a motion asking the court to lift the automatic stay so that it can move forward with the foreclosure (more below). A good rule of thumb is to seek help from a knowledgeable attorney whenever significant assets are at risk.

What Happens to Property in Chapter 7 Bankruptcy?

Chapter 7 bankruptcy is what most people think about when they think about bankruptcy. It's called "liquidation" bankruptcy because it cancels your debts, but you might have to let the bankruptcy court liquidate (sell) some of your property for the benefit of your creditors.

When you file Chapter 7, most property you own automatically becomes part of your "bankruptcy estate," under the control of the bankruptcy court. The bankruptcy trustee will have the authority to sell property you can't protect in the bankruptcy estate and use the proceeds to pay your creditors.

Every state lets you claim some or all of your bankruptcy estate as exempt, meaning you get to keep it. As a general rule, exemption laws allow you to keep necessities, such as furniture, clothing, personal effects, tools of the trade, cars, books, TVs, and home computers. Most states also allow you to keep at least some equity in the house you live in when you file for bankruptcy; this is known as a homestead exemption. When home equity is low, most people don't lose property to the bankruptcy trustee.

RESOURCE

Check the exemptions in your state. The type and amount of property you can exempt exempt varies by state. You can find the exemptions in your state on Nolo.com at www.nolo.com/legal-encyclopedia/bankruptcy-exemptions-state.

Keep in mind that if you don't own the property outright—for instance, you're making payments and the lender can take the property back if you stop paying—the exemption will protect your property's equity amount. If you have no equity, you can keep the property without using an exemption. For example, if your car is worth $20,000, but the remaining car loan balance is $20,000, you have no equity and wouldn't need to use an exemption to keep it. You'd still need to be current on your payments to avoid repossession and pay back the loan after bankruptcy.

Even though you might have to give up nonexempt property to help pay off your debts, many people don't have any nonexempt property.

But if you own a luxury item outright—such as a boat, an RV, a valuable coin collection, corporate securities, an ownership interest in a business, or an expensive car in which you have considerable equity— the trustee will likely sell it to repay your debts. Finding out what your state will allow you to protect in bankruptcy should be one of the first things you do when deciding whether bankruptcy will be right for you.

What Happens to Debts in Chapter 7 Bankruptcy?

Once the bankruptcy trustee has paid creditors whatever money is available, your remaining qualifying debt will be canceled (discharged). The debts you'll remain responsible for paying include:

- student loans (with rare exceptions)
- most back taxes
- back child support and alimony
- criminal fines and penalties (state or federal)
- liabilities arising from willful and malicious actions such as assault or theft
- liabilities for personal injury or death arising from drunk driving
- debts arising from acts the creditor proves were fraudulent (for instance, misstatements on a loan application)
- traffic tickets, and
- HOA (homeowners' association) fees that accrue after you file for bankruptcy.

Using Chapter 7 Bankruptcy to Keep Your House

You can use Chapter 7 bankruptcy to save your house if both of the following are true:

- You are current on your mortgage payments when you file, and
- Your equity in the house is protected by the exemption laws available to you in your state.

If you are not current on your payments, Chapter 7 bankruptcy will be only a temporary remedy unless you can modify your loan (which isn't guaranteed). The lender will be able to proceed with a foreclosure within two or three months. Instead, you should explore Chapter 13 bankruptcy, which provides a way for you to keep your house by spreading out your missed payments over several years. (See Ch. 5.)

Staying Current on Payments

Suppose you are current on your payments but expect to fall behind very shortly. Perhaps your mortgage interest rate is due to reset higher, or you've reached the principal cap on an interest-only loan. It could be that you have just lost some work hours or been laid off.

In these and similar situations, filing for Chapter 7 could be a big help. Except for a few categories of debt, such as those mentioned above, you can eliminate virtually all your unsecured debt, such as credit card debt, personal loans, medical debts, money judgments, and car repossession deficiencies, in about four months. You can even stop paying them before you file (but be sure that you qualify first—it can be hard to catch up once you fall behind). Once your unsecured debt load is eliminated or greatly reduced, you will have a much better chance of paying your mortgage.

Protecting Equity

In every Chapter 7 case, the bankruptcy trustee looks for property to sell for the benefit of the creditors. The trustee will only be interested in selling the property that would produce money for the creditors. In other words, property that you own outright or in which you have equity. The trustee will subtract the following from the property's value:

- the amount the trustee must pay a secured lender (your mortgage or car loan)
- the exemption amount the trustee would need to refund to you, and
- the costs to sell the property.

If a reasonable amount of money would remain, the trustee will go forward with the property sale. Selling property worth less than the amount owed to a secured lender or fully protected by an exemption wouldn't net any money for creditors. In that case, the trustee wouldn't sell it and you'd get to keep it (you'd still have to pay any outstanding loans against it).

> CAUTION
>
> **Once you file, you might not be able to change your mind.** If you file for Chapter 7 and then discover that you won't be able to keep your house because it has too much equity, you probably won't be allowed to back out and dismiss your bankruptcy case. Your right to dismiss your bankruptcy case isn't based on what you'd like to do—the judge will determine what would be best for your creditors. If the creditors would receive a distribution from your house's sale, the bankruptcy might go forward. You'd receive the amount you're entitled to exempt, and your creditors would be paid out of the remaining proceeds.

Most states let you keep at least some home equity when you go through Chapter 7 bankruptcy. Protection for home equity varies dramatically from state to state. As of March 2021, you get $500,000 in Massachusetts (if you declared a homestead; $125,000 otherwise), $605,000 in Nevada, $450,000 in Minnesota ($1,125,000 if it's used for agriculture), and just $15,500 in Alabama. Some states allow you to choose between the state and federal list—you'd pick the list that's most advantageous to you. And in California, you can choose between two state lists. (If you haven't resided for at least two years in the state where you file for bankruptcy, however, you must use the exemptions for the state where you resided previously.)

If your equity is less than the protected amount and you're current on your payment, you should be able to keep your house when you go through Chapter 7 bankruptcy.

> **EXAMPLE:** Stuart and Stephanie have built up $25,000 of equity in their house, and they've managed to stay current on the mortgage payments. But credit card and medical debts (their young son has been ill) have piled up alarmingly, and they're considering bankruptcy.
>
> They live in Maine, which lets a family with dependents keep $95,000 of equity under the state's homestead exemption. If they filed for bankruptcy, the trustee would not sell their house because after paying off the mortgage, only $25,000 would remain. The trustee would have to give that portion to Stuart and Stephanie because it's within Maine's $95,000 homestead exemption. Nothing would be left for creditors.

However, if you have a significant amount of unprotected equity, the bankruptcy trustee will use it for your creditors.

> **EXAMPLE:** Petra owns a house in South Carolina. The house carries a mortgage of $300,000 but is valued at $500,000, giving Petra $200,000 in equity. In South Carolina, you can protect only $63,250 worth of equity in your house. Petra has a problem. She has creditors threatening to sue her, but she can't borrow against her equity because she can't afford

to pay another loan. She's managed to keep current on her mortgage payments, but she won't be able to keep that up if her creditors sue her and garnish her wages. If Petra filed for Chapter 7 bankruptcy, the bankruptcy trustee would sell her house, pay off the mortgage, give Petra her $63,250 exemption amount and use the rest to pay Petra's creditors. If there were anything left over, Petra would get that as well. If this is not the result Petra wants—and it probably isn't—she should not file for Chapter 7 bankruptcy.

RESOURCE

How much home equity can you keep? If you have home equity and you want to find out how much your state protects or what other property is protected under your state's exemption laws, visit Nolo.com and in the "Bankruptcy" section choose "Bankruptcy Exemptions" or go straight to www.nolo.com/legal-encyclopedia/bankruptcy-exemptions-state.

You Can't Eliminate Payments on a Second or Third Mortgage

When property values fall, second and third mortgages are frequently left unsecured. In other words, the property no longer has sufficient value to guarantee their payment.

After the 2008 economic downturn, many properties were worth less than the amount the homeowner owed. Although this situation has reversed itself as of this writing, new events, such as the COVID-19 pandemic, could spark another drop in home values.

If your home is worth less than what you owe on your first mortgage, you can wipe out a subsequent mortgage, such as a second or third, in a Chapter 13 bankruptcy. This option is not available in a Chapter 7 case. A homeowner who keeps a house in a Chapter 7 bankruptcy must pay all loans secured by the property, regardless of the property's value. It isn't because Chapter 7 doesn't wipe out the mortgage—it still does. It's because the lender retains a lien right allowing for foreclosure if the debt isn't paid and the court doesn't remove the liens in Chapter 7.

> **EXAMPLE:** Paige owes $200,000 on a first mortgage, $100,000 on a second mortgage, and $50,000 on a third mortgage. Her house is worth $275,000, leaving the second mortgage partially unsecured, and the third mortgage wholly unsecured. If she files for Chapter 7 bankruptcy and keeps the home, she'll have to continue paying all three mortgages to keep the house. If, however, she files for Chapter 13 bankruptcy, she can file a motion asking the court to strip off the wholly unsecured third mortgage. (Partially secured mortgages remain in Chapter 13 bankruptcy. Only completely unsecured mortgages will qualify for discharge.)

Using Chapter 7 Bankruptcy to Delay a Foreclosure Sale in Good Faith

The instant you file for bankruptcy, all foreclosure proceedings must cease. So if you file for bankruptcy at 11:59 a.m., a foreclosure sale at 12:00 p.m. would be void. Because of this instant relief, many people turn to bankruptcy as a last resort when their efforts to work something out with their lender have failed to materialize. As mentioned, a Chapter 7 bankruptcy filing will give you two or three months of relief before the foreclosure can proceed again, but it's not a permanent fix.

As a general rule, filing for Chapter 7 bankruptcy is a bad idea if you have little or no debt to discharge and your only reason for filing is to buy some extra time in your house. You won't be able to get another Chapter 7 discharge for eight years, so why waste it to get a little extra time? Also, the courts frown on filers using bankruptcy for tactical purposes. However, if you are facing foreclosure, you also probably have some serious debt issues. If your Chapter 7 would eliminate that debt as well as buy you some more time in your home, the equation changes and Chapter 7 bankruptcy becomes a valid option you could file in "good faith."

How Much Time You'll Get

A Chapter 7 bankruptcy takes about three to four months (sometimes longer) from filing to the date of discharge (cancellation) of your debts. Unless the judge gives the lender permission, no foreclosure sale can take place during that time.

However, the lender can file a formal request (motion) asking the bankruptcy court to lift the automatic stay and let the foreclosure sale proceed. Lenders usually must provide at least 25 days' advance notice of the hearing on their motion unless they get the judge's permission to shorten that time. Generally, the lender must hire a lawyer to file the motion, so it is a relatively expensive procedure. For this reason, some lenders skip the expense, let the bankruptcy proceed, and simply reschedule the foreclosure sale once it's complete. That would leave your three- to four-month delay intact.

A lender who thinks it's worthwhile to ask the court to let the foreclosure go ahead usually files a motion 30 to 45 days after you file. A court will schedule the hearing about 25 to 30 days later and will likely grant the motion to lift the stay unless you can show that any of the following apply:

- The proposed foreclosure is illegal in some way.
- The lender hasn't complied with state procedural requirements (see Ch. 7).
- The party bringing the foreclosure hasn't produced the necessary paperwork or evidence to show it has the authority to seek the foreclosure.
- There is substantial equity in the property that you cannot protect with an exemption. In this case, the trustee would likely sell the property.

If the court lifts the stay, the lender will then be free to resume the foreclosure process. If the court refuses to lift the stay, the foreclosure will be stalled until you receive your bankruptcy discharge.

After the discharge (or after the court lifts the stay), the lender can proceed with the foreclosure. Unlike Chapter 13 bankruptcy, Chapter 7 doesn't force the lender to let you make up your missed payments over time or preserve your right to keep ownership of your house.

Timing Your Filing

Sometimes you don't have the luxury of deciding when to file for Chapter 7 bankruptcy. If your wages are about to be garnished, you'll most likely file as soon as possible. However, if there's no emergency, it sometimes helps to wait until your filing has the best possible effect on delaying your foreclosure sale. In most cases, this means waiting to file until just before the sale date.

Keeping Money Saved Before Filing for Bankruptcy

If you're sure you'll be giving up your house sooner or later, it makes financial sense to keep living in it and give it up later. If you are current on your mortgage when you make this decision, you'll likely be able to save at least three or four months' worth of mortgage payments before foreclosure proceedings even begin. And depending on how long you have before the actual sale, you will probably be able to save at least several more months' worth of mortgage payments. (More on this in Ch. 9.)

However, if you would like to file for Chapter 7 bankruptcy, you should first figure out whether you'll be able to keep what you've saved before you file, or whether you'll have to give it up to be used by the trustee to pay down your unsecured debt. This issue doesn't arise for any money you save after you file your Chapter 7 bankruptcy; it applies only to what you have in the piggy bank on the day you file.

You can keep your savings through the bankruptcy process if you can claim it as exempt. Every state has its own rules about how much money is exempt from creditors—in other words, how much you are allowed to keep when you go through bankruptcy. And there is a separate set of federal exemption rules; in states that allow it, you can pick whichever system works better for you. However, most states don't allow you to keep much—if any—savings. But that's not always the case.

For example, in California, under the exemption system that just about everybody uses when there is no home equity to protect, you can protect roughly $30,000 worth of any property of your choosing, including cash in a bank account. You can also keep such commonly owned items as household furnishings and personal effects, as well as $8,725 in the tools you need in your profession and $5,850 of vehicle equity. So, if you have $10,000 in the bank, you could keep that $10,000 and still have enough remaining to protect other property.

To find out how much money you are allowed to keep when filing for Chapter 7 bankruptcy, check your state's page in the appendix.

It might be that the exemptions available to you in your state won't let you keep the cash you've saved as well as all your other property. In that case, you'll have to pick and choose what property you keep and what you give up. For example, if you have $50,000 worth of home equity, and your state makes you choose between the home equity and your savings account, you might have to give up the savings account. In the end, the only way to know how much property (and cash in the bank) you can keep in a Chapter 7 bankruptcy is to review the exemptions.

EXAMPLE 1: Jon lives in California. He has no home equity. He has not been paying his $2,500 mortgage for seven months. With the money earned from his job, he has put $2,500 a month in a bank account, giving him savings of $17,500. In addition to hand-me-down furniture and everyday personal effects, Jon's only other property is a classic 1967 Chevrolet Camaro Rally Sport worth $20,000.

In one of the two available exemption systems in California, Jon can exempt $5,850 worth of motor vehicle equity and $30,825 of any other property using the wildcard exemption. Jon wants to hold on to his Camaro but will have to use $14,150 of the wildcard exemption to supplement the $5,850 motor vehicle exemption.

That leaves him $16,675 from the wildcard exemption. Because there is no specific exemption for a bank savings account (as there is for a motor vehicle, for example), Jon can exempt only $16,675 of his savings. He'll have to give up the rest ($825) as nonexempt property to be used by the bankruptcy trustee to pay down his unsecured debt. If he is eligible to make retirement plan contributions, he might be able to exempt his cash by depositing $825 into an IRA account. He can also use the money for necessary items before filing, such as food, utilities, and clothing, but he should keep good records in case the trustee asks about the funds.

EXAMPLE 2: Angela lives in Massachusetts in a house she inherited. She has home equity of $200,000, but she doesn't have enough income to borrow against her equity and she has a lot of credit card debts. Bankruptcy seems like the best way out. Angela learns that the Massachusetts homestead exemption fully protects her equity. Unfortunately, the Massachusetts exemption system provides very little protection for savings, so if Angela has saved money before filing for bankruptcy, she'll have to give it up if it isn't used for necessary purchases before filing.

Suppose Angela had no home equity to protect. In that case, she could use the federal exemptions (an alternative system to the Massachusetts state exemptions) to protect her savings because the federal exemptions provide $13,900 "wildcard" protection for any property (including a bank account) for single filers and $27,800 for joint filers.

The Chapter 7 Bankruptcy Process: An Overview

Chapter 7 bankruptcy is a very straightforward process. It typically consists of six steps:

Step 1: Before filing, complete a mandatory credit-counseling course by phone or online.

Step 2: File the official bankruptcy forms listing all your property and creditors and providing information about your financial transactions during the previous two years (fillable forms are available at www.uscourts.gov/forms/bankruptcy-forms).

Step 3: Mail the bankruptcy trustee appointed to the case a copy of your most recently filed income tax return, plus any other documents the trustee asks for—usually bank statements and paycheck stubs.

Step 4: About 30 days after you file, attend a creditors' meeting. The creditors' meeting occurs in a small hearing room and is conducted by the trustee. Creditors seldom appear. At this meeting, you must answer any questions the trustee has about the information in your papers and provide other information the trustee thinks is relevant. A typical meeting lasts five minutes or less. You are not required to have a lawyer represent you. Still, you'll have to answer the trustee's questions about matters reasonably related to your financial situation.

Step 5: No later than 60 days after the creditors' meeting, you must attend mandatory budget counseling (by phone or online) and file a simple form telling the court that you have completed it. You'll attach a certificate of completion from the counseling agency.

Step 6: Wait until the court sends you a written discharge of your debts. That will come about 60 to 75 days after the creditors' meeting. During that period, creditors can, but seldom do, object to a discharge (cancellation) of your debt. The trustee arranges for you to turn over nonexempt property if you have any.

The Chapter 7 Bankruptcy Timeline	
Before you file	Mandatory credit counseling
Filing date	Papers filed to start the bankruptcy
About a month after you file	Creditors' meeting held
Up to 60 days after the creditors' meeting	Mandatory budget counseling
60 days after the creditors' meeting	Court sends written discharge of your debts

Do You Qualify for Chapter 7 Bankruptcy?

To qualify for Chapter 7 bankruptcy, you must pass the means test. It's a two-step process. Here is how it works.

Means Test: The Six-Month Gross Income Test

You'll qualify for Chapter 7 bankruptcy if your average gross household income is below your state's annual median household income. You'll double your gross household income earned during the full six months before filing to the state annual median income.

Most courts define a household as including all members of an economic unit; that is, an arrangement where income and expenses are shared for the benefit of all. For example, domestic partners and their children are one economic unit, as are groups of people living together as "families." Roommates, on the other hand, are typically not considered an economic unit, assuming they handle their income and expenses separately and only share the rent. Similarly, arrangements in which a debtor lives with parents, but the income and expenses are not shared, are not considered economic units. A few courts reject the economic unit definition of "household" and instead look to whether a household member is the bankruptcy debtor's dependent.

To see whether you qualify under this income test, add up all your gross income for your household for the six calendar months immediately preceding the current month. Then multiply the total by two.

Figuring Your Gross Income

Total household income for last six calendar months $ _____

× _____ 2

Average annual income   = $ _____

Then compare this figure to the median household income for your state. You can find the most current figures on the website of the U.S. Trustee at www.justice.gov/ust (choose "Means Testing Information" and then click on the appropriate date range under "Data Required for Completing the 122A Forms and the 122C Forms").

If you pass the means test, you are halfway there. You also have to provide information about your current income and living expenses (called Schedules I and J). You should be fine if your living expenses are reasonable and use up virtually all your monthly income. If the schedules show that you have more income per month than you need for living expenses, the trustee might seek to dismiss your case.

> **EXAMPLE:** Preston and Megan live in Kansas with their two children. In September, their gross income from all sources (which includes bonuses, commissions, overtime, and even lottery winnings) for the months of March through August totals $36,600. They multiply that figure by two to arrive at an annual figure of $73,200. They go to the U.S. Trustee website and learn that Kansas's median annual household income for a family of four is $94,036. Because their annual gross household income is less, they pass and qualify for a Chapter 7 debt discharge.

TIP

If you wait, you might qualify later. If your income is higher than the median income for your state based on your gross income for the previous six months, but your income has recently gone down, you might consider waiting another month or two to file. The delay could render your income low enough to produce an average below your state's median.

Means Test: Deducting Expenses

If your household income is above the median for your state and household size, you might still qualify after taking the second half of the means test. You'll have to show that your allowable expenses and certain standard deductions leave you with inadequate funds to repay a substantial portion of your unsecured debts. (An unsecured debt is a debt that isn't guaranteed by collateral—for example, credit card debt.)

If you pass, you can file for Chapter 7 bankruptcy. If you don't pass, you might qualify for Chapter 13 bankruptcy. But check with a bankruptcy lawyer first. An experienced bankruptcy lawyer might be able to help you pass the means test.

The Actual Income and Expenses Test

Again, even if you pass the income or means test, some bankruptcy courts will require you to file for Chapter 13 bankruptcy rather than Chapter 7 bankruptcy. The court will consider whether your actual income will exceed your actual expenses in the future. The court will examine the income and expense schedules filed with the bankruptcy case. If your income exceeds your expenses, you might have to pay the excess to creditors in a Chapter 13 case.

Will You Need a Lawyer?

Will you need a lawyer to represent you in Chapter 7 bankruptcy? Opinions on this differ.

Those who feel you can go it alone point to the fact that there's no court appearance for the vast majority of filers (although you will have to appear at the meeting of creditors) and no legal advocacy is needed.

If you decide to represent yourself, be aware that the legal system holds you to the same legal standards as a licensed attorney. You are responsible for knowing and correctly following the laws and for completing your paperwork properly. When you appear at the meeting of creditors, the trustee will not provide you with legal advice or help. Instead, the trustee will scrutinize your case looking for assets to take and reasons to have your expenses disallowed.

If you file under the wrong chapter, incorrectly believe you can keep particular property, or make other mistakes, you will bear the consequences. You might need to amend your papers and attend one or more extra creditor meetings for some mistakes. But other errors can be much more costly. For example, the trustee or your creditors might ask the court to deny your bankruptcy or you might lose assets or other valuable legal rights.

A bankruptcy lawyer can help you successfully navigate the bankruptcy system. Also, your attorney can advise you on whether you can keep your home. If you think you might want to represent yourself, first get a good do-it-yourself book and read it carefully (Ch. 10 has some recommendations). If you'd like to find out if your case has any tricky issues, take the free online bankruptcy quiz at www.thebankruptcysite.org/resources/do-i-need-a-lawyer-to-file-for-bankruptcy.html or meet with a bankruptcy attorney. There's no downside given that most bankruptcy lawyers will provide an initial consultation for free.

Fighting Foreclosure in Court

**How to Fight a Foreclosure (And How Long You Can Delay
the Sale of Your House)** 147

    Judicial Foreclosures 147

    Nonjudicial Foreclosures 152

When It Might Be Worth Fighting 154

    You're on Active Duty in the Military 155

    The Lender Didn't Follow State Foreclosure Procedures,
    Federal Mortgage Servicing Laws, or Mortgage Terms
    Governing Foreclosures 156

    The Foreclosing Party Can't Prove It Has the Right to Foreclose 157

    The Mortgage Servicer Made a Serious Mistake 160

    The Lender Engaged in Unfair Lending Practices 167

    The APR Test 169

    The Points and Fees Test 169

    The Prepayment Penalty Test 169

    You Have a High-Cost Mortgage 171

The Statute of Limitations Has Expired 172

    When Does the Statute of Limitations Clock Start Ticking? 172

    Stopping a Foreclosure Using a Statute of Limitations Defense 173

    What If the Statute of Limitations Expires After Foreclosure Starts? 173

When You Can Sue for Money 174

f you live in a state that requires foreclosures to go through court (see Ch. 2 and the appendix to find out if you live in a judicial foreclosure state), you'll have the right to present your objections to the foreclosure to a judge for review. If you're facing a nonjudicial foreclosure, you'll have to file an action in court against the foreclosing party (or file bankruptcy) to have a judge review the foreclosure.

In judicial foreclosure states, you might have a decent shot at delaying or stopping a foreclosure, even if you don't file for bankruptcy, in any of the following situations:

- The foreclosing party brought the foreclosure based on false information. For example, say the servicer credited your payments to someone else, and you were never behind. Or the lender substantially overstated the amount you had to pay to reinstate your mortgage, depriving you of your reinstatement rights under state law.
- You can prove that the foreclosing party didn't follow state procedural requirements for bringing a foreclosure. For example, the lender failed to properly serve you a notice of intent to foreclose that state law requires.
- The foreclosing party isn't legally entitled to bring a foreclosure action. For example, state law says that only the promissory note's actual holder can foreclose, and the foreclosing party doesn't meet that description.
- The person signing the affidavits or other documents in support of the foreclosure did not have personal knowledge of the information in the documents (in other words, the person signing was a robosigner).
- The notary public attesting to the validity of a signature in the documents did not follow regulations governing notarization.
- The original lender or mortgage originator engaged in unfair lending practices through fraudulent behavior or by violating a state or federal law concerning certain mortgage provisions or disclosures to borrowers.

As you'll see, to successfully fight a foreclosure in court you will probably need to hire an attorney to represent you. The foreclosing party will have an attorney, and trying to do battle with an attorney in court when you aren't one yourself can be an exercise in futility. If you absolutely have to represent yourself, though, some resources are available that can help you, and they're discussed in Ch. 10.

How to Fight a Foreclosure (And How Long You Can Delay the Sale of Your House)

As you might expect, contesting a judicial foreclosure is very different than fighting a nonjudicial foreclosure. (If you don't know which kind you're likely to come up against, see Ch. 2 or your state's page in the appendix.) And the amount of delay you're likely to get depends on the procedure, too.

Judicial Foreclosures

In a judicial foreclosure, the foreclosing party (the plaintiff) must file a lawsuit to get the foreclosure started. You'll get notice of the suit when the summons and complaint are delivered to (served on) you. These papers will advise you of the lawsuit and give you a deadline to respond if you choose to contest the foreclosure. The amount of time you get to respond to the suit typically ranges between 20 and 30 days, though it varies, depending on state law. The summons you receive with the complaint will say how much time you have to file an answer in your case.

Whether you respond is up to you. Either way, the plaintiff will have to prove that the foreclosure is legal. But if you don't respond, the chances are excellent that the foreclosure will go through. The paperwork that the plaintiff will use to try to prove its case will typically include a copy of the promissory note and mortgage or deed of trust you signed when you got the loan. You might also see copies of notices, signed agreements, internal accountings of payments both made and missed, and written statements under oath (called "declarations" or, if sworn before a notary public, "affidavits") from the plaintiff and mortgage servicer officials who claim to have knowledge of:

- your missed payments
- the plaintiff's compliance with your state's laws regarding foreclosure procedures, and
- the circumstances through which the plaintiff came to own the mortgage.

As a general rule, if you don't point out errors or omissions in the paperwork or process, the court will accept the documents as evidence that will support a foreclosure judgment and order for sale.

If you do respond, you have the opportunity to tell a judge why you think a foreclosure isn't warranted. To fight a judicial foreclosure, you have to file a written answer to the lawsuit. You must present your defenses and explain why the plaintiff shouldn't be able to foreclose. If you answer the suit, you'll definitely get some additional time to live in your home. And, if you have strong evidence that the plaintiff or servicer made a mistake in the foreclosure procedures, you might even be able to force it to start the foreclosure over, which will substantially prolong the process.

In the answer, you need to address all of the allegations in the complaint. For each numbered paragraph in the complaint, you should admit, deny, or say you don't have sufficient information to admit or deny (and therefore you deny) the allegations contained in that particular paragraph. You may also ask that the plaintiff prove its claims, like how much it says you owe and the fees it says are due. Be aware that if you admit an allegation, the plaintiff doesn't have to prove it. You'll also need to raise any defenses and affirmative defenses in your answer, such as the plaintiff doesn't have standing (the right to foreclose), as well as any counterclaims, like the servicer violated federal mortgage servicing laws when you applied for a loan modification, for example.

Once you file an answer to the suit, the plaintiff can't get a default judgment (an automatic win) against you from the court. Instead, because the plaintiff can't get a default judgment, it will probably file a motion for summary judgment. This kind of motion asks the court to decide the case without a trial because the critical facts aren't in dispute, any defenses you've raised lack merit, or you didn't show wrongdoing on the part of the plaintiff or servicer. You'll have to file a response to this motion explaining your legal argument based on statutes and case law and serve it to the other parties if you don't want the court to grant a judgment of foreclosure. The court may then hold a hearing on the matter.

If the material facts in the case aren't in dispute—say you're far behind in payments and you don't have any valid defenses to the foreclosure—the court will likely grant the motion for summary judgment, permitting the plaintiff to foreclose. Foreclosures are often stalled only until a court grants summary judgment. But if the court thinks you've raised some compelling points, the judge will deny the plaintiff's motion, and the case will move on. Following discovery, which might happen before or after the summary judgment motion, you'll have to show the judge at trial why the plaintiff shouldn't be allowed to foreclose based on the issues you've raised, generally by questioning witnesses and presenting evidence.

If the plaintiff convinces the court during the trial that a foreclosure is appropriate, the judge will order a foreclosure sale and possibly set the sale date. But if you argue your case convincingly, the judge might dismiss the foreclosure, probably "without prejudice," which means the plaintiff can still foreclose—but it has to start the process over.

It's impossible to guess exactly how long it will take for your case to wind its way through the court system if you decide to challenge the foreclosure, but the process is likely to last at least several months. In fact, in some states, a foreclosure can take years, especially when the borrower fights the foreclosure and has a valid defense. But if you don't file an answer to the suit, you'll likely have a month or so before the court grants a default judgment and orders your home sold at a foreclosure sale.

What Is Discovery?

"Discovery" is the stage of litigation that allows both sides to learn about evidence in each other's possession. Both you and the plaintiff can get information from each other using discovery tools, such as:

- written interrogatories (questions about case-related facts that the other side must answer in writing)
- requests for the production of documents (a demand requiring the other party to turn over specified documents)
- depositions (the other side testifies under oath in front of a court reporter), and
- property inspections (one side views real estate or property, such as a car, that's in the other side's possession).

Borrowers sometimes make discovery demands in their answer or when opposing a motion for summary judgment on the basis that discovery is necessary to expose specific facts about the case or facts that the plaintiff claims are true. Going through the discovery process might add several months to a foreclosure. But you'll have to show that discovery might lead to relevant evidence or that the facts you need to justify your opposition to the foreclosure are exclusively within the knowledge and control of the plaintiff. Otherwise, the court might go ahead and grant summary judgment.

If you decide to answer the foreclosure complaint without a lawyer's assistance and represent yourself in court proceedings, you'll need to devote a substantial amount of time to conducting research, getting your paperwork in order, and preparing your arguments. Also, sometimes filing an answer isn't the best option. Say you're facing a judicial foreclosure and you have an argument that requires you to file another type of pleading to preserve your rights; filing an incorrect response might cause you to lose an important right. For instance, if the lender made an error, like failing to serve you with the foreclosure lawsuit properly, you can dispute the court's jurisdiction by filing a motion to dismiss. If you win, the foreclosure has to start over. But if you file an answer, you likely stipulate (agree) that the court has the right to hear the case, and the foreclosure goes ahead. Litigation is complicated, and most people fare better after getting help from a lawyer. If you can't afford a lawyer, you may contact a legal services program in your area to find out if you qualify for free legal help. You can find a list of various legal aid programs on the Legal Service Corporation's website at www.lsc.gov.

Were the Affidavits in Your Foreclosure Case Robosigned?

In a judicial foreclosure, the lender must prove that it owns the mortgage loan and that the borrower defaulted. Typically, the lender does this by submitting documents and a written statement signed under oath (called an "affidavit") by a person who has reviewed the documents and has some personal basis for believing the facts in those documents are true. The idea is to prevent foreclosures when the foreclosing party can't prove that it owns the loan or the homeowner isn't in default to the degree asserted in the foreclosure papers.

In 2010, it came to light that several large banks routinely used affidavits signed by employees who signed thousands of affidavits a month, spending about 30 seconds on each affidavit, and who didn't have a clue regarding the veracity of the affidavit or the documents in question—hence the name "robosigners."

A foreclosure is invalid if a supporting affidavit is false and any affidavit completed by a robosigner is false by definition. After the issue of robosigning came to light, banks and servicers adjusted their procedures, and some states passed laws imposing penalties for robosigning. In judicial foreclosures, judges now take a much closer look at the affidavits and underlying paperwork and will refuse to sign off on a foreclosure if the documents are suspicious. Although, the foreclosure will probably continue once the paperwork is in order. In nonjudicial foreclosures, a homeowner can bring a lawsuit to stop a foreclosure if false affidavits or other documents were recorded as part of the foreclosure process.

Nonjudicial Foreclosures

In nonjudicial foreclosures, the only way to raise a defense to the foreclosure (other than filing for Chapter 13 bankruptcy) is to file an action in state court seeking a motion for a temporary restraining order (TRO) and preliminary injunction to enjoin (stop) the foreclosure sale while your claims are being litigated. Most people also ask the court for a permanent injunction.

In your application for a TRO, you must convince the judge that you'll suffer "irreparable injury" if the foreclosure happens. Most courts will agree that losing your home to foreclosure causes irreparable harm. Courts often grant a TRO without a formal notice or hearing, which means the foreclosing lender might not have much time to prepare a response. If the lender doesn't respond, the judge probably will grant the TRO. But you could have to post a bond to protect the lender from economic harm if you eventually lose the case, which can be expensive. You might be able to get the bond requirement waived under some circumstances, like if your income is low enough or if the court decides that the lender's interest is adequately protected. Some courts have decided that a bond isn't required in a foreclosure because the lender has a secured interest in the property and will eventually be permitted to proceed with foreclosure if the court rules against the borrower. This is especially true in cases where the property value exceeds the amount that the borrower owes. Or you could propose paying the bond by making payments such as at your regular monthly mortgage payment amount or in an amount that would offset any expense the lender might incur or, in some cases, in a de minimus (minimal) amount. The TRO will typically last until a hearing in which the court may issue a preliminary injunction that would stop the foreclosure pending a full trial on the matter.

At the preliminary injunction hearing, the court will review each party's documentation, typically the same type of documents used in a judicial foreclosure. You'll have the burden of proving that the foreclosing party didn't follow state or federal laws or the terms of the loan contract. You'll need to show the judge at the preliminary injunction stage that the foreclosure should be put on hold until you can produce your full case at trial. You might use declarations or affidavits from you and other witnesses to establish the facts you believe entitle you to stop the foreclosure. At this hearing, the court must decide whether you're likely to prevail if the case goes to trial, and the injury that you would suffer from the foreclosure outweighs the injury that the lender is suffering by not getting paid.

If the judge decides these issues in favor of the lender, the TRO will end, and the court will deny your motion for a preliminary injunction. While you can still proceed with your lawsuit, the foreclosure will likely go ahead because an injunction isn't in place to prevent it. At this point, it's a long shot, but you might be able to ask a higher court to overrule the denial.

But if you can convince the judge to halt the foreclosure until you can produce your case at trial, the judge will issue a preliminary injunction. The injunction might order the lender to fix any mistakes it made in the process, or it might just keep the TRO in effect. The lender might then try to settle with you, give up on the current foreclosure and start over, or meet any conditions the court sets and then ask the court to lift the injunction. Otherwise, you'll go to trial.

Recording a Lis Pendens

"Lis pendens" is Latin for "suit pending." If you don't record a lis pendens notice in the county records and, for whatever reason, a foreclosure sale happens, the buyer (unless it is the lender or someone closely associated with the lender), who's called a "bona fide purchaser for value," will be presumed to have had no notice of your pending suit and will receive good title to the property.

Again, it's impossible to guess exactly how long it will take for your case to wind its way through this process. If you have a valid argument, it could take at least several months. But if the only basis for your challenge is that the lender made a minor procedural violation, you'll probably gain only a few weeks of delay even if you win. You'll most likely need to hire an attorney to succeed in your lawsuit. Unfortunately, litigation is always expensive, probably many thousands of dollars, particularly when you have the burden of proof. So unless the lawyer thinks you have a very good case, you might not want to bother with a lawsuit.

If, however, you think you have a strong defense to the foreclosure and want to keep your home, the risk could be worth it. Because the law is complicated and court procedures vary quite a bit, it's a good idea to hire a lawyer if you can. If you can't afford a lawyer, you might be able to get free legal help from a legal aid office if you meet specified criteria. You can find a list of various legal aid programs on the Legal Service Corporation's website at www.lsc.gov.

TIP

Delaying foreclosure with a foreclosure mediation program. If you participate in a state or county foreclosure mediation program, you might be able to delay the foreclosure and force the lender to discuss loss mitigation options with you. You can learn more about how mediation programs work in Ch. 4.

When It Might Be Worth Fighting

If it's clear that the foreclosing party failed to follow the law and deprived you of an important right, it might be worth it to go to court and contest the foreclosure. After all, if you could get the foreclosure lawsuit dismissed or significantly delayed, you might be able to stay in your house much longer than you would otherwise. And that, of course, could have significant financial and emotional benefits. (See Ch. 9.)

Often, however, you can't really tell whether a foreclosure is illegal unless you have access to internal bank documents. You most likely won't be able to access these documents unless you file a lawsuit and seek production of the documents in discovery proceedings.

Other Strategies for Fighting Foreclosure

This section lists the most common circumstances in which you might want to contest a foreclosure in court. But many others exist. Over the years, attorneys have come up with a panoply of theories to contest foreclosures, drawing on the common law—law fashioned in cases decided by our courts. None of these theories are widely used; however, it's possible that one might be useful in your case.

For example, you might be able to block foreclosure by arguing that your loan terms are unconscionable—that is, so unfair that they shock the conscience of the judge. In one case, for example, the borrower spoke very little English, was pressured to agree to a loan that he obviously couldn't repay, wasn't represented by an attorney, and was unaware of the harsh terms attached to the loan (such as an unaffordable balloon payment).

Check *Home Foreclosures*, published by the National Consumer Law Center, for more information on these common law defenses.

You're on Active Duty in the Military

If you're on active military duty, you have some special protections under the Servicemembers Civil Relief Act (SCRA). Foreclosure on a mortgage you took out before you were on active duty must be a judicial foreclosure, no matter what the custom is in your state. You can waive this requirement, but the waiver must be in writing and be executed while you're on active duty or afterward.

If a foreclosure starts while you're on active duty, you can stay (postpone) the action for a period of not less than 90 days by requesting it from the court in writing. (See Ch. 4 for more detail on these and other SCRA laws that protect servicemembers.)

The Lender Didn't Follow State Foreclosure Procedures, Federal Mortgage Servicing Laws, or Mortgage Terms Governing Foreclosures

Because every foreclosure means that someone loses a home, courts usually require the foreclosing party to strictly follow the law and respect the terms of the mortgage or deed of trust. If they don't, you can call them on it.

But if the foreclosing party makes a trivial violation of the rules, the judge will probably let it go. Virtually all judges overlook errors that are inconsequential, such as the misspelling of a name. And the law in some states specifically provides that certain procedural errors (often failure to provide required notices, particularly when the borrower has actual notice of sale) won't affect the right to foreclose.

If the foreclosing party's error doesn't actually cause you any harm, it's probably not worth fighting over. Most courts will overlook a violation that is technical in nature and doesn't deprive you of a fair procedure, on the principle of "no harm, no foul." For example, say the lender failed to record the notice of default in the local land records office (a typical requirement) on time, but you got your required notice on time. The court might well decide that the failure to record didn't harm you and allow the foreclosure to proceed.

More severe violations will get a more serious response from the court. Significant errors include:

- not sending a breach letter (if required by the mortgage or deed of trust)
- failing to comply with federal loss mitigation requirements
- dual-tracking a foreclosure while a modification (or another foreclosure alternative) is pending or while you were making payments under a modification agreement, and
- failing to send required foreclosure notices.

For example, if the lender failed to send you a notice of default as required by state law, the lender might have to start over because the lack of adequate notice deprived you of valuable time to resolve the problem. You might have worked out an alternative arrangement with the lender, gotten refinancing, or taken advantage of state rules permitting reinstatement or redemption of the mortgage.

Other serious errors include failing to identify the breach in a notice of default, inaccurately stating the total amount due, or not giving an appropriate amount of time to cure the default in a required foreclosure notice. You might also have a solid defense if the foreclosing party didn't serve you notice of the foreclosure in the proper way or you have a federally backed mortgage loan, like an FHA-insured mortgage, but the servicer didn't comply with federal regulations governing loss mitigation procedures for that kind of loan.

The Foreclosing Party Can't Prove It Has the Right to Foreclose

A mortgage loan consists of two basic parts: (1) a promissory note setting out the terms of the loan, and (2) a security agreement (a mortgage or deed of trust) making the real estate collateral for the loan and setting out the terms under which a foreclosure might occur after a default. When the loan changes hands, the promissory note is endorsed (signed over) to the loan's new owner. In some cases, the note is endorsed in blank, which makes it a bearer instrument under Article 3 of the Uniform Commercial Code (U.C.C.). Then, any party that possesses the note has the legal authority to enforce it. In practice, all states have adopted the U.C.C. or some form of it. Similarly, the mortgage or deed of trust is "assigned" to the new owner. Assignments are typically recorded in the land records.

In the past, attorneys representing homeowners were sometimes successful in delaying or derailing foreclosures on the grounds that loan ownership hadn't been satisfactorily established due to gaps in the chain of endorsements or assignments. The legal theory involves a concept called "standing"—that is, who has the right to foreclose. But now, lenders are more careful about addressing any gaps before starting a foreclosure. Also, courts have heard this issue often and have decided against homeowners in many situations, making it harder to prevail on an argument based on standing. Still, your case might be the exception.

What Is MERS?

The mortgage banking industry created the Mortgage Electronic Registration System, Inc. (MERS) in the mid-1990s to simplify the assignment process when one entity sells a mortgage to another. MERS isn't a lender, a servicer, or an investor. Rather, it is a large electronic database of mortgages and mortgage transactions. Mortgage documents typically refer to MERS as the "mortgagee of record" and "nominee," or agent for the purpose of making future transfers to other entities.

MERS then acts as a stand-in for the loan owner in the county land records, tracking and transferring the mortgages that are registered on its system between different owners. According to MERS, it doesn't have to record these transfers in the county land records because MERS is the loan owner's nominee. Transferring loans is easier and cheaper under this scheme.

Attorneys for borrowers have challenged foreclosures involving MERS by arguing that it lacks the legal authority to act as a nominee on behalf of the original lender and subsequent loan owners. However, these arguments haven't been very successful.

Many courts have rejected borrowers' challenges to MERS's role as a nominee, ruling that MERS had authority to act, was a legitimate organization, and that the mortgage the borrowers signed put them on notice of MERS's role in home loan transactions.

A considerable amount of litigation has also dealt with whether MERS has standing to initiate a foreclosure in its name as the plaintiff in a judicial foreclosure or as a beneficiary in nonjudicial foreclosure proceedings. For example, the Maine Supreme Court held in 2010 that because MERS doesn't own the promissory note, it lacks standing to begin foreclosure proceedings in that state (*Mortgage Electronic Registration Systems, Inc. v Saunders*, 2 A.2d 289 (Maine 2010)). The Supreme Court of Minnesota, on the other hand, decided in the case of *Jackson v. Mortgage Electronic Registration Systems, Inc.*, 770 N.W.2d 487 (Minn. 2009) that MERS does have standing to foreclose.

What Is MERS? (continued)

As a result of this type of litigation, MERS instituted a significant policy change in 2011, generally prohibiting members from conducting foreclosures in its name. Now, in most states there won't be any more new MERS foreclosures. MERS now typically assigns the mortgage or deed of trust to the foreclosing party before the foreclosure starts. In the unlikely event that MERS is the foreclosing party in your foreclosure case, you'll want to be familiar with cases involving MERS. (See Ch. 10 for more information on doing your own legal research.)

The issue of standing is complicated, and the law varies among states. In some courts, the foreclosing party must establish that it has the right to enforce the note (that is, it holds the note or is acting as the note holder's authorized representative) in order to foreclose. If your loan has been transferred multiple times or was securitized, proving just who has this right can be difficult. The original promissory note you signed is stored somewhere, but it might be difficult for a foreclosing party to come up with the original or a copy. Even if the original note is available, the endorsements might not be in order.

When it comes to assignments of mortgages, many courts follow the general rule that the mortgage follows the note. So, when the foreclosing party has the right to enforce the note, a recorded assignment of the mortgage might not be needed.

However, some states have a law that requires a valid, recorded assignment of the mortgage (or deed of trust) for the foreclosure to be lawful. Nonjudicial foreclosure states, in particular, tend to require an assignment as part of the foreclosure process.

Cases about the ownership of mortgages, deeds of trust, and promissory notes, and the legality of foreclosure proceedings, can be very difficult to argue. You'll most likely need an attorney to help you review your ability to raise a defense based on standing and argue it in court if you decide to go this route. If you do decide to represent yourself, Nolo has an excellent book on this topic. See *Represent Yourself in Court*, by Paul Bergman and Sara J. Berman. Keep in mind you're unlikely to be successful these days if you simply say that you don't know who owns your mortgage loan, you want the foreclosing party to "produce the note," or that you have a MERS loan (see "What Is MERS?" above). You'll need to know the laws in your state and how to present the arguments properly.

The Mortgage Servicer Made a Serious Mistake

Mortgage servicers sometimes make mistakes when they're dealing with borrowers. In fact, many state and federal settlements have revealed just how error-prone servicers are when handling home loans (for instance, the National Mortgage Settlement, the Ocwen National Servicing Settlement, the National SunTrust Settlement, and the Independent Foreclosure Review). You might be able to fight your foreclosure based on servicer mistakes—for example, because the servicer imposed excessive fees or told you that you owed more than you really did.

What to Look For

Many errors happen when a lender or mortgage servicer tells you how much you must pay to reinstate your mortgage. When you receive notice of an impending foreclosure and are told how much you would need to pay to reinstate the loan, the amounts must be reasonably accurate and justified by language in the mortgage documents. For example, your lender can't require you to pay a fee for a monthly reappraisal or inspection of the property if the mortgage documents don't provide for it, if you were current on your payments when the inspection was made, or if the overall number of inspections or the inspection fee itself is obviously unreasonable. You could properly contest the foreclosure on the ground that the notice you received deprived you of the right to reinstate your mortgage because of the excessive fees.

> **EXAMPLE:** Henry receives a statutory notice of default that tells him he'll have to make up five missed payments and pay costs of $2,800. The costs include $800 for a reappraisal of the property and $2,000 for ten drive-by property inspections at $200 each. While he could make up the missed payments, he can't afford the costs, so he doesn't reinstate the loan within the time allowed in the notice.
>
> An attorney advises Henry that the reappraisal and inspection fees are unreasonable, so Henry contests the foreclosure on the basis that the notice of default was faulty. The court agrees and delays the foreclosure for a month to give Henry time to reinstate the mortgage without paying the inflated fees. If Henry doesn't reinstate on time, the foreclosure will go forward.

Determining whether your mortgage agreement allows a particular cost or procedure requires careful reading of the document. The fact is, mortgages are often almost undecipherable—you need an expert to make sense of them. One area of contention is the amount the lender charges for attorneys' fees. As a general rule, such charges must be reasonable, though some state laws specifically limit the amount of attorneys' fees that can be charged in a foreclosure.

If the mortgage has been bought by Freddie Mac or Fannie Mae or insured by the FHA, the law limits what attorneys can charge for services related to mortgage defaults or foreclosures. Limits also apply to fees charged by mortgage servicers. If the fees exceed these limits, and reinstatement of the mortgage is conditioned on payment of the fees, the result depends on the kind of foreclosure proceeding:

- **In a judicial foreclosure,** the judge could dismiss the foreclosure proceedings and require the lender to start over or delay the foreclosure, giving you more time to reinstate.
- **In a nonjudicial foreclosure,** a violation of attorneys' fee limits could be the basis for you to ask the court for an order (injunction) halting the foreclosure proceedings.

Rules on Force-Placed Insurance

Most mortgages and deeds of trust require the homeowner to maintain adequate insurance on the home so that the lender's interest is protected in case of fire or other casualty. This type of insurance also covers the loss of your personal property if stolen, damaged, or destroyed. If you let your homeowners' insurance coverage lapse, the mortgage servicer can purchase insurance coverage at your expense. This is called "force-placed" or "lender-placed" insurance. This type of policy does not cover your personal belongings. Force-placed insurance policies tend to be costly because of uncertainty about what might happen to the home if the borrower isn't keeping up with the bills.

Under mortgage servicing regulations that went into effect January 10, 2014, the servicer must send two notices to you before imposing force-placed insurance. The servicer must send the first notice at least 45 days before purchasing a force-placed insurance policy. The servicer must then send a second notice (a reminder notice) no earlier than 30 days after the first notice and at least 15 days before charging you for force-placed insurance coverage. This notice must include the cost of the force-placed insurance or a reasonable estimate of the cost.

If you obtain hazard insurance on your own and provide proof to the servicer, the servicer must cancel the force-placed insurance within 15 days of receiving evidence of existing insurance, and refund any premiums charged for duplicate coverage.

In addition to errant attorneys' fees, other common errors that your servicer might have made that could lead a court to stop a foreclosure are:

- misapplying your mortgage payments (like not crediting a payment to your account or applying the payment to the wrong account)
- buying homeowners' insurance for the property and billing you for it even though you already carried (and were current on) the

insurance required by your mortgage agreement (see "Rules on Force-Placed Insurance," below)

- failing to pay your property taxes, resulting in your owing fines to the government, even though you were paying into an escrow account and the servicer was responsible for paying the taxes
- considerably overstating the amount you must pay in a reinstatement or payoff quote
- charging you late fees and property inspection fees even though you were current on your mortgage payments or charging unreasonably high fees
- overcharging you for other fees or charging unreasonable types of fees
- failing to properly implement a loan modification, and
- engaging in coercive collection practices and falsely claiming that certain amounts are due.

How to Get Information About Errors

The more information you can get from your mortgage servicer, the better. A federal law called the Real Estate Settlement Procedures Act (RESPA) provides a way for you to challenge common types of errors such as improper charges, improper calculation of interest, or the failure to credit payments properly. It also gives you a way to get the information you need to make such a challenge.

Start by sending the servicer what's known under RESPA as a qualified written request. In it, you identify the borrower, the account, and the information you're after. Under amendments to Regulation X (which implements RESPA) that went into effect January 10, 2014, your inquiry might be categorized as a "request for information" or a "notice of error." (12 C.F.R. § 1024.36, 12 C.F.R. § 1024.35.) These categorizations expand on the previous qualified written request requirements. Different time frames for the servicer to respond to you apply, depending on the type of request you send.

TIP

Send your request to the correct address. The servicer can require that you send your inquiry to a particular address. Check for the correct address on the servicer's website, your periodic statements or coupon books, or on notices that the servicer sent you regarding early intervention and loss mitigation.

Request for Information

Within five business days of receiving a request for information, the servicer must provide you with written acknowledgement that it received your request. Within 30 business days, the servicer must provide the information you requested or explain why it isn't available, plus give you the name and contact information of someone you can follow up with. (The servicer must respond within ten business days if the information you're seeking is the identity, address, or other relevant contact information for the owner or assignee of your mortgage loan.) The 30-day period may be extended for an additional 15 days if, within that 30-day period, the servicer notifies you of the extension and the reasons for delay in responding.

Notice of Error

The servicer must provide a written acknowledgment within five business days of receiving a notice of error asserting certain types of mistakes, like the servicer didn't:

- accept your payments
- apply or credit payments properly
- pay taxes or insurance, or
- provide accurate information regarding loss mitigation options and foreclosures.

Other errors that would trigger this process include the servicer's imposition of fees or charges without a reasonable basis, as well as other errors relating to the servicing of your mortgage loan. Errors related to the origination, underwriting, or a subsequent sale or securitization, however, wouldn't trigger the servicer's obligation to respond under RESPA.

The servicer must correct the error, provide notification of the correction, and give contact information for you to follow up (or let you know that no error occurred along with the reasons for this determination). The time period in which the servicer must do this depends on the type of error you asserted in your notice.

- If you complained that the servicer failed to provide an accurate payoff statement upon your request, it must respond not later than seven business days after it gets your notice.

- If your notice asserts that the servicer improperly started the foreclosure during the 120-day preforeclosure waiting period, moved for a foreclosure judgment or order of sale, or conducted a foreclosure sale in violation of federal mortgage servicing laws on loss mitigation procedures (basically, if you've asserted that the servicer dual-tracked your loan), it must respond prior to the date of a foreclosure sale or within 30 business days after it got your notice, whichever is earlier.

- For all other types of errors, it must respond not later than 30 business days after it gets your notice of error.

- The 30-day period may be extended for an additional 15 days if, within that 30-day period, the servicer notifies you of the extension and the reasons for the delay in responding. The servicer can't get the extension if the notice of error pertains to a payoff statement request or certain errors pertaining to loss mitigation and foreclosure.

When the Servicer Doesn't Have to Comply

If the servicer determines that it doesn't have to comply with your error resolution or information request for some reason—for example, the notice of error or request for information is essentially the same as one you previously sent or your request is overbroad—it must notify you no later than five business days after making that determination and give you its reason for the determination.

What Happens to Credit Reporting and a Pending Foreclosure During Your Request?

While this process is going on, the servicer can't report to a credit reporting agency that a payment is overdue if it relates to your notice of error. If you send a request for information, however, it can continue to report overdue payments.

In most situations, if you request information or send a notice of error after a foreclosure has begun, the servicer can continue with foreclosure proceedings. It must stop the foreclosure, however, if your notice of error is based on the 120-day preforeclosure waiting period or dual-tracking restrictions. In those situations, the issue must be resolved before the servicer can continue with the foreclosure, unless the servicer receives the notice of error seven or fewer days before the foreclosure sale. If that's the case, the servicer only has to make a good faith attempt to respond to your notice of error, orally or in writing, and either correct the error or state the reason it determined that no error occurred.

Remedies If the Servicer Doesn't Follow the Rules

If the servicer fails to comply with the law, you can sue for statutory damages of $2,000, reimbursement for your attorneys' fees, and compensation for your other losses. (12 U.S.C. § 2605.)

RESOURCE

Sample request for information and notice of error. You can find samples of these letters on the CFPB's website at www.consumerfinance.gov. Search for "How do I dispute an error or request information about my mortgage?" Then, click on the "sample letter" links.

The Lender Engaged in Unfair Lending Practices

You might be able to fight your foreclosure by proving one or more violations of federal or state laws designed to protect you against illegal lending practices.

Two federal laws protect against unfair lending practices associated with residential mortgages and loans: the Truth in Lending Act (TILA) and the Home Ownership and Equity Protection Act (HOEPA). Technically, HOEPA is part of TILA. Both allow you to sue for money damages, including a refund of any financing costs you paid. Both of them also let you cancel your mortgage under some circumstances. Canceling the mortgage would usually work to defeat the foreclosure if you could arrange for a refinance to return the remaining loan principal to the lender.

As powerful as these statutes might sound, most lenders are aware of them and either comply with their requirements or structure their loans so that they don't apply. Still, your case might be the exception.

The Right to Rescind the Loan

For the purpose of fighting a foreclosure, the most important provision of these laws is that you might, for some types of loans and some types of violations, be able to retroactively cancel or rescind your loan. This right is referred to as the "right to an extended rescission."

Both laws require a lender to give you a three-day rescission period when you take out the loan. But your right to rescind is extended for three years if it later comes to light that the lender violated an important part of the law. TILA also permits rescission by way of recoupment even after the three-year period expires, if state law allows it. (Recoupment is a defense to a collection action, like a foreclosure.) So, if one or both of these laws cover the mortgage being foreclosed, and you can show a material violation of these laws, you can cancel the loan and, by doing that, defeat the foreclosure. But those are a couple of big "ifs." Let's take them one at a time.

What Loans Are Covered

Under TILA, the right to extended rescission applies only if you did not use the mortgage loan to buy or build your primary residence. So a first mortgage, which you used to buy your house, isn't covered. But a home equity loan, equity line of credit, or refinancing loan would be. The law is aimed at predatory lenders who use loans to skim the equity from borrowers' homes, particularly those of older, minority, and low- income homeowners.

But lenders of second or third mortgages rarely foreclose—so the right to rescind is unlikely to help you with foreclosure. It might, however, help you if you refinanced your first mortgage and the holder of the new mortgage is foreclosing.

HOEPA initially applied only to high-cost loans that were closed-end consumer credit (that is, loans repayable under specific terms over a specified term). Beginning on January 10, 2014, pursuant to the Dodd-Frank Act, the coverage of HOEPA expanded. Under rules promulgated by the Consumer Financial Protection Bureau, most types of mortgage loans secured by a consumer's principal dwelling, including purchase-money mortgages, refinances, closed-end home equity loans, and open-end credit plans (home equity lines of credit or HELOCs) are now potentially subject to HOEPA coverage. However, significantly, HOEPA's right to rescind doesn't apply to mortgages taken out to purchase a home or a refinancing of that mortgage loan by the same creditor if no new money is advanced.

HOEPA imposes additional requirements on high-cost mortgage loans, which means those made at high rates or excessive costs and fees. A mortgage loan is considered high-cost if the borrower's principal dwelling secures the loan and one of the following is true:

- The loan's annual percentage rate (APR) exceeds a certain threshold.
- The amount of points and fees paid in connection with the transaction exceed a particular threshold.

- The prepayment penalties the lender charges under the loan or credit agreement exceed a specific amount (or can be charged after a certain time period).

The APR Test

A loan is considered a high-cost mortgage if its APR on the date the interest rate is set exceeds the Average Prime Offer Rate (an annual percentage rate that is derived from average interest rates, points, and other loan pricing terms) for a comparable transaction on that date by more than:

- 6.5 percentage points for first-mortgage loans, generally
- 8.5 percentage points for first-mortgage loans, if less than $50,000 and secured by personal property (such as an RV, a boat, or a manufactured home that is considered personal property), or
- 8.5 percentage points for subordinate loans (second or third mortgages, HELOCs, etc.). (12 C.F.R. § 1026.32.)

The Points and Fees Test

As of January 1, 2021, a mortgage is also considered to be a high-cost mortgage if its points and fees exceed:

- 5% of the total loan amount if the loan is equal to or more than $22,052, or
- the lesser of 8% of the total loan amount or $1,103 if the loan is less than $22,052.

These figures are adjusted annually. (12 C.F.R. § 1026.32.)

The Prepayment Penalty Test

A loan is a high-cost mortgage if the lender charges a prepayment penalty:

- more than 36 months after the loan is taken out, or
- in an amount that exceeds 2% of the amount prepaid.

If the loan is indeed a high-cost mortgage, a prepayment penalty isn't allowed. (12 C.F.R. § 1026.32.)

What Is a Material Violation of TILA and HOEPA

To be able to rescind your loan, you must also show that the lender materially violated the law—in plain English, that it violated a significant provision of the law.

Material violations of TILA. Lenders violate this law when they don't make the disclosures it requires, for example, the notice of your right to cancel, as well as the annual percentage rate, the finance charge, the amount financed, the total payments, the payment schedule, and more. Typically, these terms are found in the documents you receive when taking out the loan. The numbers must be accurate to within very narrow tolerances. Depending on the type of loan, the disclosed annual percentage rate (APR) must be within one-eighth of one percentage point of the actual APR. The total finance charge can't be understated by more than $100 in most cases and by not more than $35 if the creditor has started foreclosure proceedings. (15 U.S.C. § 1635(i)(2), 12 C.F.R. § 1026.18(d), 12 C.F.R.§ 1026.23(g).)

Material violations of HOEPA. The violations must be something that deprived you of the benefits of HOEPA. A lender that makes a HOEPA loan must comply with various notice provisions. The lender is also subject to restrictions on fees and practices. For example, late fees are limited to 4% of the past-due payment and balloon payments are generally prohibited except under limited circumstances. (12 C.F.R. § 1026.34(a)(8), 12 C.F.R. § 1026.32(d).) Ultimately, a violation of HOEPA's disclosure requirements or the inclusion of a prohibited term triggers an extended right to rescind the loan.

Who Can Be Held Responsible for TILA and HOEPA Violations

TILA and HOEPA apply not only to the original lender or mortgage originator, but also to any person or entity who became an owner through an assignment. In other words, downstream mortgage holders are held accountable for the actions of the original lenders. Downstream mortgage holders can escape liability only if they can demonstrate that a reasonable person exercising ordinary due diligence could not have determined that the loan was covered by HOEPA.

How to Rescind a Loan

To rescind a loan under TILA, you must give the creditor, not the mortgage servicer, a written notice of rescission. In 2015, the U.S. Supreme Court ruled that in order to comply with the three-year deadline to rescind, the borrower only needs to send a rescission notice; the borrower does not need to file suit within the three-year period. (See *Jesinoski, et ux. v. Countrywide Home Loans, Inc.*, 135 S.Ct. 790 (2015).)

If the rescission is successful, the lender must return everything you paid except for payments of loan principal, and you must return the portion of the loan principal that hasn't yet been repaid. In other words, when you rescind a loan, you can get out from under the loan (and the foreclosure), but you can't keep the loan proceeds. You'll need to refinance, sell the home, or find another source of funding to repay the principal.

RESOURCE

More information on TILA and HOEPA. Any attorney you hire to fight your foreclosure should be intimately familiar with TILA and HOEPA and know how those laws could help you in fighting your foreclosure. If you are representing yourself, consider buying a copy of *Home Foreclosures* and *Truth in Lending*, published by the National Consumer Law Center (www.nclc.org).

You Have a High-Cost Mortgage

A number of states have special protections for people facing foreclosure on high-cost mortgages. If your state has a high-cost mortgage statute and the lender has violated any of its provisions, you might be able to raise that violation as a defense in your foreclosure case. If your state has a high-cost mortgage statute, you'll find a summary on your state's page in the appendix, including any provisions that might help you fight your foreclosure.

The Statute of Limitations Has Expired

A "statute of limitations" sets a time limit for initiating a legal claim. If your lender starts a foreclosure after the statute of limitations has passed, the foreclosure is invalid. So, when applicable, the statute of limitations is a strong defense against foreclosure for both nonjudicial and judicial actions.

As discussed earlier in this book, a typical home loan transaction involves two main documents: the promissory note, which evidences the borrower's debt obligation, and the security instrument, usually a mortgage or deed of trust, which designates the real estate as collateral for the loan. Some states set a six-year limitations period for foreclosure based on the right to enforce a promissory note under the Uniform Commercial Code (U.C.C.) (§ 3-118). In other states, the statute of limitations for written contracts is the applicable statute. Or a more specific statute of limitations could control your case, perhaps a statute of limitations for foreclosure. In some cases, the applicable statute of limitations might be the one for enforcing a security interest in land, such as a secured interest created by a mortgage or deed of trust.

So, the statute of limitations period for foreclosure can be very different from state to state. Again, a six-year limitations period based on the right to enforce a note under the U.C.C. is common. But the statute of limitations might be ten to twenty years, or shorter or longer, depending on where you live.

When Does the Statute of Limitations Clock Start Ticking?

When the statute of limitations starts to run depends on state law and the circumstances. For an individual payment, the statute of limitations clock begins when the default, like a missed payment, happens. The limitations period is usually calculated from the date of the last payment or the due date of the first missed mortgage payment. Again, this depends on your state's law. Some courts treat each missed payment like a new default, which restarts the clock.

For the full loan, the statute of limitations generally starts on the loan's maturity date, often 15 or 30 years after the first payment due date. Before the maturity date, the borrower has the right to pay the loan back in installments.

The limitations period can also start when the lender accelerates the loan. Acceleration occurs following the loan default. When the loan is accelerated, the full loan balance becomes due immediately, and the lender can foreclose if the borrower doesn't pay off the entire outstanding balance.

Stopping a Foreclosure Using a Statute of Limitations Defense

If the statute of limitations has expired, you have a basis to fight the foreclosure. But you'll have to assert this defense in front of a judge to defeat the lender's claim, which is easier in a judicial foreclosure than a nonjudicial one; otherwise, the defense is deemed waived.

What If the Statute of Limitations Expires After Foreclosure Starts?

If the statute of limitations runs out after the foreclosure process has already started, then the statute of limitations isn't a defense to the foreclosure. So, even if a foreclosure takes years to complete, if the statute of limitations expires while the foreclosure is in process, the foreclosure can still go through. To comply with a statute-of-limitations law, the lender just has to start the foreclosure before the deadline passes.

The statute of limitations will also apply to any subsequent foreclosure, even if a prior foreclosure is canceled or dismissed. Generally, the lender would have to start another foreclosure within the period provided for in the statute of limitations. But if the lender revokes the loan's acceleration (called "decelerating" or "de-accelerating" the loan), the statute of limitations usually starts over.

Specific actions can decelerate a loan that the lender previously accelerated. For example, if you make a payment, the statute of limitations might restart. Also, the statute of limitations generally restarts if the lender gives you notice that it's canceling the acceleration and allowing you to keep making payments. However, at least one court, in Florida, ruled that simply dismissing a prior foreclosure action decelerates the loan. (*Bartram v. U.S. Bank*, 211 So. 3d 1009 (Fla. 2016)). And in New York, the Court of Appeals ruled on four foreclosure cases involving deceleration. It said that a lender's voluntary withdrawal of a foreclosure action decelerates the loan, and subsequent foreclosure actions aren't time-barred. (*Freedom Mortgage Corp. v. Engel*, ---N.E.3d--- (Feb.18, 2021). But entering into a repayment plan or if the lender considers you for loss mitigation probably won't revoke acceleration. Precisely what constitutes deceleration of a loan varies depending on state law.

If you think you might want to raise a statute of limitations defense, you'll most likely need an attorney to help you review your state's laws and argue it on your behalf.

When You Can Sue for Money

A number of state and federal laws also give you the right to sue violators for compensation for your monetary losses. But the violations don't mean you can stop the foreclosure itself. The reason? Mortgages have become investment vehicles, and for the system to work, investors must be able to rely on the legitimacy of their investments. If all bad behavior by a mortgage broker, servicer, or lender could retroactively be used to devalue an investment, investors would never invest.

For instance, say that a mortgage broker recklessly encouraged you to take out a mortgage you couldn't afford, telling you that you could refinance in a year or two and make the mortgage more affordable then.

You might think that a court would make things right by denying the foreclosure and ordering the lender to rewrite your loan to make it affordable. Unfortunately, this sort of relief is usually not available. But if you can cast doubt on the legality of your mortgage or the foreclosure proceedings, you might have the leverage against your lender you need to get a modification. (See "The Lender Didn't Follow State Foreclosure Procedures, Federal Mortgage Servicing Laws, or Mortgage Terms Governing Foreclosures" and "The Foreclosing Party Can't Prove It Has the Right to Foreclose," above.)

The legal doctrine of "promissory estoppel" is another tool borrowers sometimes use to seek monetary damages from banks that broke their promises to homeowners. Under promissory estoppel, someone who makes a promise is prevented (estopped) from reneging on that promise if the person to whom the promise was made reasonably relied on the promise by taking some action (or failing to take action) and suffered monetary damages as a result.

In one class-action lawsuit, the named plaintiff claimed that her lender promised her a permanent mortgage modification if she completed a trial period during which she made modified payments to the bank. The plaintiff made the payments required during the trial period, but the bank refused to give her the permanent modification as promised. The homeowner complained that she had reasonably relied on the bank's promise, made the payments, and suffered money damages (the amount of the modified payments, which she would not have made without the bank's promise of a permanent modification) when the bank reneged on its promise.

The case ultimately settled. The bank involved in the suit agreed to provide the borrowers with:

- an opportunity to reapply for a new loan modification
- paid counseling assistance from qualified, independent, non-profit organizations
- foreclosure stays, in most circumstances, to prevent foreclosure while they applied for a modification, and
- a waiver of certain fees and costs if the loan was modified.

This case's outcome doesn't mean, of course, that your lender will easily settle if you sue it based on a promissory estoppel theory or that the court in your case will allow you to proceed with a claim of promissory estoppel. While foreclosing lenders are increasingly being held accountable for their actions, this type of dispute is very fact sensitive, especially when it comes to whether you reasonably relied on the lender's promise to your detriment. If you think you have a claim of promissory estoppel against your lender or mortgage servicer, you should speak with an attorney.

If You Decide to Leave Your House

Let the Foreclosure Proceed 179

Be Community Minded 182

Be Wary of Leaving the Home Before the Foreclosure Sale 182

Sell the House in a Short Sale 184

    Advantages of a Short Sale 185

    Disadvantages of a Short Sale 185

    Will You Be Able to Work Out a Short Sale? 187

Offer the Lender a Deed in Lieu of Foreclosure 193

    Will the Lender Accept a Deed in Lieu? 193

    Fannie Mae and Freddie Mac Deeds in Lieu of Foreclosure 194

Avoiding Deficiency Judgments 194

Income Tax Liability for Deficiencies 195

Once it appears that foreclosure is inevitable, people sometimes pack up their belongings and their families and immediately look for a new place to live. They fear losing reliable shelter and want to find another home as soon as possible where they'll feel secure. Staying in a house facing foreclosure can be terrifying if you think you might end up out on the street. And it could be unbearably depressing if you're reminded every day that you won't be living there indefinitely.

While these reactions to foreclosure certainly are understandable, foreclosure can actually be a time of opportunity. You will almost certainly have enough time to find a new place to live. Meanwhile, it could prove to be a big financial advantage to stay put for a while—maybe a long while.

Giving Up the House: Your Options

- **Sell your home:** If you have equity in your home (the house is worth more than you owe), you might be able to sell it quickly by pricing it aggressively, which means low, and then pay off the loan. You might even be able to leave with some money in your pocket.
- **Let foreclosure work for you:** Stay in the house as long as possible without making any payments to save money for a future move.
- **Short sale:** If you're "underwater" (you owe more than the home is worth), put the house up for sale and persuade the lender to accept a potential buyer's offer and let you off the hook for the loan.
- **Deed in lieu of foreclosure:** Persuade the lender to let you sign over the deed in exchange for canceling a foreclosure.
- **Walk away:** Move out when it suits you and let the foreclosure proceed. Works best when your lender can't sue you for a deficiency. (Though if you do this, you might become the victim of a zombie foreclosure. See below for more on this subject.)
- **Work out a mortgage modification:** Apply for a modification, even if you think your efforts will ultimately prove unfruitful, to avoid being labeled a "strategic defaulter" when you apply for a mortgage in the future and gain some extra time to live in the home.
- **File for Chapter 7 or Chapter 13 bankruptcy:** Eliminate any deficiencies or taxes you owe as a result of the foreclosure or other remedies.

So try to put fear and negativity aside as you assess your options to come up with the best choice for your circumstances. This chapter lays out the basic approaches to giving up your house and the advantages and disadvantages of each.

Let the Foreclosure Proceed

If you don't fight the foreclosure or take any of the other steps discussed in this book, the foreclosure will move forward on a schedule that your lender and servicer's workloads and policies, and the laws of your state, dictate. Specific information for your state is in the appendix.

The single most important point to understand is that *you don't have to leave your house just because the lender has started foreclosure proceedings.* In most states, you'll probably be able to stay long enough to plan for the future by saving all or some of the money that you're no longer putting toward the mortgage.

> **EXAMPLE:** Joshua and Ellen got in over their heads and now can't afford the $3,000 monthly payment on their mortgage. They decide to let the house go. They already know that federal mortgage servicing regulations require the lender to wait 120 days after they quit making payments before officially starting the foreclosure. They then turn to their state's page in the appendix to see how much more time they have. They learn that:
> - They will receive what's called a notice of default in their state. This notice gives them an additional three months to make things right. If they don't (and remember, they plan to let the house go), they will have another 20 days' notice before the house is sold.
> - They can file for Chapter 7 bankruptcy and delay the sale by three additional months. Bankruptcy will also let them leave without owing the lender anything. (They otherwise could face a deficiency judgment in their situation.)
> - After the foreclosure sale, they'll probably be able to stay in the house for a month or so.

Altogether, they'll have around a year of living in the house without making payments, and if they can save at least $2,000 a month, they will have roughly $25,000 in the bank when they set out to seek a new place to live. (See Ch. 9 for more details on how this all works.)

Foreclosure Moratoriums

The Department of Housing and Urban Development (HUD), the Department of Veterans Affairs (VA), the Department of Agriculture (USDA), and Federal Housing Finance Agency (FHFA) set foreclosure moratoriums for federally backed mortgage loans, including FHA-insured, VA-guaranteed, USDA loans, and Fannie Mae- and Freddie Mac-backed loans through at least June 30, 2021, due to the coronavirus crisis. Also, many states and localities imposed a foreclosure suspension when the pandemic began. Many of these moratoriums have expired, but some are still in place. To find out whether any moratoriums are ongoing in your area, talk to a foreclosure lawyer. You can also find the latest developments at www.nolo.com/legal-updates/legal-updates-for-foreclosure.

Natural disasters, new state laws, and further federal regulations could also lead to additional foreclosure moratoriums in the future.

And, if you're unlucky enough to have your foreclosure fall around the holidays, lenders sometimes impose moratoriums on evictions following foreclosures at Christmastime. In the past, most major lenders also tended to hold off on conducting foreclosure sales during this time, but that's no longer the case.

How much time you'll get to remain in your house and how much money you can save, depend on these factors:

- how soon in the whole process you decide to stop making payments
- if you apply for a loan modification, how long the process takes before your servicer issues a denial and proceeds with foreclosure (probably about 30 days, longer if you're entitled to an appeal period)

- whether judicial or nonjudicial foreclosure is used in your state (judicial foreclosures usually take longer than nonjudicial ones)
- whether any foreclosure moratoriums are in effect (see above)
- whether your state's law gives you the right to live in the home during a post-sale redemption period
- whether part of your strategy involves filing for bankruptcy before the foreclosure sale, which provides an additional two to three months' delay, and
- if you file for bankruptcy, how much money you can keep under your state's exemption laws.

These variables are discussed in detail in Ch. 9, and your state's page in the appendix will give you an estimate of how long you can remain in your home.

Walking Away From Your House

What about just walking away from your house? If you do, sooner or later, the lender will foreclose on the property and sell it. You might think this won't concern you; you'll be gone, onto the next phase of your life. You might—or might not—be correct, depending on your potential tax liability and potential liability for the unpaid part of the loan. Some people could be better off emotionally by shutting their old house out of their minds and finding a new home in some different location. But for most people, this option makes the least sense.

If you want to use the foreclosure to your best advantage, at least consider remaining in the home for as long as possible—payment free—and, depending on the circumstances, think about filing for bankruptcy to rid yourself from any liabilities arising from your former home ownership. And if tax liability is an issue, you should do your best to file for bankruptcy before the foreclosure sale or be prepared to prove that you were insolvent at the time of the foreclosure sale.

Be Community Minded

The longer you stay in your home throughout the foreclosure process, the better off your lender, the ultimate purchaser, and your neighborhood will be. Neighborhoods full of vacant homes are often plagued by theft and vandalism.

If the owners of those homes stayed put and continued to maintain them, everyone's home values would likely be higher. The point is that you are earning your keep by remaining on the property until a new owner is ready to assume occupancy.

Be Wary of Leaving the Home Before the Foreclosure Sale

If you decide to leave your home before the foreclosure sale occurs, you could end up in a zombie foreclosure. With a "zombie foreclosure," sometimes called "zombie title," you move out after foreclosure starts, but the process is canceled, the sale is never held, or the home's title is never officially transferred to a new owner. As a result, certain debts continue to accrue in your name and follow you like the walking dead.

Zombie foreclosure numbers tend to be high in states where the foreclosure process takes a long time, such as in judicial foreclosure states like Florida, New York, and New Jersey. Homeowners who are eager to move on with their lives sometimes abandon their homes when the foreclosure process drags on. Zombie foreclosures also often occur in lower-income areas where the lender isn't anxious to assume responsibility for the upkeep of the property and wants to save on taxes, as well as other costs. If squatters occupy the property or it falls into severe disrepair, the lender could simply wash its hands of the property. Or the lender might have other reasons for not following through with the foreclosure, such as it already has too much inventory or the costs of foreclosing don't justify completing the foreclosure.

In this situation, because title is never transferred out of your name, you remain liable for any property taxes, HOA dues, and maintenance on the property. Debts associated with these responsibilities can go unpaid for years. They'll then come back to haunt you even though you have no idea that the foreclosure process was never completed because the lender wasn't legally required to inform you that the foreclosure stopped or it might not be able to locate you after you moved out.

Zombie Homes in Wisconsin

The Wisconsin Supreme Court decided in 2015 that lenders couldn't let "zombie" homes linger in the foreclosure process indefinitely. In the case of *Bank of New York Mellon v. Carson*, 2015 Wisc. 15 (Feb. 17, 2015), the bank obtained a foreclosure judgment but never held a foreclosure sale. The homeowner had moved out of the home around the time the foreclosure started and was subsequently fined for building code violations after the property fell into disrepair. The homeowner then sued the bank to force it to finish the foreclosure by selling her home at a foreclosure sale.

The Court of Appeals ultimately sided with the homeowner and decided that the bank must proceed to a sale if it obtains a judgment of foreclosure on an abandoned (empty) home. (Previously, a bank could let an abandoned house linger indefinitely in the foreclosure process.) The Wisconsin Supreme Court subsequently upheld this decision and ruled that the sale must occur within a reasonable amount of time. For a while, this ruling meant that a lender couldn't simply walk away from a vacant Wisconsin property in foreclosure, leaving the homeowner with the problem of a zombie home.

But the Wisconsin legislature responded in 2016 by passing a law that states a lender foreclosing on an abandoned home must do one of the following things within 12 months after the court enters a foreclosure judgment: hold a foreclosure sale, or release the mortgage lien and vacate (cancel) the judgment of foreclosure. (Wis. Stat. § 846.102.) So, instead of finishing the foreclosure, the lender can cancel the proceedings and walk away from the property, leaving the borrower to face the problem of a zombie home.

Say you leave your property, and title is never transferred out of your name. The following things, among others, could happen months or even years later:

- The tax collector could come looking to collect back property taxes.
- An HOA might file a lawsuit to recover unpaid assessments.
- You could be threatened with fines for not complying with housing codes and ordinances.
- The local government could send you a bill for yard maintenance, repairs, trash removal, or graffiti scrubbing.

The risk of a zombie foreclosure provides yet another reason to remain in your home as long as possible. You'll be much more likely to avoid becoming the victim if you stay through the entire foreclosure process and wait for an official notice to vacate before moving out.

If you choose to move out early, you should confirm that the lender completes the foreclosure sale and transfers the home's title out of your name. Review the land records at the county recorder's office (in person or, in some cases, online) to make sure a new deed has been recorded. If the home remains in your name, you should be aware that you're still on the hook for expenses related to the property, such as property taxes and HOA dues.

Sell the House in a Short Sale

In a short sale, you sell your house before it's auctioned off in foreclosure for an amount that falls short of what you owe on it. For a short sale to work, all lenders, like first and second mortgage holders, must agree to receive less than they're entitled to under the terms of the loans you signed.

Advantages of a Short Sale

The main benefit of a short sale is that, if the lender agrees, it allows you to get out from under your mortgage without liability for the loan amount that's left unpaid. You also won't have a foreclosure or a bankruptcy on your credit record. The general thinking is that your credit won't suffer as much as it would were you to let the foreclosure proceed or file for bankruptcy to get out from under any liability you might incur in the course of the foreclosure.

Your credit rating will take a major hit regardless of which option you choose—short sale, foreclosure, or bankruptcy.

 RESOURCE

For more information on how these options will affect your credit, see Ch. 1 or get *Credit Repair: Make a Plan, Improve Your Credit, Avoid Scams* by Amy Loftsgordon and Cara O'Neill (Nolo).

Disadvantages of a Short Sale

Short sales have some drawbacks when compared to letting a foreclosure happen or filing for bankruptcy.

No Chance to Stay and Save

If you sell your house, you'll be expected to leave as soon as escrow closes. But if you let the foreclosure happen and stay in the property until you're formally told to leave by written notice, you can build savings that you can draw on in the future to put toward rental housing. (Again, see Ch. 9 for more about this strategy.)

It's difficult to accomplish a short sale if you don't get started as soon as you learn about the pending foreclosure, especially if you have to deal with several mortgage holders. Needless to say, if you don't complete the short sale before the foreclosure sale, you'll have nothing to sell.

Potential Deficiency Judgment

In a short sale, the sale price is "short" of the full amount you owe to the lender; the difference between the total debt owed and the sale price is the "deficiency." For example, say your lender approves a short sale in the amount of $200,000, but you owe $250,000. The deficiency is $50,000. In many states, the lender is prohibited from getting a deficiency judgment following a foreclosure. However, most states don't prohibit the lender from getting a deficiency judgment after a short sale. (California is one of the few states that does specifically prohibit deficiency judgments following short sales.) (Cal. Civ. Proc. Code § 580e.) If you want to avoid a deficiency judgment following a short sale, you'll have to make sure that the short sale agreement expressly states that the transaction is in full satisfaction of the debt and that the lender waives its right to the deficiency. Or you might be able to negotiate a reduced deficiency.

Potential Tax Liability

A short sale could generate an unwelcome surprise: taxable income based on the amount the sale proceeds are short of what you owe. While in recent years, homeowners have been able to exclude forgiven debt related to a short sale (or a foreclosure or deed in lieu of foreclosure) from their federal taxable income under the Qualified Principal Residence Exclusion, established by the Mortgage Forgiveness Debt Relief Act of 2007, you can only do this if you took out the mortgage to buy, build, or substantially improve your home (or to refinance debt incurred for these purposes), and the debt was forgiven in calendar years 2007 through 2025, or discharged after that if you entered into a written agreement before January 1, 2026. On the other hand, if you borrowed against your principal residence and used the money for any other purpose, such as to buy a second house, pay college tuition for a child, or take a vacation, and you end up not paying it back in full, the amount your lender writes off, typically whatever amount wasn't paid back, is considered forgiven debt. Although the concept isn't intuitive, the IRS treats forgiven debt as taxable income, subject to regular income tax.

EXAMPLE: Jess owes $150,000 on her first mortgage and $50,000 on the second, which she borrowed to pay for her daughter's first year of tuition at an exclusive Eastern college. Jess loses her job and is facing foreclosure. She arranges to sell the house in 2020 for $140,000 and gets permission from her first lender to pay off the first mortgage for $135,000 and permission from her second mortgage lender to pay off the second mortgage for $5,000.

The $15,000 the first mortgage holder will write off (forgive) isn't considered taxable income because Jess used it to acquire the house. But the amount the second mortgage holder will write off, $45,000, is forgiven debt and considered taxable income to Jess because it wasn't used to buy or improve her principal residence.

If you face this situation and can prove to the IRS you were legally insolvent at the time of the short sale, you won't have to pay the tax (see "Income Tax Liability for Deficiencies," below). Insolvency is when your total debts are more than the value of your total equity in your real estate and personal property. You can also get rid of this kind of tax liability by filing for Chapter 7 or Chapter 13 bankruptcy if you file before escrow closes. Of course, if you're going to file for bankruptcy anyway, there isn't much point in pursuing a short sale because the bankruptcy will negate any benefit to your credit rating from completing a short sale. Also, forgiven debt might affect your state taxes.

Will You Be Able to Work Out a Short Sale?

Historically, short sale deals have often fallen apart because of the amount of time required to obtain the lender's approval. When the housing crisis happened, so many people requested short sales that lenders simply couldn't keep up with the volume. Sellers and buyers often got frustrated and chose to give up on the deals before the sales were approved. Since then, many lenders have increased their personnel and streamlined the process to better handle increased requests for short sales, often because the law requires them to.

Under federal mortgage servicing regulations, you have 120 days after falling delinquent before the servicer can start the foreclosure. You can apply for a short sale during this time. If you don't submit an application then and the foreclosure starts, you can still apply. So long as you submit your loss mitigation application more than 37 days before a scheduled foreclosure sale, the servicer can't move for foreclosure judgment or order of sale, or conduct a foreclosure sale, while it evaluates your application. Generally, the servicer must complete its evaluation within 30 days.

After its evaluation, the servicer might give you the opportunity to enter into a listing or marketing period agreement (assuming you don't already have an offer). During the listing or marketing period, the servicer won't pursue a foreclosure. If you don't obtain an approved short sale transaction by the end of the marketing or listing period, the servicer can proceed with the foreclosure. (An "approved short sale transaction" is a short sale transaction that has been approved by all relevant parties, including the servicer, other lienholders, or insurers, if applicable, and the servicer has received proof of funds or financing.)

California Prohibits Dual Tracking of Short Sales and Foreclosures (Sort of)

Under California's Homeowner Bill of Rights, your servicer can't continue with foreclosure proceedings once a short sale is approved. (Cal. Civ. Code § 2924.11.) But because the protection doesn't kick in until the short sale is approved in writing by all parties, the servicer can initiate a foreclosure or continue with a foreclosure if you're considering a short sale, are negotiating with a buyer, or even have a short sale offer. It's not until the lender, and all other parties, such as junior lienholders, actually sign off on the deal that the dual tracking ban kicks in.

Still, California provides more protection than most other states when it comes to dual tracking and short sales. If you hope to complete a short sale in a short time frame, contact a local real estate agent with substantial experience in this area to discuss whether a short sale of your home is a realistic goal and, if it is, to start the process right away.

Strict timelines are in place for homeowners with Fannie Mae or Freddie Mac mortgages. (To find out if Fannie Mae or Freddie Mac owns your loan, go to www.knowyouroptions.com/loanlookup or https://loanlookup.freddiemac.com.) Under Fannie Mae and Freddie Mac guidelines, mortgage services are required to:

- acknowledge receipt of a short sale offer within five business days
- notify you within five business days if outstanding documentation is needed (provided you don't qualify for a streamlined process that doesn't require further documentation), and
- review and respond to a short sale offer within 30 calendar days from receipt of the offer.

And keep in mind that the loss mitigation requirements under federal mortgage servicing laws (see Ch. 4) apply to short sale requests.

Still, sometimes it's difficult to get a short sale processed in time. Short sale negotiations often occur in rushed settings because many homeowners start thinking about short sales only when they're about to lose their houses to foreclosure. And you might need a bona fide offer from a buyer before you can find out whether the lender will go along with it.

The Terms

A short sale will benefit you only if your lender (or lenders) are willing to accept the amount a buyer is willing to pay and let you off the hook for the rest. For example, if you owe $300,000 and you can sell your house for just $200,000, you're unlikely to be successful in negotiating a short sale.

Clearly, the closer the offer is to the amount you owe on the loan, the quicker the lender will sign off on the sale. It would be nice if a hard and fast line existed for how much a lender will forgo. Real estate agents and HUD-approved housing counselors should have a pretty good idea of the kind of deals lenders are accepting in your area.

You'll want to work with a real estate professional anyway when you're trying to get your house sold at a price that will be acceptable to all lenders and lienholders. A real estate agent's negotiating help can be critical because the lender might agree with the proposed offer or make a counteroffer. This process could go back and forth until everyone is satisfied or the deal falls through.

> **EXAMPLE:** Toby and Tyler face foreclosure on their first mortgage and decide a short sale is their best option. They contact a real estate agent, who tells them that they should list their house for at least 85% of their mortgage debt—or $225,000—for the sale to be acceptable to the lender. The 85% figure is based on the agent's knowledge of the going rate for lender acceptance of short sales.
>
> As the foreclosure sale date grows nearer and the house goes unsold at the 85% figure, Toby and Tyler finally get an offer that would pay 75% of their mortgage; they accept, contingent on approval by the lender. The agent takes the offer to the lender and quickly receives a rejection. The buyer raises his offer to 80%, and the lender agrees.

When a Short Sale Might Make Sense

- You can sell your house for a price that the lender (or lenders) will likely sign off on.
- You don't plan to file for Chapter 7 or Chapter 13 bankruptcy (because if you're hoping a short sale will preserve your credit record, a bankruptcy would undermine that goal).
- All your lenders are willing to let you off the hook for the deficiency (the amount by which the sales price falls short of what you owe).
- You have time before the scheduled foreclosure sale to find a buyer and to explore other options, like filing for bankruptcy. A relatively quick foreclosure time frame can be a problem in states that don't give you much notice before the sale. Keep in mind you get 120 days before the foreclosure starts to explore options to avoid foreclosure.

Convincing Multiple Lienholders

Multiple lenders (or anyone else who has a legal claim or "lien" on your property) can fatally complicate short sales. If you have only one mortgage, you have only one lender to convince. If you have two or more mortgages or other types of home loans or liens on your property, you must convince all of the lienholders. So the more lienholders there are in your picture, the harder it will be to complete a short sale, especially if the property's value has substantially decreased. In this scenario, a sale will probably produce little or no money for a second or third lienholder (typically, the holder of a tax lien, home equity loan, or line of credit). If these other lenders won't get anything out of the short sale, they don't have any incentive to release their liens (legal claims on the property) so that a new buyer can have clear title.

And more important to you, they won't absolve you from liability for what you owe them—which defeats a central purpose of the short sale.

> **EXAMPLE 1:** Carlos has a first mortgage on his property of $240,000, a second mortgage of $30,000, and $15,000 out on a home equity line of credit. He can sell the house for only $230,000. All of that money would typically go toward the first mortgage. The second mortgage and line of credit lenders wouldn't get anything. They would rather let the foreclosure go through and sue Carlos for the deficiency than accept a small percentage of what they're owed and agree to not sue him for the balance. Without their agreement, he won't be able to sell the house with clear title, because the property would still be subject to the liens of the other mortgage holders.

> **EXAMPLE 2:** John owes $225,000 on his first mortgage, $50,000 on his second mortgage, and $25,000 on a home equity loan. He falls behind on his mortgage payments and decides to put the house up for sale. John receives an offer of $260,000. This amount will more than please the first mortgage owner because its $225,000 loan will be paid off in full. The second mortgage owner won't be so happy because it will get only $35,000 of the $50,000 it's owed. But considering the fact that it wouldn't get anything if the house went into foreclosure ("junior" liens are wiped out in foreclosures brought by senior lienholders) and would have to sue John to collect what's due, it agrees to the sale.

Unfortunately, when the home equity lender hears that it won't get anything, it nixes the sale. And without all lienholders agreeing to the sale, it can't happen. So John goes back and asks the second mortgage holder to take $25,000 (half of what it's owed) and offers $10,000 to the home equity lender. The second mortgage holder is even unhappier now because its share is being reduced, but it still wants the sale to go through, so it agrees. In the end, John manages to negotiate a deal where everyone gets something but not as much as they would like.

Scam Alert

Some companies operate scams aimed at defrauding homeowners who are trying to put together a short sale. Make sure you're dealing with a reputable real estate company and with the company that's servicing the loan (the company to which you've been sending your payments). You should also be getting guidance from a HUD-approved housing counselor (see Ch. 4).

Here's how a scam might work. A business calling itself a mortgage company offers to buy your home in a short sale and pay off the lender. You sign the deed over to the company. The company then convinces you that it will deal with the lender (for one reason or another) and that you should move out because the lender won't participate in a short sale unless you do. Then, instead of paying the lender, it turns around and sells the house to an unsuspecting buyer (or rents it out), pockets the proceeds, and walks away when the lender moves forward with the foreclosure. You're not only out of your house, but you've paid nothing to the lender and are on the hook for the entire mortgage balance.

For more information on foreclosure rescue scams, see Ch. 1 and check this book's companion page (see "Get Legal Updates and More at Nolo.com" in the introductory chapter, "Your Foreclosure Companion").

Offer the Lender a Deed in Lieu of Foreclosure

If you want to simply hand over ownership of your house to the lender and get your loan canceled in exchange, you can propose something called a "deed in lieu of foreclosure." If your lender agrees, it will accept a deed to your property and, in exchange, promise not to initiate foreclosure proceedings or to drop them if they've already begun. You don't have to sell the house; the lender will do that.

Will the Lender Accept a Deed in Lieu?

Getting a lender to accept a deed in lieu of foreclosure can be a hard sell. The problem is that the lender wants cash, not real estate.

On the other hand, if the lender thinks it's a better deal to take your offer than to incur the expense of a foreclosure, it will be a done deal. As with short sales, it will be helpful for you to work with a HUD-approved housing counselor. (See Ch. 4.)

Before the lender accepts a deed in lieu of foreclosure, it might require you to put your home on the market for a while, three months is typical. Banks would rather have you sell the house than have to sell it themselves.

You can't do a deed in lieu of foreclosure if you have multiple mortgages or liens on the property, such as those arising from delinquent taxes, work on your home, or money judgments. You must be able to deed clear title to the whole property. In other words, you can't do two deeds in lieu of foreclosure and split the property between the first and second mortgage lenders or other lienholders.

Even if the lender approves a deed in lieu of foreclosure, ideally, you'll want to have an agreement, in writing, that the lender won't go after you for any deficiency before you decide to complete the transaction. While it used to be standard practice for lenders to release borrowers from any further liability on the debt after a deed in lieu of foreclosure, now your lender might try to hold you liable for the deficiency—or at least part of it. (In most cases, the deficiency amount will be the difference between the total indebtedness and the fair market value of the property at the time of the deed in lieu of foreclosure.) If your lender insists that you pay all or part of the deficiency, you can try to negotiate a lower amount or arrange to repay the deficit over time.

Again, if the lender forgives some or all of the deficiency, you might face tax consequences.

Fannie Mae and Freddie Mac Deeds in Lieu of Foreclosure

Fannie Mae and Freddie Mac allow some delinquent and current borrowers to give up their properties with deeds in lieu of foreclosure (sometimes called "mortgage releases").

For the most part, if a borrower meets the eligibility requirements, any deficiency will be waived. To learn if you qualify, go to www. fanniemae.com, www.freddiemac.com, or call your loan servicer. But some borrowers might have to make a cash contribution or sign a promissory note. (Some servicemembers with permanent change of station (PCS) orders are exempt from this requirement.) Fannie Mae and Freddie Mac offer up to $6,000 to second lien holders to expedite the process and, in some cases, borrowers can receive up to $3,000 in relocation assistance.

With Fannie Mae, you might be able to stay in the home rent-free for three months after the mortgage release is complete if you meet certain criteria (for example, the home is your primary residence). Or you could sign a 12-month lease and pay rent at market rate if you meet specific criteria, such as you have a verifiable income.

Avoiding Deficiency Judgments

The laws of most states allow the lender to come after you for a "deficiency"—that is, the amount by which the foreclosure sale proceeds fall short of the borrower's total debt. But some states protect homeowners from liability for deficiencies from mortgages that were used to purchase the homes or in other circumstances following a foreclosure sale. (See the appendix for your state's rule.) Few states offer protection against deficiency judgments following a short sale or deed in lieu of foreclosure.

You don't need to worry about a deficiency if either of the following applies:

- Your state's law prohibits deficiency lawsuits.
- The lender agrees, as part of accepting a short sale or deed in lieu of foreclosure, not to come after you for any deficiency.

But if your state does allow deficiency lawsuits, or you have a second or third mortgage, you could be on the hook for a lot of money even after you lose your house. You can wipe out that debt by filing for Chapter 7 bankruptcy. (See Ch. 6.)

Some foreclosure advisers will tell you that deficiency lawsuits are rare and not to worry about them. While this was true in the past, it's not the case anymore. Lenders are more likely to pursue deficiency judgments now than they used to be, particularly if you have assets that could be recovered. In any event, it's hard to know whether your lender will seek a deficiency judgment. Even if you don't end up in a lawsuit, do you want to take the chance? Bankruptcy is your ultimate safety net when it comes to any liability arising from your former home ownership.

Income Tax Liability for Deficiencies

If you default on your mortgage, you or the lender might eventually sell the property at a foreclosure sale or through a short sale, or you'll give up the home with a deed in lieu of foreclosure, for less than what you owe. And you might be asked to pay income tax on the difference if the lender doesn't come after you for this amount. The theory is that you're receiving a gift of this amount because you don't have to pay it back. (The lender forgives the debt.)

The IRS learns of the forgiven deficiency when it receives an IRS Form 1099-C from the lender. This is a form on which a creditor reports income derived because the creditor canceled (forgave) your debt after a foreclosure, short sale, or deed in lieu of foreclosure.

Whether you'll owe federal taxes depends on the circumstances. (Also, forgiven debt might affect your state taxes.) Here are the basic rules.

Loans for your principal residence. Congress passed the Mortgage Forgiveness Debt Relief Act in 2007, and Section 108(a)(1)(E) was added to the Internal Revenue Code, creating the Qualified Principal Residence Indebtedness exclusion. Under this law and its various extensions, if you have mortgage debt forgiven in calendar years 2007 through 2025, or debt later discharged pursuant to a written agreement entered into before January 1, 2026, you can exclude up to $750,000 ($375,000 if married and filing separately) starting December 31, 2020. Before December 31, 2020, taxpayers could exclude as much as $2 million ($1 million if married filing separately) of that forgiven debt from their federal taxable income. You must have used the money you borrowed to buy, build, or substantially improve your house (or to refinance debt you incurred for these purposes). The IRS has more information about forgiven mortgage debt and instructions for taxpayers at www.irs.gov. Be sure to review IRS Publication 4681, *Canceled Debts, Foreclosures, Repossessions, and Abandonments*, as well as Topic No. 431, "Canceled Debt—Is It Taxable or Not?"

Tax laws are complicated, and even if you don't qualify for the Qualified Principal Residence Indebtedness exclusion, another exception or exclusion could save you from having to pay taxes on canceled debt (see below). If you received a 1099-C form indicating your lender forgave all or part of your mortgage debt, or if you're considering completing a loan modification, short sale, or deed in lieu of foreclosure that has tax implications, talk to a tax attorney or tax accountant to get advice specific to your circumstances.

RESOURCE

Looking for a lawyer? Asking for a referral to an attorney from someone you trust can be a good way to find legal help. Also, two sites that are part of the Nolo family, Lawyers.com and Avvo.com, provide excellent and free lawyer directories. These directories allow you to search by location and area of law, and list detailed information about and reviews of lawyers.

Whether you're just starting your lawyer search or researching particular attorneys, visit www.lawyers.com/find-a-lawyer and www.avvo.com/find-a-lawyer.

Loans for other real estate. If you default on a mortgage that's secured by property that isn't your primary residence, you'll likely owe tax on any forgiven deficiency. So, for example, if you walk away from a loan on your second house in the country, expect a Form 1099 in the mail. The same is true for loans on nonresidential real estate.

Loans not used for real estate. Similarly, if you take out a home equity loan and take that world trip you've been dreaming of instead of using the money to improve your house, you could end up on the wrong side of a tax bill.

> **EXAMPLE:** Harry owes $200,000 on his second home, which is foreclosed and sold at auction for $150,000. The lender files an IRS Form 1099, reporting the $50,000 difference as taxable income to Harry.

Other ways to exclude forgiven debt from your federal taxable income. If you do face income tax liability, you have a few possible ways of getting out from under it, including the insolvency exclusion and bankruptcy. To use the insolvency exclusion, you'll have to prove to the satisfaction of the IRS that your liabilities exceed the value of your assets. Filing for bankruptcy works because debt wiped out (discharged) in bankruptcy isn't considered taxable income. You'll have to show the IRS that you filed for bankruptcy before the event that would cause the lender to file a Form 1099-C. Of course, you'll want to file for bankruptcy only if it otherwise makes sense. (Bankruptcy is discussed in Chs. 5 and 6.)

> **TIP**
>
> **You can fight back if an unpaid loan amount is treated as taxable income.** If you receive a Form 1099 attributing income to you from mortgage debt forgiveness, but you think you shouldn't owe the tax, file IRS Form 982, *Reduction of Tax Attributes Due to Discharge of Indebtedness*, with your regular tax return.

How Long Can You Stay in Your House for Free?

When You Miss Your First Few Payments 202

After You Receive a Formal Notice of Foreclosure 203

    Nonjudicial Foreclosures..204

    Judicial Foreclosures..204

The Redemption Period 206

After the Sale 206

    Eviction as an Extension of the Foreclosure Action.......................................206

Eviction Lawsuits After Foreclosure 207

A s we've mentioned throughout this book, going through a foreclosure can actually provide an excellent opportunity to save some serious money. That's because legal procedures—including foreclosures—typically take many months. While the foreclosure proceeding goes on, and then afterward (during the redemption period, perhaps, or until you're evicted), you probably won't have to move—or make any payments.

For example, if your mortgage payments are $2,000 a month, and you stay in the house for nine months without making a payment, you could save $18,000. Of course, you might not be able to save the entire amount of your mortgage payment, but even if you saved half, you would still have a considerable amount of money in the bank when the time comes to leave.

As long as you remain, you also save the house from nine months of deterioration (and possibly vandalism) it would suffer by being vacant. So, you're doing your community a great favor.

How long can you stay in your house payment-free once you decide to give it up? It's impossible to give you a precise timeline for your personal situation. Each phase of the process, from your first missed payment to your last day in the house, involves variables unique to your situation. But the information on your state's page in the appendix will give you an idea of whether you're likely to have several months, a year or more, or something in between.

This chapter explains the elements of that basic timeline in more detail. Once you have a rough idea of what to expect, it's a good idea to talk to a HUD-approved housing counselor (see Ch. 4) to get a reality check on how fast events are moving in your community.

When You Stay, Everybody Wins

You might feel a little guilty about staying in your house once you stop making payments on it or after the property is auctioned off at a foreclosure sale. But by staying, you're doing your neighbors—and probably even the lender or new owner—a favor.

It's well documented that foreclosures tend to cluster in certain communities. And when several empty houses are in a neighborhood, it's obvious. Lawns are overgrown with weeds or brown from lack of water; flyers pile up on porches. Maintenance is neglected. The signs of neglect quickly attract vandals, thieves, and transients. Graffiti appears on fences as copper pipes and appliances disappear from the vacant houses.

Some cities have actually sued lenders to recoup the costs of dealing with the problems caused by abandoned houses. The cities say they have had to pay more to their fire and police departments and have lost property tax revenue. They have also demolished some houses that were past saving and sued for the costs of demolition. Success has varied in these types of cases.

When you stay in the house until you're legally required to leave, you'll help maintain its value—and that of your neighbors' homes. So let go of the guilt and remind yourself that you're doing a good deed.

TIP

Filing for bankruptcy shortly before the sale date can buy you more time. If you file for Chapter 7 bankruptcy after the foreclosure sale has been scheduled, the sale will be delayed for several months while the bankruptcy is pending. If you file for Chapter 13 bankruptcy, you can probably delay the foreclosure sale for at least five or six months, especially if you hire a lawyer to help you. (To find out more, see Chs. 5 and 6.)

When You Miss Your First Few Payments

If you've decided that you'll ultimately have to give up your house because your mortgage payments are no longer affordable, the first step toward benefiting from a foreclosure is to stop making the payments. Open up a savings account in which to deposit as much as possible of the extra money you now have.

TIP

Don't forget about modifications. Before bailing out on your home, find out whether you qualify for a mortgage payment reduction through a modification. You don't have to be making payments on your mortgage when you first begin the modification process, and whether you ultimately plan to leave, there's no harm in seeing what you can get through a modification. Even if the modification application fails, simply engaging in the process can buy you some time to live in the property payment-free. (See Ch. 4 for more information.)

Depending on state law, you might get a preforeclosure notice telling you that foreclosure proceedings will begin within a particular period, or you might get a breach letter. As discussed in Chs. 2 and 4, under federal regulations, the servicer generally can't start formal foreclosure proceedings until you're more than 120 days delinquent and must provide you with information about loss mitigation options after you default. In all but a couple of states (check your state's page in the appendix to see what kind of notice you'll get), you'll know when the lender takes the first step toward foreclosure because you'll get a notice in the mail or served a copy of the lawsuit (see below).

If you get help from a HUD-approved housing counselor and try to work something out with your lender before a foreclosure officially starts, even though you privately think you'll probably be giving up your house, you might gain several extra months before foreclosure proceedings start. (See Ch. 4 for information about HUD-approved housing counselors.)

So, from the time you decide to stop making payments until the time you receive notice that foreclosure proceedings have begun, you can live in your home for at least four months, maybe five or six, payment-free. But that's not all. Keep reading.

After You Receive a Formal Notice of Foreclosure

Before your house can be sold at a foreclosure sale, you must get some sort of formal notice that your state's foreclosure laws require. (See Ch. 2.) The kind of notice you will get depends on where you live.

If you're in a nonjudicial foreclosure state, you might get:

- a notice of default (allowing you time to reinstate your mortgage by making up all the back payments) followed by a notice of sale (if you haven't reinstated your mortgage by the deadline)
- a combined notice of default and sale (stating that the property will be sold on a certain date unless you make up the missed payments)
- only one notice—a notice of sale announcing that the property will be sold on a certain date unless you pay off the mortgage, or
- in a couple of states, notice only by publication and posting.

If you're in a judicial foreclosure state, you'll get a summons and complaint telling you that foreclosure proceedings have been filed in the appropriate court and that you have a specific amount of time to respond.

In almost all judicial foreclosure states, if the judge orders the foreclosure sale, you'll get a notice telling you when and where the sale will take place. In Connecticut and Vermont, however, the judge can transfer title to the property as part of the judgment of foreclosure.

Will Contesting a Nonjudicial Foreclosure in Court Gain Time?

To oppose a foreclosure in a nonjudicial foreclosure state, you have to file a lawsuit. Normally, you would file a petition with the local court requesting an injunction (court order) to block the foreclosure. This might delay the foreclosure by a week or two, or longer if the court believed your argument has merit. You would have the burden of proving that the lender hadn't followed proper procedures or had made some other mistake, and it would be very difficult for you to get very far in this type of lawsuit unless you hire a lawyer. (See Ch. 7 for information on fighting foreclosure in court.)

Nonjudicial Foreclosures

How much time you have from the first formal notice that foreclosure proceedings have started to the foreclosure sale date varies widely from state to state. You can probably count on at least 30 days' notice before the sale. In most states, you'll get a couple of months. Check your state's page in the appendix to get an idea of how much notice you're entitled to get.

Judicial Foreclosures

If you're in a state where foreclosures go through court (see your state's page in the appendix), typically, you'll have 20 to 30 days to respond after the lender files its lawsuit against you. If you file a response contesting the foreclosure action, it could take several months or, if you have a good case, even years before the judge rules on whether to grant the foreclosure. Even if you don't contest the foreclosure action, the sale usually won't take place until at least a month after the judge issues the foreclosure order.

So you'll likely have a minimum of two months from the first notice to the date the court orders the sale to take place. You'll have at least double that amount of time if you decide to oppose the foreclosure in court. And, in some states that use a judicial process, foreclosures take much, much longer. According to a U.S. Foreclosure Market Report from ATTOM Data Solutions, in the fourth quarter of 2020, a few states that had extremely long average timelines for foreclosures were Hawaii (2,186 days), New York (1,465 days), Kentucky (1,390 days), Pennsylvania (1,275 days), and Massachusetts (1,223 days).

Gaining Time by Contesting a Judicial Foreclosure

One of the great benefits of living in a judicial foreclosure state is that you automatically have an opportunity to contest the foreclosure. In a judicial foreclosure, the lender (the party filing the suit) has the burden of filing all the paperwork required to prove its case. You must file a written response to the foreclosure complaint or petition, respond to any motions the lender files, attend any scheduled hearings, and voice your objections. Merely filing a written response could achieve a delay of at least several months. The more foreclosures that are occurring in that particular court, the longer it will take.

If you're able to convincingly allege one or more defects in the foreclosure process, you might be able to use these facts as leverage against the lender to negotiate an acceptable modification. In other words, you don't necessarily have to win in the court to get what you want.

If you're contesting the foreclosure to try to stay in your house permanently, you almost certainly will want to hire a lawyer because of what's at stake. But if your only goal is to slow the process down so you can stay in your house a little longer and save some money, you likely can accomplish this mission without a lawyer. Of course, you must have a reasonable basis for contesting the foreclosure. (Ch. 7 explains in considerable detail how you can challenge the legitimacy of a foreclosure.)

The Redemption Period

A statutory "redemption period" is a specific amount of time, ranging from several days to a year, that state law gives to foreclosed homeowners during which they can recover the property after a foreclosure sale. During this period, you can "redeem" the property and reclaim the home, generally by paying the successful bidder the amount of the winning bid plus interest and allowable costs or paying off the total amount of the mortgage debt. In some states, you can continue to live in the home, payment-free, during the redemption period. (See your state's page in the appendix to learn about the redemption period after a foreclosure in your state, if any.)

After the Sale

After the foreclosure sale or, depending on state law, following the post-sale redemption period, when a new deed has been recorded with a new owner's name on it, you go from homeowner to tenant. A commonly held belief is that you aren't legally a tenant unless you enter into a formal landlord–tenant relationship and agree to pay rent. In fact, with a couple of exceptions, you're considered a tenant (typically termed a "tenant at will" or "tenant by sufferance"). You may remain in your home until you're formally evicted. Though, you might decide it's in your best interest to move out earlier.

Depending on your state's law and the circumstances of your case, the eviction might be included as part of the foreclosure action, or the lender might have to file a separate lawsuit in court to evict you.

Eviction as an Extension of the Foreclosure Action

In some judicial foreclosures, the court order authorizing the sale also authorizes the sheriff to evict you following the sale, after a required brief notice is served on you.

When an eviction is an extension of the foreclosure action, it can happen quickly. Generally, if the foreclosing lender is the purchaser at the foreclosure sale, it then asks the court for what's called a "writ of possession" or a "writ of assistance." The writ is a court order telling the sheriff to remove you from the property. Typically, the sheriff will post a notice on the property's front door giving you 24 hours to leave the home. If you don't move out by the deadline, the sheriff's crew could physically remove you—and your belongings—from the property.

Cash for Keys: Getting Paid to Move Out Voluntarily

Before proceeding with an eviction, the new owner might offer to pay you a lump sum if you leave the property by a specific date and you agree to leave the property in good condition. Some former homeowners report offers as high as several thousand dollars, which, from the new owner's perspective, is cheap compared to what it would cost the owner if you dug in your heels and made a formal eviction necessary. Also, experience shows that unhappy former homeowners can do a remarkable amount of damage to a house if they think the new owner is being unreasonable.

Not all buyers of foreclosed properties are enlightened enough to make this sort of offer and might be willing to spend hundreds or even thousands of dollars in lawyer fees to get you out. That said, you should be ready to propose a move-out bonus if the new owner doesn't. And if the new owner does offer one, you shouldn't be shy about negotiating for a higher amount.

Eviction Lawsuits After Foreclosure

If the new owner of your home has to file a lawsuit in court to evict you, in most cases, you'll first get a notice demanding that you leave the property—for instance, a "notice to quit"—before the eviction officially starts. The notice will tell you how long you have before you need to move out. Generally, you'll get between three and 30 days.

If you don't leave, the new owner of your home will then file an eviction suit in court, which is often called an "unlawful detainer" or "forcible entry and detainer" action. You'll be served a summons and complaint. You have the right to contest the eviction complaint by filing a formal written response. Generally, after notice and a hearing, the court will issue an eviction judgment and an order giving you a few days to move before the sheriff is allowed to remove you. The eviction process might take a few months, which would give you some more time in your house payment-free.

But forcing the new owner of the home to evict you in court has its downside. It's often best to move out at the end of the period set out in the initial notice instead of waiting until the new owner goes to court and gets an eviction order. If you're sued, it's a matter of public record and can hurt your ability to rent or lease in the future. You'll already have bad credit due to the foreclosure (and bankruptcy, if you go that route), and many landlords subscribe to private databases that screen prospective tenants for being the subject of previous eviction lawsuits. That fact, above all others, can lead a potential landlord to turn down your application for a lease or rental agreement.

> **TIP**
>
> **Consider filing for bankruptcy.** When you're pretty sure you're going to have to give up your house, your prime concern becomes living there payment-free for as long as possible. You might be able to extend that time if you file for Chapter 7 or Chapter 13 bankruptcy. Check out Chs. 5 and 6 to find out whether you're eligible, whether you might benefit from filing for reasons other than delaying foreclosure, and other important information.

Resources Beyond the Book

HUD-Approved Housing Counselors 210

Real Estate Brokers 211

Mortgage Brokers 212

Lawyers 212

What Type of Lawyer Do You Need? 214

How to Find the Right Lawyer 214

Choosing a Lawyer 215

How Much Will a Lawyer Charge? 217

Foreclosure Websites 220

Books 221

Looking Up Foreclosure Statutes 223

How to Find Your State's Foreclosure Laws 223

How to Find Federal Mortgage Servicing Laws 226

At some point, as you make your way through the foreclosure process, you're going to want help from someone who knows the territory—a lawyer who's familiar with what local judges will approve or a real estate agent who can tell you how quickly your house will likely sell—can be an invaluable guide. This chapter provides a little guidance about who can help you, where to find them, and how to choose someone who will best suit your needs.

But sometimes you need help from other sources, perhaps because you can't afford an expert's fee, you don't like the answer you received, or you'd rather find the information yourself. So we'll also steer you to some books and websites that can provide information and guidance.

Finally, this chapter introduces some techniques for finding the foreclosure-related laws listed on your state's page in the appendix. Virtually all of these laws can be accessed online, in a law library, and quite often in a general public library.

HUD-Approved Housing Counselors

HUD-approved housing counselors provide foreclosure avoidance counseling and assistance in applying for a mortgage workout—all at no cost to you. If you're facing a foreclosure, the sooner you talk to a housing counselor, the better. You can have no better advocate if you're trying to work out a loan modification or another loss mitigation option.

These counselors can help you assess your mortgage situation and, if possible, work out a solution with your lender that will keep you in your house. Lenders—which can suffer economically from foreclosures and benefit if something can be worked out—are a principal source of funds for these agencies. (See Ch. 4 for an in-depth discussion of finding and working with a HUD-approved housing counselor.) Consider contacting one of the following:

- The federal Department of Housing and Urban Development (HUD) has a list of approved counselors. You can find a HUD-approved counselor at www.hud.gov (search for "Talk to a Housing Counselor" or go to www.hud.gov/i_want_to/talk_to_a_housing_counselor) or by calling 800-569-4287.

- The Homeownership Preservation Foundation website, www.995hope.org, offers free online counseling, among other things. Or you can call 888-995-HOPE and talk with someone.
- The National Foundation for Credit Counseling (NFCC) can put you in contact with a certified housing counselor who can offer guidance on avoiding falling behind in your mortgage payments and resolving your mortgage situation. Go to www.nfcc.org/what-we-offer/homeownership-counseling for more information.

Some homeowners become convinced that they should pay a company to step in to help them, which is almost always a mistake. No proof exists showing that private companies offering modification or other foreclosure assistance can get the job done any faster or better than a HUD-approved housing counselor. Worse, plenty of evidence shows that the forms of help these companies offer are scams in which homeowners spend large sums of money for few or no results.

Real Estate Brokers

Real estate brokers and agents can be indispensable if you're facing foreclosure and want to sell the property. One difficulty in doing a short sale is that you might need a solid offer from a potential buyer before your lender will tell you whether it will accept the terms. A local broker or agent who's familiar with a particular lender's practices will have a good idea of what kind of terms the lender will accept.

The broker can also negotiate the final terms with your lender. Finalizing a short sale can require experience with the lender (or lenders) and expertise in negotiating real estate deals.

If you don't already have a broker or agent you trust, ask around for reliable names. Most communities have well-respected and trusted real estate firms.

Real estate brokers and agents are subject to regulation by every state. To find out whether your broker or agent is licensed, check the website of your state's real estate regulatory agency.

Mortgage Brokers

If you want to refinance, a mortgage broker can help you find the best loan. Like real estate brokers and agents, mortgage brokers are regulated in all states, and licensed in most. You usually can find out whether a particular mortgage broker is licensed by visiting your state's regulatory agency website.

Use mortgage brokers for what they are best at: finding a refinancing source at the lowest available interest rate. But when it comes to understanding how the mortgage works and whether or not you can afford it, keep the old Latin phrase *caveat emptor* (let the buyer beware) firmly in mind.

Lawyers

Some tasks are just too steep for many people to handle—foreclosure law is complicated. If you think you can keep your house (see Chs. 3 and 4), hire a lawyer if you can afford it. If you are only trying to delay the inevitable, hire a lawyer if you can, but also consider handling the case (or most of it) yourself.

You almost certainly will need a lawyer if you're determined to keep your house by:

- fighting a foreclosure in court, or
- filing for Chapter 13 bankruptcy and making up missed payments over several years.

A lawyer can also:

- Inform you about all loss mitigation options. Keep in mind that certain types of loans, like FHA-insured loans, have special loss mitigation options. But not all servicers will let you know about every alternative that might be available to you. Your attorney can advise you about the available options. A HUD-approved housing counselor is also an excellent resource for this type of information.

- Help you in the loan modification process. An attorney can assess whether a servicer is following the laws governing the process. An attorney can also review the conditions of any modification that the lender offers you. The lawyer will examine the documents to ensure no illegal charges are included—like improper fees or advances—added to the total balance and that the modification is in your best interest. Keep in mind that some states, like California, don't allow an attorney to accept payment until after the attorney has completed every modification service agreed to. (Cal. Civ. Code § 2944.7.)

- Ensure that the lender follows the rules. Lenders don't always comply with the strict foreclosure requirements under state and federal law. An attorney can ensure that the lender follows relevant laws or challenge the foreclosure in court.

- Represent you in foreclosure mediation. In areas that offer foreclosure mediation, an attorney can help ensure that the lender and servicer treat you fairly.

- Even if you'll probably lose the house sooner or later, you'll likely benefit from having a lawyer if the lender or servicer violated the law.

When can you go it alone? Having a competent lawyer to represent you can always be beneficial, but the amount you'll have to pay for one can often outweigh the benefits. With that in mind, you might sensibly choose to represent yourself if you are filing for Chapter 7 bankruptcy to get rid of your other debts so your mortgage will be more affordable or so that you'll emerge from your foreclosure with a fresh start. You also might not need to talk with an attorney if you don't have a valid reason to fight the foreclosure and your goal is to live in the home throughout the foreclosure process and save money. For example, say you stopped making your payments and have no intention of resuming them. If you understand your rights, including how long you can remain in the home, and think your lender and servicer have treated you fairly under the law, then you probably have no reason to hire an attorney. Instead, put the money you'd use to pay a foreclosure attorney toward finding somewhere else to live.

What Type of Lawyer Do You Need?

Most lawyers who represent people in foreclosure actions specialize in foreclosure defense, real estate transactions, consumer protection, or bankruptcy.

How do you know what expertise a lawyer has? Your best shot is to ask directly. "How many foreclosure cases have you handled, and what were the results?" would be a great place to start. Many lawyers appreciate this approach and will give you honest answers.

As a general rule, if you want to keep your house but you have concluded that you don't want to file for bankruptcy, a foreclosure defense lawyer might be the best option. A foreclosure lawyer will be comfortable fighting the foreclosure in court, if necessary, as well as analyzing the lender's paperwork and working with the lender to keep you in your house. On the other hand, if it looks like you won't be able to work something out with the lender, a bankruptcy lawyer is likely your best choice. Bankruptcy is a highly technical area, and few nonbankruptcy lawyers know the details necessary to represent you well, so hire someone who regularly practices bankruptcy.

How to Find the Right Lawyer

If you're looking for a lawyer, it's worth it to shop around. Here are some tips.

Start with personal referrals. If you know someone pleased with the services of a foreclosure or bankruptcy lawyer, contact that lawyer first.

See whether you can get free or low-cost help. Many law schools sponsor clinics that provide free legal advice to consumers. And many places have senior law projects, with lawyers who will, without charge, help people over 55 with debt and foreclosure issues. To find something near you, do an online search for "senior legal services" in your area. Many parts of the country also have functioning legal aid offices to help people who qualify deal with foreclosures. And if you don't qualify, you might get a quality referral to a lawyer who won't charge you as much as others in the community might.

Be careful with lawyer referral panels. Most county bar associations will give you the names of lawyers who have expertise in fighting foreclosures. But some bar associations probably won't do much screening of the lawyers they list. Ask about this when you contact them.

Check out online directories. Both bar associations and commercial websites provide lists of real estate lawyers online, usually with a lot of information about each lawyer. Two sites that are part of the Nolo family, Lawyers.com and Avvo.com, provide excellent and free lawyer directories. Use Google to find other lawyers for your state or city.

Look for a bankruptcy expert. To find a good bankruptcy lawyer, consider using the National Association of Consumer Bankruptcy Attorneys' membership directory at www.nacba.org. Membership in this organization is a good sign that the bankruptcy lawyer understands the nuances necessary to save your house or keep you in it longer. Also, because foreclosure and bankruptcy are so closely related, a bankruptcy lawyer will likely be knowledgeable about foreclosures.

Choosing a Lawyer

No matter how you find a lawyer, these suggestions will help you make sure you have the best possible working relationship.

Keep in mind that you're hiring a lawyer to perform a service for you. So fight any urge you have to surrender to or be intimidated by the lawyer. You should be the one who decides what you feel comfortable doing about your legal and financial affairs.

Second, make sure you have good chemistry with any lawyer you hire. When making an appointment, ask to talk directly to the lawyer. If you don't get through, this might give you a hint as to how accessible the lawyer is.

If you can talk to the lawyer, ask some specific questions. Do you get clear, concise answers? Is the lawyer making an effort to teach you about your overall situation? If not, look for someone else. Also, pay attention to how the lawyer responds to your knowledge. If you've read this book, you're already better informed than the average client. Does the lawyer appreciate your efforts to educate yourself?

Your main goal at the initial conference is to find out what the lawyer recommends in your case and how much it will cost. Go home and think about the lawyer's suggestions. If they don't make sense or you have other reservations, look elsewhere.

Communicating With Your Foreclosure Lawyer During the Coronavirus Pandemic

Most attorneys—not just foreclosure lawyers—have adjusted their practices, making it easier for you to interact with them while adhering to social distancing protocols due to the coronavirus. Here are a few examples of how some lawyers are adjusting their practices.

- **Telepractice.** Attorney-client communications already often happen over the phone. Some law offices are still open, so attorneys and staff are available to take calls as usual. But many practices have opted to close their offices during the coronavirus pandemic. Some of those firms are rerouting calls to attorneys and staff who are working remotely.
- **Email, text, and file-sharing applications.** By using email and file-sharing applications, like Google Drive and Dropbox, you can usually avoid having to take documents to a lawyer personally. You can also scan documents or take a photo with your phone and then send them via email or text to your lawyer. Some firms allow clients to speak with their attorney or send confidential documents through a secure client portal.
- **Online appointments and videoconferencing.** Attorneys and firms are now frequently using secure videoconferencing options to talk with clients and other lawyers. Firms conduct meetings over the Internet using Skype, Legaler, FaceTime, or Zoom, for example. Most devices that have a camera—including a smartphone, laptop, or tablet—are compatible with videoconferencing applications.
- **E-signatures.** E-signatures are, for the most part, safe and reliable methods for signing paperwork, including attorneys' fee agreements.

Rest assured, many foreclosure lawyers are ready to help you through the process, no matter what it takes.

> ### High-Volume Bankruptcy Law Firms
>
> Some lawyers handle a high volume of cases for fees that are significantly less than other bankruptcy lawyers charge. These firms depend heavily on paralegals to get the work done, and the lawyer appears only briefly at the beginning of the case and at your creditors' meeting (the one personal appearance you will likely make in a Chapter 7 bankruptcy). If you choose a lawyer by price,which is understandable given the standard fees, you'll likely be trading hands-on legal representation for a cookie-cutter approach to your case that might not be in your best interest.

When shopping for a lawyer, it's common to hire the first one you talk to, unless the lawyer's fees are way out of your league or you don't get along with the lawyer. You might want to talk to a few people before making your final decision.

How Much Will a Lawyer Charge?

With a few happy exceptions, plenty! It's not a stretch to generalize that if you need an attorney to help you with your foreclosure, you will have difficulty raising the money to pay for it.

Chapter 13 Bankruptcies

Chapter 13 attorneys commonly charge $2,500 to $5,000 a case, depending on the attorney and where you live. If your matter appears unusually complex initially, the fee will run on the high side. If the fees are below a certain amount set by each court (called "no-look fees"), the court won't examine them; the attorney will have to convince the court that they're justified if they're above the no-look fee amount.

Many Chapter 13 lawyers allow you to pay a portion of the fees up front and the remainder through your Chapter 13 plan. Exactly how much a bankruptcy lawyer will require up front depends on the individual attorney or firm. On average you can expect to pay a third to half of the total fee before your case is filed—but some lawyers will charge as little as $100.

Chapter 7 Bankruptcies

Attorneys' fees for a routine Chapter 7 bankruptcy case run from $1,200 to $3,500, depending on the lawyer and the locality. You can expect the attorney to require you to pay the full fee before filing the bankruptcy, because bankruptcy legally discharges (cancels) whatever fees are unpaid as of the filing date.

Lawyers can get permission from the court to charge you for work done after you file, but they would rather not be your creditor after they have worked to get you out of debt. So, in many cases, their up-front charges take into account the work they might have to do after you file.

Filing for Chapter 7 Bankruptcy: How Much Will It Cost?	
Filing fee (unless a waiver is granted)	$338
Mandatory credit counseling (before filing) and budget counseling (after)	$50
If you fill out and file your own bankruptcy papers with the help of *How to File for Chapter 7 Bankruptcy* (Nolo), or	about $35
If you hire a nonlawyer bankruptcy petition preparer to do the paperwork, or	about $150
If you hire a lawyer to represent you	about $1,500 to $3,500
Total	$425 to $3,850

TIP

Filing for Chapter 7 bankruptcy without an attorney. You may be able to file for a simple Chapter 7 bankruptcy on your own, with the aid of a good self-help guide (see "Books," below, for recommendations). For a Chapter 13 bankruptcy, however, you'll most likely need a lawyer.

Fighting a Foreclosure in Court

If you want to fight a foreclosure in a judicial foreclosure proceeding or a separate court action in a nonjudicial foreclosure proceeding, plan on paying an up-front retainer of several thousand dollars.

Other Tasks

One way to get help from a lawyer—and pay less—is to pay only for specific tasks. Some lawyers will agree to perform certain limited tasks for you instead of taking responsibility for the whole matter. This is called offering "unbundled" services. For example, if you file for bankruptcy without a lawyer's help, and then your lender asks the court to let it proceed with a foreclosure, you might be able to hire a lawyer to oppose the lender's request.

The fee will vary depending on the complexity of the task and the lawyer's enthusiasm for providing unbundled services. As a general rule, you should hire an attorney for an unbundled service whenever the amount of the dispute justifies the fee. If a creditor objects to the discharge of a $500 debt, and it will cost you $400 to hire an attorney, you might be better off trying to handle the matter yourself, even though this increases the risk that the creditor will win. But if the dispute is worth $1,000 and the attorney will cost you $400, hiring the attorney makes better sense.

But keep in mind, most attorneys won't take on a case for a few hundred dollars—it's not worth their time. Another reason many attorneys don't like to work on a piecemeal basis is because they worry that they might be on the hook if something goes wrong in another part of your case. Also, the bar associations of many states discourage lawyers from providing unbundled services.

You Might Be Able to Afford a Lawyer If You're Not Paying Your Mortgage

A lawyer can often be retained for the equivalent of one or two mortgage payments. Because a lawyer can help you gain many extra months of foreclosure delay and living in your home payment free, hiring a lawyer can be cost effective.

Foreclosure Websites

If you're facing foreclosure, or worry that you might be facing one soon, you'll find easy-to understand information about foreclosure and your options at these websites:

- **Nolo's Foreclosure Law Section** (www.nolo.com/legal-encyclopedia/foreclosure). Learn everything you need to know about foreclosure, including how it works, how to avoid it, and your options if you are in danger of losing your home.
- **Federal Reserve System** (www.federalreserve.gov/consumers communities/foreclosure.htm). The Federal Reserve System has established regional Foreclosure Resource Centers throughout the country. Click your region to get consumer information and foreclosure resources in your area.
- **Federal Trade Commission (FTC)** (www.ftc.gov). The FTC publishes fact sheets and press releases for consumers on foreclosure scams. Search for "mortgage relief scams."
- **Homeownership Preservation Foundation** (www.995hope.org). The Homeownership Preservation Foundation is a nonprofit that offers free foreclosure counseling. The website also provides information and help for people who can't make their mortgage payment, have received a modification, or are victims of a mortgage scam.
- **MakingHomeAffordable.gov** (www.makinghomeaffordable.gov). This government website provides comprehensive information about interacting with your mortgage company, mortgage assistance options, information you'll need when applying for mortgage assistance, and tips to avoid foreclosure. The website also provides information about finding HUD-approved housing counseling agencies.
- **National Consumer Law Center (NCLC)** (www.nclc.org). The consumer section of NCLC's website has helpful information and links on foreclosure, predatory lending, and foreclosure scams.

- **National Foundation for Credit Counseling (NFCC)** (www.nfcc.org). The NFCC website has a national directory of local member agencies—nonprofit credit counseling agencies staffed by NFCC-trained, and certified counselors. NFCC housing counselors can assist with foreclosure and other homeowner issues.
- **U.S. Department of Housing and Urban Development (HUD)** (www.hud.gov). The HUD website has a section on foreclosure that includes tips on avoiding foreclosure, assistance for FHA-insured homeowners, links to government-assisted rental programs, links to local and state resources, and a national directory of HUD-approved housing counselors who provide assistance free of charge.

Books

If you're facing foreclosure, we encourage you to read every book on this topic that you can put your hands on. Every book will have something different to offer. Each author will be giving you the benefit of personal experiences, tips on strategy and tactics, and opinions on the best approach to dealing with foreclosure.

In addition to the books referenced in previous chapters, we recommend the following books:

- *How to File for Chapter 7 Bankruptcy,* by Cara O'Neill and Albin Renauer (Nolo). As the title says, this book explains everything you need to know about filing for Chapter 7 bankruptcy.
- *Chapter 13 Bankruptcy: Keep Your Property & Repay Debts Over Time,* by Cara O'Neill (Nolo). This is a guide to the whole Chapter 13 process.
- *The New Bankruptcy: Will It Work for You?* by Cara O'Neill (Nolo). If you're not sure whether or not bankruptcy is the right way to go for you and your family, this book will highlight the pros and cons and help you evaluate your situation.

- *Credit Repair: Make a Plan, Improve Your Credit, Avoid Scams,* by Amy Loftsgordon and Cara O'Neill (Nolo). If you want to take steps to make your credit better, this is the book for you. It provides all the steps that have traditionally been necessary to raise your credit score.
- *Home Foreclosures and Mortgage Servicing and Loan Modifications.* Authored by the staff of the National Consumer Law Center, these are the best books out there for in-depth legal research on the subjects of foreclosure and loss mitigation. They cover many of the areas we've addressed—and some we have not— in considerably more detail, including:
  - how to negotiate preforeclosure workout agreements, and current workout options with Fannie Mae, Freddie Mac, HUD, VA, and RHS
  - the best discussion anywhere on how to challenge mortgage servicer abuses
  - foreclosure litigation, including power of sale, due on sale, and substantive and procedural defenses
  - raising loan broker and loan originator-related claims against the mortgage holder
  - special rights to stop foreclosure of FHA, VA, and RHS mortgages
  - mobile home foreclosures, and
  - tax liens and tax foreclosures.

  They come with access to a companion website containing many forms, foreclosure laws, and other materials you will need if you want to fight a foreclosure or do your own workout with your lender. For more information, visit www.nclc.org.

Looking Up Foreclosure Statutes

As discussed throughout this book, federal mortgage servicing laws provide various loss mitigation protections to homeowners when it comes to foreclosure. And each state has its own foreclosure procedures—and homeowner protections—for those who are delinquent on mortgage payments. After reviewing these laws, you'll better understand what steps are involved and your rights during the process.

The first step in finding federal and state foreclosure laws is to learn the references to these laws, called "citations." By using the citations, you can find and read the laws (called "statutes") that apply to mortgage servicing and foreclosure. You can then read for yourself your state's laws on such matters as:

- your loss mitigation rights
- restrictions on starting or continuing a foreclosure, like whether you're protected against dual tracking
- how much and what type of notice you'll get before your home is sold at a foreclosure sale
- how much time you have to reinstate your mortgage after a default
- how much time you get to redeem the property after the foreclosure (applicable in some states), and
- whether your lender can sue you for a deficiency judgment and, if so, under what conditions.

How to Find Your State's Foreclosure Laws

Your state's page in the appendix lists references to the laws governing foreclosures in your state. You can also generally find the citations for your state's foreclosure laws online by searching for "(your state's) foreclosure laws" or similar language. Or you can check the links to state-specific articles in our Summary of State Foreclosure Laws at www.nolo.com/legal-encyclopedia/summary-state-foreclosure-laws.html.

The easiest way to access state laws is online. To find your state's laws, search for "[your state] statutes" or "[your state] laws." Make sure you're reading the most recent, official laws. Often, when it comes to official statutes, the URL will end in ".gov" or the statutes will be on an official state legislature webpage. You can also usually find the statutes at a law library or even at a public library.

Once you find your state's statutes, you can use the citations to find the specific laws you want to read. Statutes are usually organized hierarchically by numbered title, article, chapter, and section.

RESOURCE

More information on legal research. Legal research is its own subject; if you want to delve into it more deeply, see *Legal Research: How to Find & Understand the Law*, by the Editors of Nolo (Nolo).

Here's an example of the steps you could use to find the Vermont foreclosure statutes once you have the citations, which are Vermont Stat. Ann., Title 12, Chapter 172, Sections (§§) 4931 through 4954.

Step 1: Find the relevant set of statutes online. Run an online search for "Vermont's statutes." Again, make sure you look at the most recent statutes. In your list of results, you'll find a link called "Vermont Laws— Vermont Legislature" on the Vermont General Assembly's website. Clicking on that link will take you to a page listing Vermont's statutes. Then look for the relevant title, chapter, and sections that you want to review.

Step 2: Find and click on the appropriate title. For this example, it's "Title 12." Clicking on Title 12 opens up a list of chapters.

Step 3: Scroll down until you reach the applicable chapter. Look for the chapter that contains §§ 4931–4954, Vermont's foreclosure statutes. It's "Chapter 172: Foreclosure of Mortgages." Then, click on that chapter.

Step 4: Look for and review the foreclosure sections. In this example, it's §§ 4931–4954. Read each section to learn Vermont's various foreclosure laws.

Most other states arrange their statutes in a similar manner: by title, chapter, and section. Use the same method to find the statutes referenced on your state's page. (You can use a similar method when looking up federal laws, using the title, chapter, and section.) Some states arrange their statutes in a slightly different manner. For example, if you were looking for Section 2323.07 of the Ohio Revised Code, you would use the first two numbers to find the correct title ("Title 23"). Click on that title, and then Chapter 2323. Next, find the statute numbered "2323.07."

In New York, the citation to the foreclosure laws reads: N.Y. Real Prop. Acts. Law, Sections 1301 to 1391. You would find these statutes by first browsing the list of legal topics until you found "Real Property Actions and Proceedings." Click on that topic and then browse until you find the article (Article 13) that contains "Sections 1301 to 1391 (Action to Foreclose a Mortgage)."

Your state could use a slightly different model from any of these. You might have to use a little ingenuity to get to the right statutes. As a general rule, the number at the left of the citation will be the number you use to start your search, whether it is the title, article, or chapter number. If for some reason the citation number doesn't work, look for a subject heading dealing with foreclosure, real estate, or real property, or if you are in a judicial foreclosure state, civil procedure.

Foreclosure Statutes Can Be Hard to Read

Especially in Eastern states, foreclosure statutes come from English law adopted here in the 18th century. The language is very different from modern English, even modern legal English, and can be hard to understand.

Also, for reasons that escape us, they aren't organized very well. Sometimes one relevant statute will be found in one section of the law while a closely related one will appear elsewhere. For example, some foreclosure laws are found in the code dealing with court procedure, while other laws are found in the part of the code dealing with real estate. So, be prepared to look in several different parts of the code.

How to Find Federal Mortgage Servicing Laws

Under Regulation X, which implements the federal Real Estate Settlement Procedures Act (RESPA), most mortgage servicers must take specific steps and provide specific protections to borrowers facing foreclosure (see Ch. 4). Again, the first step in finding the federal foreclosure laws is to learn the citations.

The Consumer Financial Protection Bureau website (www.consumer finance.gov/compliance/compliance-resources/mortgage-resources/ mortserv) lists many of these citations. You can also find them online by searching for "federal mortgage servicing laws," "federal foreclosure laws," or similar language.

To read these federal laws, you might want to visit the Library of Congress's legal research site (www.loc.gov/law/help/guide.php), which provides links to federal regulations and federal statutes. Or go to a law library or local public library.

Glossary

Acceleration. Requiring a borrower to pay off the loan balance. Under a provision commonly found in promissory notes, if the borrower misses some payments, the lender can demand that the borrower pay the total loan amount immediately. The loan must be accelerated before the lender can foreclose. In many states, the borrower gets a chance to reinstate the loan (and cancel the acceleration) by paying the arrears, plus costs and interest.

Adjustable-rate mortgage (ARM). A mortgage or deed of trust providing that the interest rate on the underlying promissory note can be adjusted up or down at specified intervals tracking the movement of a federal interest rate or another index.

Administrative expenses. In a Chapter 13 bankruptcy repayment plan, the trustee's fee, the debtor's attorneys' fees, and other costs that a debtor must pay in full. Administrative costs are typically 10% of total payments under the plan.

Amortization. Paying off a loan with regular payments over a set period. Part of each payment is applied to principal and to interest.

Amount financed. The amount of money you are getting in a loan, calculated under rules required by federal law. This is the amount of money you are borrowing after certain financing costs and fees are deducted. The amount financed is far less than the total amount you pay back, because the total amount of the loan includes the interest on the amount financed.

Annual percentage rate (APR). The interest rate on a loan expressed under rules required by federal law. To determine the true cost of a loan, it's more accurate to look at the APR than the stated interest rate.

Appraisal. An expert's evaluation of what a particular item of property is worth in the marketplace. Colloquially, the term is used to describe any opinion about a property's value. For instance, real estate agents and brokers often informally appraise property, even though they aren't licensed appraisers.

Arrears. Overdue loan payments. With a mortgage loan, the arrears might include any missed payments, interest on the missed payments, and the costs the lender incurred in trying to collect the debt.

Assignee liability. Liability of an assignee (an entity that has been assigned ownership of a mortgage or deed of trust) for unlawful or abusive acts of the original lender or mortgage originator. Assignee liability can be important in lawsuits against a foreclosing party for violations of federal or state laws prohibiting predatory lending practices. In most cases, assignees are off the hook for those practices if they conducted a reasonable investigation into the history of the loan.

Assignment. A document showing that ownership of a mortgage or deed of trust (and the underlying promissory note) has been transferred (assigned) from the original owner to a new owner (assignee).

Automatic stay. An automatically-issued injunction when someone files for bankruptcy. The automatic stay prohibits most creditor collection activities, such as filing or continuing lawsuits, making written requests for payment, or notifying credit reporting bureaus of an unpaid debt.

Balloon payment. A large lump-sum payment due as the last payment on a loan. For instance, if you borrow $10,000, your note might require you to pay $5,000 of the loan over a three-year period, plus a balloon payment for the amount remaining at the end of that period.

Bankruptcy code. The federal law that governs the operation of bankruptcy courts and establishes bankruptcy procedures. It's in Title 11 of the United States Code.

Bankruptcy petition preparer. Any nonlawyer who helps someone with bankruptcy. Bankruptcy petition preparers (BPPs) are regulated by the U.S. Trustee. Because they are not lawyers, BPPs can't represent you in bankruptcy court or provide legal advice.

Capitalization. Treating items owed on a loan as part of a new principal balance. For example, when missed payments on a mortgage are added to the mortgage principal, to be paid off over time, they are capitalized. If missed payments are capitalized and the loan is reamortized, the lender will recalculate the monthly payment using the existing interest rate and new principal balance.

Chapter 7 bankruptcy. A liquidation bankruptcy, in which the trustee sells the debtor's nonexempt property and distributes the proceeds to the debtor's creditors. At the end of the case, the debtor receives a discharge of all remaining debts, except those that can't legally be discharged.

Chapter 12 bankruptcy. A type of bankruptcy designed to help small farmers reorganize their debts.

Chapter 13 bankruptcy. A type of consumer bankruptcy designed to help individuals reorganize their debts and pay all or a portion of them over three to five years.

Chapter 13 plan. A document filed in a Chapter 13 bankruptcy that shows how all of the debtor's projected disposable income will be used over a three- to five-year period to pay all mandatory debts—for example, back child support, taxes, and mortgage arrearages—as well as a percentage of unsecured, nonpriority debts, such as medical and credit card bills.

Closed-end loan. Any loan that must be paid off within a specific period of time. Loans that don't have to be paid off within any particular time—for example, credit card debt—are open-ended.

Collateral. Property that a borrower pledges as security for a loan. If a creditor accepts property as collateral for a loan under a security agreement, and the agreement is properly recorded, the creditor has a lien on the collateral and can repossess it if the conditions of the security agreement (typically, making monthly payments on the loan) aren't met.

Complaint. A formal document that initiates a lawsuit.

Confirmation hearing. A court hearing conducted by a bankruptcy judge at which the judge decides whether a debtor's proposed Chapter 13 plan is feasible and meets all legal requirements.

Conforming loan. A mortgage loan that is small enough to be bought or guaranteed by Fannie Mae or Freddie Mac. See "Jumbo loan."

Conventional loan. A mortgage loan issued to a borrower with an excellent or very good credit rating. Conventional loans do not include those insured by the federal government or subprime loans.

Cramdown. In a Chapter 13 bankruptcy, the act of reducing a secured debt to the replacement value of the collateral securing the debt.

Credit and debt counseling. Counseling that explores the possibility of repaying debts outside of bankruptcy and covers credit, budgeting, and financial management. Consumers must go through credit counseling with an approved provider before filing for bankruptcy.

Credit bureau. Another name for a consumer reporting or credit reporting agency. The three major credit bureaus, Equifax, Experian, and TransUnion, gather and sell information about a consumer's credit history to certain categories of people or organizations. Individuals are entitled to one free credit report per year from each bureau, not including the person's credit score.

Credit report. Also called a "consumer report" or a "credit record," this kind of report documents the credit history and current status of a borrower's monthly payment obligations and contains public information such as bankruptcies and court judgments. Chapter 7 bankruptcies remain on a credit report for ten years, Chapter 13 bankruptcies and other negative information for seven years.

Credit score. A "credit score" is a number that supposedly summarizes your credit history. The score is based on a number of factors, including your debt payment history, how much debt you currently have, how long you've had credit, and how recently your major credit transactions occurred. Lenders use credit scores to decide whether to grant a loan and at what interest rate. FICO scores (the most popular basic credit score) generally range from 300 to 850; a score in the mid-700s or more generally gets you the best loans at the best rates.

Creditor. A person or an institution to whom money is owed.

Creditors' meeting. A meeting that someone filing for bankruptcy must attend, at which the trustee and creditors can question the debtor about property, court documents, and debts.

Curing a default. See "Reinstating a mortgage."

Current market value. The price that property could be sold for.

Current monthly income. As defined by bankruptcy law, a bankruptcy filer's total gross income (whether taxable or not), averaged over the six-month period immediately preceding the month in which the bankruptcy is filed. The current monthly income is used to determine whether or not the debtor can file for Chapter 7 bankruptcy, among other things.

Debt consolidation. Refinancing debt into a new loan. Homeowners sometimes convert relatively short-term unsecured debt into debt secured by the home—putting the house at greater risk if they default in payments on the consolidated debt.

Debtor. Someone who owes money to another person or business. Also, the generic term used to refer to anyone who files for bankruptcy.

Deed in lieu of foreclosure. An arrangement under which a homeowner can get out from under a mortgage loan and prevent a foreclosure, by signing the deed to the home over to the lender in exchange for the lender's agreement not to foreclose. Typically, the lender agrees to not hold the homeowner liable for the remaining amount of the mortgage loan.

Deed of trust. In about half the states, a loan that is secured by real estate is termed a "deed of trust." Deeds of trust are like mortgages. However, unlike mortgages, deeds of trust typically have a power of sale clause that lets the lender foreclose nonjudicially without court supervision.

Default. Failing to meet the requirements of an agreement. Defaults that lead to foreclosure typically involve the failure to make payments, but other types of defaults are possible, such as the failure to maintain necessary homeowners' insurance or keep the property in proper condition.

Default rate. An interest rate that replaces a contractual interest rate if a borrower defaults on a loan. If the default rate is set out in the mortgage loan agreement, it will typically be considerably higher than the contract rate.

Deficiency. The amount a homeowner owes the lender after a house is sold at a foreclosure sale or short sale for less than the actual debt. With a deed in lieu of foreclosure, the deficiency is the difference between the borrrower's debt and the property's fair market value. In most states, the lender can recover a deficiency from the borrower.

Discharge. A court order, issued at the conclusion of a Chapter 7 or Chapter 13 bankruptcy case, which legally relieves the debtor of personal liability for debts that can be discharged in that type of bankruptcy.

Dischargeable debt. A debt that is wiped out at the conclusion of a bankruptcy case, unless the judge decides that it should not be.

Disposable income. In a Chapter 13 bankruptcy, the difference between a debtor's current monthly income and allowable expenses. This is the amount that the bankruptcy law deems available for a repayment plan.

Equity. The amount of cash you would pocket if you sold your house and paid off all the liens (for example, mortgages, property taxes, money judgments, mechanic's liens, and tax liens). For example, if you owe $300,000 on your house on first and second mortgages, the IRS has a tax lien on the house for $50,000, you sell your home for $390,000, and costs of sale are $20,000, you will get $20,000. That's your equity.

Equity stripping. The practice of giving high-cost second mortgages to homeowners, reducing the borrower's equity. Some of these loans violate federal or state truth-in-lending laws, and homeowners might be able to cancel (rescind) the loans later or sue the lender. See "Home Ownership and Equity Protection Act (HOEPA)."

Exempt property. Property described by state and federal laws (exemptions) that a debtor is entitled to keep in a Chapter 7 bankruptcy. Exempt property cannot be taken and sold by the trustee for the benefit of the debtor's unsecured creditors.

Exemptions. State and federal laws specifying the types of property that creditors are not entitled to take to satisfy a debt and the bankruptcy trustee is not entitled to sell for the benefit of the debtor's unsecured creditors.

Fannie Mae (Federal National Mortgage Association). A government-chartered corporation set up to buy mortgages from original lenders and, sometimes, repackage them for private investors. Congress authorized Fannie Mae to stimulate the growth of the housing market by making capital available for new loans. Investors and lenders that deal with Fannie Mae must follow various guidelines regarding mortgage servicing and foreclosure practices.

Federal exemptions. A list of exempt property in the federal Bankruptcy Code. Some states give debtors the option of using the federal rather than the state exemptions.

Federal Home Loan Mortgage Corporation. See "Freddie Mac."

Federal Housing Administration (FHA). A federal agency that insures first mortgage lenders against loss when a loan is made following FHA regulations. The FHA doesn't lend money; it only insures the loan. The FHA also certifies nonprofit housing counselors.

Federal National Mortgage Association. See "Fannie Mae."

Filing date. The date a bankruptcy petition in a particular case is filed. With few exceptions, debts incurred after the filing date are not discharged.

Forbearance. A lender's willingness to let you skip all or a portion of your monthly payments for a brief period, usually three to six months. You'll have to pay the skipped amounts later by making a lump-sum payment, with a repayment plan, in a payment deferral program, or through a modification in which the lender adds the unpaid amounts to the balance of the loan.

Foreclosure. The legal process by which a creditor with a claim (lien) on real estate forces a sale of the property to collect on the debt. Foreclosure typically occurs when a homeowner defaults on a mortgage. See "Judicial foreclosure" and "Nonjudicial foreclosure."

Foreclosure "rescue" scams. Scams on people who are facing foreclosure. The scam artist learns about impending foreclosures from public filings, advertisements, and postings and contacts homeowners with promises of help that typically result in the homeowner's losing the house, equity, or money.

Forgiven debt. Debt that is written off as uncollectable by the creditor. Forgiven debt—the amount you don't have to pay back—is generally taxable as income, and the creditor is required to send you (and the IRS) a Form 1099-C stating the amount. Three major exceptions: You won't have to pay tax if you are insolvent when the debt is written off, the debt is discharged in bankruptcy, or you qualify for an exclusion, such as the Qualified Principal Residence Indebtedness exclusion because you took out the mortgage to buy, build, or substantially improve your home (or to refinance debt incurred for these purposes) and the debt was forgiven in calendar years 2007 through 2025, or later discharged pursuant to a written agreement entered into before January 1, 2026.

Freddie Mac (Federal Home Loan Mortgage Corporation). Like Fannie Mae, a government-chartered company set up to buy mortgages from original lenders and, sometimes, repackage (securitize) them for private investors.

Ginnie Mae (Government National Mortgage Corporation). A quasi-governmental agency that guarantees pools of FHA- and VA-insured loans that have been packaged into securities for investment purposes.

Good faith. In a Chapter 13 bankruptcy case, when a debtor files with the sincere purpose of paying off debts over the period of time required by law rather than for manipulative purposes—such as to prevent a foreclosure that by all rights should be allowed to proceed.

Government mortgage guarantors. Special government programs that provide mortgage insurance or guarantees to lenders who make purchase-money mortgage loans to certain homebuyers. These programs are offered through the federal government (the Federal Housing Administration, the Rural Housing Service, and the Veterans Administration), or by a state housing finance agency.

Home equity loan. A loan made to a homeowner on the basis of the equity in the house and secured by the house in the same manner as a first mortgage.

Home Ownership and Equity Protection Act (HOEPA). A federal law that provides special protection to homeowners who obtain home mortgage loans at high interest rates or with exceptionally high fees. The protection includes fines and penalties recoverable in a lawsuit against the lender and sometimes a defense to foreclosure in state or federal court.

Homestead. In bankruptcy, a state or federal exemption applicable to property where the debtor lives—usually including boats and mobile homes.

Homestead declaration. A form filed with the county recorder's office to put on record your right to a homestead exemption. Only a few states require recording. In most states, the homestead exemption is automatic—you are not required to record a homestead declaration to claim the homestead exemption.

Injunction. A court order prohibiting a person or an entity from taking specified actions—for example, bankruptcy's automatic stay (in reality an automatic injunction), which prevents most creditors from trying to collect their debts.

Interest. The cost of borrowing money over time. Interest on a loan is always described as percentage of the loan payable over a period of time, as in 7% per year. In agreements for the purchase of homes and cars, the interest is computed and amortized over the period of the loan, which makes the amount owed on the secured debt a lot higher than the base loan itself. For instance, if you buy a car for $20,000 and borrow the money over seven years, the amount payable on the note is $20,000 plus the amount of interest that you'll pay over the seven years.

Interest-only loan. A type of mortgage loan where the borrower makes payments only on the loan's interest for a limited period of time. The mortgage payments are much lower than they would be if the payments were applied to the loan as a whole. When the interest-only period ends the borrower must begin making much higher payments to cover both principal and interest. It is the sudden increase in required mortgage payments that pushed many homeowners into foreclosure.

Insolvent. When a person's or business's assets are worth less than their debts.

Joint debtors. Married people who file for bankruptcy together and pay a single filing fee.

Judgment proof. Description of a person whose income and property are such that a creditor can't (or won't) seize them to enforce a money judgment—for example, a dwelling protected by a homestead exemption or a bank account containing only a few dollars.

Judicial foreclosure. A type of foreclosure used in about half the states in which the foreclosing party files a lawsuit in the county where the property is located seeking a judgment saying that the property can be sold in a foreclosure sale because the homeowner has defaulted on the mortgage. A couple of states use what are called "strict foreclosures," which allow the judge to order title to the property transferred to the foreclosing party without the need for a sale. A few other states have hybrid processes, in which the foreclosure proceeds nonjudicially under a power of sale clause but is subject to some court supervision.

Judicial lien. A lien created by recording a court money judgment against the debtor's property—usually real estate.

Jumbo loan. A loan for an amount that exceeds the conforming loan limit and that usually costs a point or two higher in interest rates as a result. See "Conforming loan."

Lease and buy-back. A scheme in which you deed your home to a third party and then lease it back. Most often it's a scam—the third party pockets your payments and borrows against the property, and the house ends up in foreclosure.

Lien. A legal claim against property that must be paid before title to the property can be transferred. Liens on real estate can also often be collected through foreclosure, depending on the type of lien. Examples of liens include mortgage liens, tax liens, and mechanic's liens.

Lien avoidance. A bankruptcy procedure in which certain types of liens can be removed from certain types of property. Liens that are not avoided survive the bankruptcy even if the underlying debt is canceled—for instance, a lien remains on a car even if the debt evidenced by the car note is discharged in the bankruptcy.

Lifting the stay. When a bankruptcy court allows a creditor to continue with debt collection or other activities that are otherwise banned by the automatic stay. For instance, the court might allow a landlord to proceed with an eviction or a lender to repossess a car because the debtor has defaulted on the note.

Loan term. The "loan term" is the period during which the loan is due to be repaid in full. Most mortgage loans have 15- or 30-year terms. Many predatory consumer loans (payday loans, car title loans, and refund anticipation loans) have very short terms, which increases the annual percentage rate the lender charges. Foreclosure rescue scams also sometimes employ short-term loans with exorbitant interest payments.

Market value. The highest price someone would pay and the lowest price the seller would accept on a property on the open market. Market value is used to determine the amount of equity a homeowner has in the property, which can determine whether it makes sense to fight foreclosure or to file for bankruptcy. Market value also is often crucial in determining whether a mortgage holder can recover a deficiency after a foreclosure sale. For example, assume a property sells for $250,000, the former homeowner owes $350,000, and a court later determines that the property's market value was actually $300,000 (which could have been realized if the minimum bid at the foreclosure auction had been set higher). In that event, if the state's laws use the property's actual market value to limit deficiency awards, the court will issue a deficiency judgment for $50,000.

Materialmen's and mechanic's liens. Liens imposed by statute on real estate when suppliers of materials, labor, and contracting services used to improve the real estate are not properly compensated.

Means test. A formula that uses predefined income and expense categories to determine whether a debtor whose income is more than the state median family income should be allowed to file for Chapter 7 bankruptcy.

Median family income. The figure at which there are as many families with incomes below it as there are above it. The U.S. Census Bureau publishes median family income figures for each state and for different household sizes. In bankruptcy, the median family income is used as a basis for determining whether a debtor must pass the means test to file for Chapter 7 bankruptcy, and whether a debtor filing for Chapter 13 bankruptcy must commit all projected disposable income to a five-year repayment plan.

Meeting of creditors. See "Creditors' meeting."

MERS. MERS stands for "Mortgage Electronic Registration Systems," an entity listed as the mortgagee of record for about half the mortgages in the United States. MERS operates a database of mortgage transactions conducted by its members, supposedly obviating the need to use county real property recording systems.

Modification. Altering one or more terms of a mortgage, such as reducing the interest rate or increasing the term of the loan.

Mortgage. A contract in which a loan to buy real estate is secured by the real estate as collateral. If the borrower defaults on loan payments, the lender can foreclose on the property.

Mortgage broker. An individual, usually licensed by the state, who arranges financing for a potential home purchaser by seeking the mortgage products for that particular person.

Mortgage or loan holder. The person or company that currently owns the loan and has the right to foreclose.

Mortgage servicer. A type of business that mortgage owners hire to administer their loan portfolios. The mortgage servicer typically accepts and records payments, negotiates a workout in case of a default, and supervises the foreclosure process if attempts at loss mitigation fail.

Mortgage-backed security. A type of investment backed by mortgage loans that have been packaged into pools or trusts, with payments on the underlying mortgages generating the return for investors. By selling original mortgages to Fannie Mae and Freddie Mac (and other players in the secondary mortgage market, where the packaging occurs) lenders generate more funds for future lending.

Mortgagee. The mortgagee is the lender or other entity that owns the rights and responsibilities granted in a mortgage by the borrower (mortgagor). Typically, the mortgagee is the party who is authorized by state law to bring a foreclosure action.

Mortgagor. Someone who borrows money and signs a mortgage.

Motion to lift stay. A formal request in which a creditor asks the bankruptcy court for permission to continue a court action or collection activities in spite of the automatic stay.

Negative amortization. "Negative amortization" occurs when payments do not cover the amount of interest due for a loan period. During the housing boom, a popular type of loan that permitted negative amortization was what's called a "Payment-Option ARM." This type of adjustable rate mortgage allows the borrower to choose among several payment options each month: a payment of principal and interest, an interest-only payment, or a payment of less than the interest owed that month. If the borrower selects the last option, the amount of unpaid interest is added to the principal, which increases the total amount owed (negative amortization) and results in the borrower paying interest on interest. This drastically increases the total amount owed and the cost of the loan. Typically, if the balance exceeds a certain limit, for example 110% or 125% of the original loan amount, the lender ends the option payments. Negative amortization loans are not readily available anymore.

Negative equity. "Negative equity" is when a property's market value is less than the total owed on all the liens recorded against it. The popular term for negative equity is "upside down" or "underwater." In the bankruptcy context, negative equity can be very helpful in that you can get rid of liens that are no longer secured by equity even though they were secured when you obtained the loans. For example, say you have a first mortgage of $200,000, a second mortgage of $100,000 and a third mortgage of $50,000. Also assume that your home sank from a value of $400,000 to $175,000. In this case you have a negative equity of $175,000 (the difference between your home's value ($175,000) and the amount of the liens created by all three mortgages, or $350,000). Your first mortgage of $200,000 is partially covered by your home's value of $175,000, but you have no equity to secure the second and third mortgages. In this situation, Chapter 13 bankruptcy can remove the second and third mortgage liens from your house's title.

Nonbankruptcy federal exemptions. Federal laws that allow a debtor who has not filed for bankruptcy to keep creditors away from certain property. The debtor can also use these exemptions in bankruptcy if the debtor is using a state exemption system.

Nondischargeable debt. Debt that survives bankruptcy, such as back child support and most student loans.

Nonexempt property. In bankruptcy, property that is unprotected by the exemption system available to the debtor. In a Chapter 7 bankruptcy, the trustee will sell nonexempt property for the benefit of the debtor's unsecured creditors. In a Chapter 13 bankruptcy, debtors must propose a plan that pays their unsecured creditors at least the value of their unsecured property.

Nonjudicial foreclosure. A foreclosure that proceeds outside of court under a power of sale clause, usually included in a deed of trust. (Some states use mortgages that include a power of sale clause.)

Nonpriority debt. A type of debt that is not entitled to be paid first in Chapter 7 bankruptcy and does not have to be paid in full in a Chapter 13 bankruptcy.

Non–purchase-money security interest. In the foreclosure context, a loan that uses your home as collateral for any purpose other than to buy it—for example, a home equity loan that is used to improve the home or pay for a vacation, college tuition, or medical emergency.

Notice to quit. A formal written notice, given to the occupant of real estate, to leave the premises within a specified period of time or face a judicial proceeding (often called an "unlawful detainer" or "forcible entry and detainer" proceedings) in which a judge can order the sheriff to physically evict the occupant. In some states, a homeowner who continues to occupy the home after a foreclosure must be given a notice to quit before eviction proceedings can go forward. In other cases, the foreclosure order will include a writ of assistance, which is an order of the court directing the sheriff to remove the foreclosed homeowner from the home.

Open-ended loan. A loan without a definite term or end date. Authorized charges on credit cards are open-ended loans.

Origination fee. A fee paid to a lender for processing a loan application. This fee is commonly called "points" and is charged as a percentage of the loan amount.

Originator. The entity the loan documents identify as the party making the loan, typically a bank or credit union.

Partially secured debt. A debt secured by collateral that is worth less than the debt itself—for instance, when a person owes $15,000 on a car that is worth only $10,000.

Personal financial management counseling. A class intended to teach good budget management. Every consumer bankruptcy filer must attend such a class to get a Chapter 7 or Chapter 13 bankruptcy discharge.

Personal property. All property not classified as real property, including tangible items, such as cars and jewelry, and intangible property, such as stocks and pensions.

Predatory lending. In the foreclosure context, lending money under terms that are likely to cause a default in payments because of the expense of the loan compared to the borrower's income, or due to hidden fees and costs that are not properly disclosed. Certain categories of predatory loans are prohibited by federal and state law, and homeowners can sometimes use a violation of those laws to defend against a foreclosure or sue for fines and penalties.

Prepetition counseling. Mandatory debt and credit counseling that occurs before the bankruptcy petition is filed. Compare personal financial management counseling, which occurs after the petition is filed.

Priority debt. In Chapter 7 bankruptcy, a type of debt that is paid first if the debtor has any assets available to pay creditors. Priority debts include alimony and child support, fees owed to the trustee and attorneys in the case, and wages owed to employees. With one exception (back child support obligations assigned to government entities), priority claims must be paid in full in a Chapter 13 bankruptcy.

Projected disposable income. In bankruptcy, the amount of income a debtor will have left over each month, after deducting allowable expenses, payments on mandatory debts, and administrative expenses from his or her current monthly income. This is the amount the debtor must pay toward unsecured nonpriority debts in a Chapter 13 plan.

Proof of service. A document signed under penalty of perjury by the person serving a document showing how the service was made, who made it, and when.

Property inspection fee. A charge imposed by a loan servicer for a cursory inspection (often just a drive-by) to determine the physical condition or occupancy status of mortgaged property after the borrower defaults. This fee might be unreasonably high and an unreasonable number of inspections could be made.

Real Estate Settlement Procedures Act (RESPA). A federal law designed to protect consumers from unnecessarily high settlement charges and certain abusive practices in the residential real estate market. RESPA provides a way for a borrower to challenge a stated loan balance provided by the servicer and to get information about how the loan has been processed. It also requires that certain disclosures be made to borrowers.

Real property. Real estate (land and buildings on the land, usually including mobile homes attached to a foundation).

Reamortization. Recalculating loan payments on different terms. For example, if you have paid for ten years on a 15-year loan, your lender might extend the loan for another ten years at a lower interest rate, lowering your monthly payments. Similarly, lenders sometimes add missed payments to the principal loan (that is, capitalize the missed payments). This reamortization can cause the monthly payments to increase because of the increase in the principal and the interest on it.

Redemption right. In foreclosure, the former homeowner's right to buy back the house after a foreclosure sale by reimbursing the new owner the amount of the purchase price or paying off the full debt. In some states, even after a foreclosure sale, the new owner can't take possession until the redemption period has passed. For example, if the state's law gives the former owner up to six months to redeem the mortgage after the sale and the right to live in the home during this time, the new owner can't take possession until that time has passed and no redemption has been made.

Refinance. Using a new loan to pay off the current loan to get a better interest rate and perhaps pull some of your equity out of the house.

Reinstating a mortgage. Getting current on your mortgage by making up missed payments, including interest, and reimbursing the lender for various costs and fees incurred during the time you were in default. This process is sometimes referred to as "curing the default."

Repayment plan. A loss mitigation option to catch up on the overdue amount. The typical repayment plan provides for amortizing missed payments (and associated interest, costs, and fees) over a period of time by increasing the monthly mortgage payment to include the extra payments. Also refers to the plan proposed by a debtor in a Chapter 13 bankruptcy.

Rescission. The act of canceling a loan agreement and asking a court to restore borrower and lender to the positions they were in before it was signed. In some cases, federal and state laws allow a borrower to rescind a mortgage loan transaction within three business days after signing the papers. This period can sometimes be extended for years if the lender violated certain federal laws. The right of rescission can sometimes be used as a defense to a foreclosure.

Reverse mortgage. A type of loan designed for people who are 62 or older and have considerable equity in their homes. The reverse mortgage lender provides the borrower with a lump sum, line of credit, or a set monthly payment (or a combination of a line of credit and monthly payments) based on the amount of the equity in the home. Once a triggering event occurs, such as the borrowers' death, the lender will typically foreclose, sell the house, and recoup what it is owed on the loan. Reverse mortgages are heavily regulated.

Second mortgage or deed of trust. A mortgage on property that is already mortgaged or subject to a deed of trust. It comes after a prior mortgage in priority of payment.

Secondary market. The process by which original mortgage lenders sell their loans to buyers (often Fannie Mae and Freddie Mac), who, sometimes, package the loans into securities with different risk ratings and resell them to individual and corporate investors with the help of Wall Street brokerages and bond-rating firms.

Secured creditor. The owner of a secured claim.

Secured debt. A debt secured by collateral.

Secured interest. A claim to property used as collateral. For instance, a lender on a car note retains legal title to the car until the loan is paid off.

Secured property. Property that is collateral for a secured debt.

Securitization. The process of converting a mortgage lender's ownership interest in an original mortgage into an investment vehicle that can be handily sold on Wall Street as another type of security.

Serial bankruptcy filing. The practice of filing and dismissing one bankruptcy after another to obtain the protection of the automatic stay, even though the bankruptcies themselves offer no debt relief— for instance, when a debtor files successive Chapter 13 cases to prevent foreclosure even though there are no debts to repay. Courts will ban the debtor from further filings.

Short sale. A sale of a house in which the sale price is less than the loan secured by the house. The homeowner must get the lender's approval for a short sale.

State exemptions. State laws that specify the types of property creditors are not entitled to take to satisfy a debt, and the bankruptcy trustee is not entitled to take and sell for the benefit of the debtor's unsecured creditors.

Statutory lien. A lien imposed on property by law, such as tax liens and mechanic's liens, as opposed to voluntary liens (such as mortgages) and liens arising from court judgments (judicial liens).

Stay. See "Automatic stay."

Strict foreclosure. A type of judicial foreclosure used in a couple of states in which the court not only orders that the foreclosure take place, but also transfers title to the foreclosing party without requiring the property to be put up for sale at an auction.

Strip down of lien. In a Chapter 13 bankruptcy, when the amount of a lien on collateral is reduced to the collateral's replacement value. See "Cramdown."

Subprime mortgage loan. A loan that carries a higher interest rate than a comparable loan, generally because of the borrower's low credit rating.

Summons and complaint. Legal documents that are served on a homeowner to initiate a lawsuit—for example, a judicial foreclosure or an eviction. The "summons" tells the homeowner how and when to respond to the lawsuit. The "complaint" sets out the reasons why the court should, for example, issue a foreclosure judgment or evict a former owner after the sale.

Tax lien. A statutory lien imposed on property to secure payment of back taxes—typically income and property taxes.

Trustee. An official appointed by the bankruptcy court to carry out the administrative tasks associated with a bankruptcy and to collect and sell nonexempt property for the benefit of the debtor's unsecured creditors. The third party who typically administers a nonjudicial foreclosure is also called a "trustee." A deed of trust gives the trustee the authority to foreclose and sell the home to pay off the loan balance at the request of the lender if the borrower defaults. State law can limit who can act as a foreclosure trustee. In theory, the trustee is a neutral third party, but the trustee is usually chosen by and often affiliated with the lender.

Truth in Lending Act (TILA). A federal law that requires most lenders to give borrowers standard disclosures of the cost and payment terms of the loan. The Home Ownership and Equity Protection Act (HOEPA) is part of the Truth in Lending Act. If the lender violates TILA or HOEPA, the homeowner might be able to stop foreclosure by rescinding the loan, depending on its type and whether it qualifies for protection under these federal laws.

Undersecured debt. A debt secured by collateral that is worth less than the debt.

State Information

Alabama	249	Montana	279
Alaska	251	Nebraska	280
Arizona	252	Nevada	281
Arkansas	253	New Hampshire	283
California	254	New Jersey	284
Colorado	256	New Mexico	286
Connecticut	258	New York	288
Delaware	259	North Carolina	290
District of Columbia	260	North Dakota	291
Florida	261	Ohio	292
Georgia	262	Oklahoma	293
Hawaii	263	Oregon	294
Idaho	264	Pennsylvania	295
Illinois	265	Rhode Island	296
Indiana	266	South Carolina	297
Iowa	267	South Dakota	298
Kansas	268	Tennessee	299
Kentucky	269	Texas	300
Louisiana	270	Utah	301
Maine	271	Vermont	302
Maryland	272	Virginia	304
Massachusetts	273	Washington	305
Michigan	274	West Virginia	306
Minnesota	276	Wisconsin	307
Mississippi	277	Wyoming	308
Missouri	278		

The information here summarizes some of the important features of each state's law on foreclosures. When you use it, please keep in mind the following point.

This is only a summary of your state's laws and does not tell the entire story. It is intended for owners of single-family residences and doesn't address special laws for agricultural land or the rights of tenants in foreclosed homes owned by their landlords.

 RESOURCE

More state-specific foreclosure information. The Foreclosure Center on Nolo.com has lots of state-specific foreclosure articles, and we are adding to the collection every day. You can find detailed articles on state foreclosure procedures, state foreclosure prevention mediation programs, state protections for homeowners in foreclosure, and other developments in state law.

This discusses only the most common method of foreclosure in your state. For example, it provides information about nonjudicial foreclosures for the states where they are the most common procedure, even though judicial foreclosures are allowed in those nonjudicial states in some circumstances.

Laws change. Foreclosure laws and procedures are complex and subject to change by legislatures and to interpretation by courts. For these reasons, you should use the information in this book as a starting point for additional research using the resources described in Ch. 10. Citations to each state's statutes are included so you can look up the laws themselves.

You can cross-check the information in this appendix with the summaries of state law in *Home Foreclosures* by the National Consumer Law Center (see Ch. 10). Also check for updates on this book's "Online Companion Page" using the link in the introductory chapter, "Your Foreclosure Companion."

For bills pending in your state's legislature or recently signed into law by your state's governor, visit your state legislature's website and search for the terms you're interested in, like "foreclosure." Remember, a bill does not become law until it is signed by your state's governor. Most proposed laws will never make it to your governor's pen.

Alabama

Foreclosure laws change! Check for updates at www.nolo.com/legal-updates.

Topic	State Rule
Most common type of foreclosure process	Nonjudicial under a power of sale in a mortgage
Notice of the foreclosure	Foreclosing party must publish notice in a newspaper once a week for three consecutive weeks; no requirement that the homeowner be served by mail. However, mortgages in Alabama often contractually require the foreclosing party to notify the borrower (usually by mail) about foreclosure proceedings.
Reinstatement of loan before sale	Not available (except as permitted by the terms of the mortgage)
Redemption after sale	Generally, available for one year after foreclosure sale. But if the loan originated on January 1, 2016, or after, a homestead exemption was claimed in the tax year during which the sale occurred, and proper notice about the right to redeem was given at least 30 days before the sale, then 180 days after the sale. If notice not provided before the sale, the redemption period doesn't start until the bank provides notice about the right to redeem, but homeowners can't redeem, under any circumstances, more than one year after the foreclosure sale. Borrower must surrender the property to the buyer within ten days after a written demand is made or lose the right of redemption.
Special protections for foreclosures involving high-cost mortgages	None
Special state protections for service members	If a service member dies while deployed overseas, the lender must wait at least 180 days before starting a foreclosure against the surviving spouse or the service member's estate provided that the surviving spouse or the estate notifies the lender and asks for a delay (and the mortgage was taken out after August 1, 2009). Ala. Code §§ 35-10-70, 35-10-71
Deficiency judgments	May be obtained by filing a lawsuit.
Cash exempted in bankruptcy	Using the wildcard exemption, $8,225 for one person, $16,450 for a married couple (will not protect wages, salaries, or other compensation).

Alabama (continued)

Topic	State Rule
Notice to leave after house is sold	Entitled to a written ten-day notice to leave before eviction proceedings may be brought.
Foreclosure statutes	Ala. Code §§ 35-10-1 to 35-10-30, 6-5-247 to 6-5-257

Alaska

Foreclosure laws change! Check for updates at www.nolo.com/legal-updates.

Topic	State Rule
Most common type of foreclosure process	Nonjudicial under a power of sale in a deed of trust
Notice of the foreclosure	Notice of default must be recorded not less than 30 days after default and not less than 90 days before sale. The notice of default must be sent by certified mail to the borrower within 10 days of recording or personally delivered to the borrower within 20 days after recording. Before the sale, the foreclosing party must publicly post and publish a notice of sale (in a newspaper and on the Internet).
Reinstatement of loan before sale	Available any time before sale, but lender can refuse to reinstate if it filed two or more prior notices of default and the borrower cured the defaults
Redemption after sale	Not available after a nonjudicial foreclosure, unless the deed of trust specifically provides a right of redemption
Special protections for foreclosures involving high-cost mortgages	None
Special state protections for service members	Servicemembers Civil Relief Act protections extended to members of the Alaska National Guard and Alaska Naval Militia while on active duty for the state by order of the governor. Alaska Stat. § 26.05.135
Deficiency judgments	Not allowed after a nonjudicial foreclosure
Cash exempted in bankruptcy	Under federal bankruptcy exemptions, $13,900 for one person, $27,800 for a married couple.
Notice to leave after house is sold	New owner must give former owner a notice to quit (leave) before filing a civil lawsuit to gain possession.
Foreclosure statutes	Alaska Stat. §§ 34.20.070 et seq.

Arizona

Foreclosure laws change! Check for updates at www.nolo.com/legal-updates.

Topic	State Rule
Most common types of foreclosure process	Nonjudicial under power of sale in deed of trust
Notice of the foreclosure	Foreclosing party must record a notice of sale at least 90 days before the sale date and must mail it by certified mail to borrower within five business days after recording. The notice of sale must also be published in a newspaper for four consecutive weeks and posted on the property at least 20 days before sale, as well as posted in the courthouse building.
Reinstatement of loan before sale	Available until 5:00 p.m. on the day before date of sale (other than a Saturday or legal holiday).
Redemption after sale	Not available after a nonjudicial foreclosure
Special protections for foreclosures involving high-cost mortgages	None
Special state protections for service members	Federal protections under the Servicemembers Civil Relief Act extended to National Guard ordered to active duty by governor in certain circumstances. Ariz. Rev. Stat. Ann. § 26-168
Deficiency judgments	Not allowed after a nonjudicial foreclosure if the property is 2½ acres or less and is a single- or two-family residence. For most other properties, allowed if lawsuit is filed within 90 days of foreclosure sale.
Cash exempted in bankruptcy	$300 for one person, $600 for a married couple.
Notice to leave after house is sold	New owner may begin an eviction action following the foreclosure sale after making a demand for possession.
Foreclosure statutes	Ariz. Rev. Stat. §§ 33-721 to 33-730 (judicial), 33-801 to 33-821 (nonjudicial), 12-1281 to 12-1283, 12-1566

Arkansas

Foreclosure laws change! Check for updates at www.nolo.com/legal-updates.

Topic	State Rule
Most common type of foreclosure process	Nonjudicial under power of sale in a mortgage
Notice of the foreclosure	Foreclosing party must mail a notice to the borrower that includes information about loan modification assistance, among other things, at least ten days before starting a foreclosure. Foreclosing party must record a notice of default and intent to sell, and then mail a copy by certified and first-class mail within 30 days after recording the notice. Notice must also be published in a newspaper for four consecutive weeks prior to sale, posted at the courthouse, and published by a third-party on the Internet.
Reinstatement of loan before sale	Allowed prior to sale
Redemption after sale	Not available after a nonjudicial foreclosure
Special protections for foreclosures involving high-cost mortgages	An intentional violation of the Arkansas Home Loan Protection Act renders the loan agreement void. The lender then has no right to collect, receive, or retain any principal, interest, or other charges at all with respect to the loan, and the borrower may recover any payments made under the agreement. Ark. Code Ann. §§ 23-53-106
Special state protections for service members	Lender may not foreclose on a military service member for nonpayment or any breach occurring during military service without a court order if certain conditions are met. Applies to National Guard members called into active service by the governor for more than 180 days. Ark. Code Ann. § 12-62-716
Deficiency judgments	Allowed for difference between the: indebtedness and the fair market value of the property or the indebtedness and the foreclosure sales price (whichever is less). Lawsuit must be filed within 12 months of sale.
Cash exempted in bankruptcy	$200 for one person, $500 for head of household, $1,000 for married couple wherein one is the head of household. Under federal bankruptcy exemptions, $13,900 for one person, $27,800 for a married couple.
Notice to leave after house is sold	The new owner can initiate an eviction action following the sale.
Foreclosure statutes	Ark. Code Ann. §§ 18-50-101 to 18-50-116

California

Foreclosure laws change! Check for updates at www.nolo.com/legal-updates.

Topic	State Rule
Most common type of foreclosure process	Nonjudicial under power of sale in deed of trust
Notice of the foreclosure	Servicer must personally contact (or meet the requirements for attempting to contact) borrowers to explore options for avoiding foreclosure 30 days before recording the notice of default. Servicer must inform the borrower of the right to request copies of the promissory note, deed of trust, payment history since the borrower was last less than 60 days past due, and any assignment, if applicable, to demonstrate the right to foreclose. The servicer then records a three-month notice of default in the county recorder's office and mails a copy to the borrowers within ten business days following recordation. After three months expires (or up to five days prior), the servicer records a notice of sale and mails a copy to the borrowers at least 20 days before the sale date. The sale date can't be earlier than three months and 20 days after the recording date of the notice of default. The notice of sale is also posted on the property, in a public place, and published in a newspaper.
Reinstatement of loan before sale	Allowed up to five business days before the sale date
Redemption after sale	Not available after a nonjudicial foreclosure. But "Homes for Homeowners" law (expiring January 1, 2026, unless extended) gives designated individuals, like eligible tenants and nonprofit organizations, the right to bid on a one- to four-unit single-family residence up to 45 days after the trustee sale closes unless a prospective owner-occupant is already the successful purchaser.
Special protections for foreclosures involving high-cost mortgages	Cal. Fin. Code § 4973 makes a number of abusive loan practices unlawful. Section 4978 provides remedies that include authority for a judge to reform the loan to comply with the law. These provisions don't apply to mortgages held by the secondary market (Fannie Mae, Freddie Mac) or to assignees that have no reason to know of the loan origination violations. Cal. Fin. Code § 4979.8

California (continued)

Topic	State Rule
Special state protections for service members	Protections similar to those under the federal Servicemembers Civil Relief Act extended to members of the National Guard called or ordered into active state service by the governor or into active federal service by the President of the United States. Also applies to reservists who have been called to full-time active duty. Cal. Mil. & Vet. Code §§ 400 to 409.13
Deficiency judgments	Not allowed after a nonjudicial foreclosure
Cash exempted in bankruptcy	$1,550 up to $30,825 depending on amount of homestead exemption used (no doubling; California 703 exemption system).
Notice to leave after the house is sold	New owner must give former homeowner three-day notice to quit (leave) and file an unlawful detainer lawsuit to evict.
Foreclosure statutes	Cal. Civ. Code §§ 2923.5, 2924 to 2924l; Cal. Code Civ. Proc. §§ 580a through 580d

Colorado

Foreclosure laws change! Check for updates at www.nolo.com/legal-updates.

Topic	State Rule
Most common type of foreclosure process	Nonjudicial under power of sale in deed of trust. The foreclosing party must file proof of debt ownership and the default with a public trustee, who oversees the process. The mortgage holder must separately obtain a court order in a Rule 120 proceeding authorizing the sale and give the public trustee a copy of the order before the sale date.
Notice of the foreclosure	At least 30 days before filing the Notice of Election and Demand, and at least 30 days after the default, the borrower must be served with information about state hotline, how to contact the foreclosing party's loss mitigation department, and a statement that it is illegal for anyone acting as foreclosure consultant to charge borrower up-front fee or deposit for foreclosure-related services. After the Notice of Election and Demand has been recorded (110 to 125 calendar days before the sale date), the public trustee must mail a combined notice of sale, right to cure, and right to redeem to the borrower within 20 calendar days after the recording date. The trustee must mail the notice again between 45 and 60 days before the sale date. Notice of the Rule 120 motion must be mailed to the borrower and posted on the property not less than 14 days prior to the response deadline.
Reinstatement of loan before sale	Available until noon the day before the sale provided the borrower files a notice of intent to cure with the public trustee no later than 15 calendar days before the sale date.
Redemption after sale	Available to some lienholders but not to borrower
Special protections for foreclosures involving high-cost mortgages	None
Special state protections for service members	Colorado law provides certain protections against foreclosure for any person who is called to state military service or called to state defense force active duty in certain circumstances for over 30 days. Colo. Rev. Stat. § 28-3-1406
Deficiency judgments	Allowed, but the borrower can raise a defense against the action for a deficiency judgment if the foreclosing party did not bid the fair market value of the property, minus unpaid property taxes and certain other expenses.

Colorado (continued)

Topic	State Rule
Cash exempted in bankruptcy	None
Notice to leave after house is sold	The new owner must make a demand for possession. If the former owner does not vacate, then the new owner files the lawsuit to evict.
Foreclosure statutes	Colo. Rev. Stat. §§ 38-38-100.3 to 38-38-114

Connecticut

Foreclosure laws change! Check for updates at www.nolo.com/legal-updates.

Topic	State Rule
Most common type of foreclosure process	Judicial ("foreclosure by sale") or; strict foreclosure in which court transfers title directly to foreclosing party without ordering a sale
Notice of the foreclosure	After the foreclosing party files the foreclosure lawsuit, borrower has 15 days after the return date to file an answer. The foreclosing party must give notice to the borrowers about the foreclosure mediation program along with the complaint and summons.
Reinstatement of loan before sale	Not available (except as permitted by the terms of the mortgage)
Redemption after sale	Up until court confirms sale or until the "Law Day" in a strict foreclosure.
Special protections for foreclosures involving high-cost mortgages	None relevant to foreclosure. But certain homeowners who are underemployed or unemployed can ask the court for protection from foreclosure and modification of mortgage terms to give relief from paying of arrearages.
Special state protections for service members	None
Deficiency judgments	May be obtained in foreclosure by sale, and within 30 days after the redemption period expires (the Law Day) in a strict foreclosure.
Cash exempted in bankruptcy	Using the wildcard exemption, $1,000 for one person, $2,000 for a married couple. Under federal bankruptcy exemptions, $13,900 for one person, $27,800 for a married couple.
Notice to leave after house is sold	Former owner will be required to move out after the sale under an order of ejectment issued by the court. Check with the marshal to see how much time you have to move out.
Foreclosure statutes	Conn. Gen. Stat. §§ 49-1 to 49-31v; Connecticut Superior Court Rules 23-16 through 23-19

Delaware

Foreclosure laws change! Check for updates at www.nolo.com/legal-updates.

Topic	State Rule
Most common type of foreclosure process	Judicial
Notice of the foreclosure	If the home is an owner-occupied residential property that is one to four units, the foreclosing party must mail the borrower a 45-day notice of intent to foreclose before starting the foreclosure lawsuit. Borrower has 20 days to respond to lawsuit. Foreclosing party must include a mediation notice with complaint. After court grants a judgment of foreclosure, borrower gets a ten-day notice of sale. Notice of sale must also be posted publicly and published in a newspaper two weeks prior to sale.
Reinstatement of loan before sale	Not available (except as permitted by the terms of the mortgage)
Redemption after sale	Available until court confirms sale
Special protections for foreclosures involving high-cost mortgages	None
Special state protections for service members	None
Deficiency judgments	May be obtained by filing a separate lawsuit after a court has issued a foreclosure judgment.
Cash exempted in bankruptcy	$500 if head of family
Notice to leave after house is sold	Eviction of former homeowner may be continued as part of the foreclosure action.
Foreclosure statutes	Del. Code Ann. tit. 10, Chapter 49, §§ 5061 through 5067

District of Columbia

Foreclosure laws change! Check for updates at www.nolo.com/legal-updates.

Topic	State Rule
Most common type of foreclosure process	Nonjudicial under power of sale in deed of trust; however, due to issues with the District of Columbia's mediation program, more foreclosures are judicial.
Notice of the foreclosure	Foreclosing party must mail a notice of default along with a mediation notice giving 30 days to elect mediation. If the borrower does not elect mediation (or participates in mediation but does not work out an agreement with the foreclosing party), the foreclosure may proceed. The foreclosing party then sends a notice of the intention to foreclose (including sale information) 30 days before the sale to borrower and sends a copy of the notice to the mayor. The 30-day period begins when the mayor receives notice.
Reinstatement of loan before sale	Allowed up to five business days before the sale, once in two consecutive years
Redemption after sale	Not available
Special protections for foreclosures involving high-cost mortgages	None
Special state protections for service members	None
Deficiency judgments	May be obtained by filing a lawsuit
Cash exempted in bankruptcy	Using the wildcard exemption, $850 for one person, $1,700 for a married couple (up to $8,925 and $17,850 depending on amount of other exemptions used).
Notice to leave after house is sold	New owner may file a lawsuit to evict former homeowners from the property after giving notice to quit. A summons must be served seven days before trial regarding possession.
Foreclosure statutes	D.C. Code Ann. §§ 42-815 through 42-816

Florida

Foreclosure laws change! Check for updates at www.nolo.com/legal-updates.

Topic	State Rule
Most common type of foreclosure process	Judicial
Notice of the foreclosure	Borrower gets 20 days to respond to complaint. Foreclosing party must publish notice of sale in a newspaper for two consecutive weeks at least five days before sale. The judge has the discretion to refer foreclosure for mediation as permitted by law.
Reinstatement of loan before sale	Not available (except as permitted by the terms of the mortgage)
Redemption after sale	Available until the court clerk files a certificate of sale or as specified in the judgment, whichever is later
Special protections for foreclosures involving high-cost mortgages	None
Special state protections for service members	If a military service member took out the mortgage before going on active duty (state or federal), lender cannot foreclose during the time of service or within 30 days thereafter unless a court issues an order ahead of time allowing it. Fla. Stat. Ann. §§ 250.5201 to 250.5205
Deficiency judgments	Allowed as part of the foreclosure action if borrower is personally served. The deficiency judgment is within the sound discretion of the court; however, in the case of an owner-occupied residential property, the amount may not exceed the difference between the judgment amount and the fair market value of the property on the date of sale. Foreclosing party may also file a separate lawsuit for a deficiency. Foreclosing party has one year to request the deficiency judgment.
Cash exempted in bankruptcy	Using the wildcard exemption, $1,000 for one person, $2,000 for a married couple ($5,000 and $10,000 if homestead exemption isn't used).
Notice to leave after house is sold	The eviction process is part of the foreclosure action and the right to possession is included in the judgment. It is not usually necessary to file an independent action for possession. The foreclosing party files a motion for a writ of possession. When the motion is granted, the clerk of court issues the writ of possession and the sheriff posts the writ to the property. (The writ gives 24 hours to move out.) If the occupant does not vacate, the sheriff executes the order.
Foreclosure statutes	Fla. Stat. Ann. §§ 702.01 through 702.11, 45.031 and 45.0315

Georgia

Foreclosure laws change! Check for updates at www.nolo.com/legal-updates.

Topic	State Rule
Most common type of foreclosure process	Nonjudicial under power of sale in a Security Deed (deed of trust)
Notice of the foreclosure	Foreclosing party must mail notice to borrower 30 days before sale. Additional notice by publication in a newspaper of general circulation is required.
Reinstatement of loan before sale	High-cost home loans may be reinstated until title is transferred. For other types of loans, the security deed may provide the right to reinstate.
Redemption after sale	Not available
Special protections for foreclosures involving high-cost mortgages	Additional notices required for high-cost loans. Georgia Fair Lending Act, Ga. Code Ann. §§ 7-6A-1 to 7-6A-13
Special state protections for service members	None
Deficiency judgments	If the foreclosure was nonjudicial, no deficiency judgment until a court confirms that the property was sold at its fair market value. (Foreclosing party must file a report of sale with the court within 30 days of the foreclosure sale.)
Cash exempted in bankruptcy	Using the wildcard exemption, up to $1,200 for one person and $2,400 for a married couple (up to $11,200 and $22,400 depending on amount of homestead exemption used).
Notice to leave after house is sold	The purchaser must first make a demand for possession, and then can begin eviction proceedings.
Foreclosure statutes	Ga. Code Ann. §§ 44-14-160 to 44-14-191

Hawaii

Foreclosure laws change! Check for updates at www.nolo.com/legal-updates.

Topic	State Rule
Most common type of foreclosure process	Judicial. In the past, most foreclosures in Hawaii were nonjudicial. However, many lenders have switched to judicial foreclosures to bypass Hawaii's Mortgage Foreclosure Dispute Resolution (MFDR) Program. This could change if the legislature amends the MFDR Program.
Notice of the foreclosure	Borrower has 20 days to respond after being served with summons and complaint. For judicial foreclosures, the foreclosing party must publish a notice of sale in a newspaper once each week for three consecutive weeks, with the sale taking place no sooner than 14 days after the date of the publication of the third public notice advertisement; or the Notice of Sale may be published not less than 28 days before the date of the public sale on a state website. (If the public notice is published on a website, the notice must also be published at least once in a newspaper not less than 14 days prior to the public sale.)
Reinstatement of loan before sale	Not available in a judicial foreclosure (except as permitted by the terms of the mortgage)
Redemption after sale	Not available
Special protections for foreclosures involving high-cost mortgages	None
Special state protections for service members	Protections similar to the federal Servicemembers Civil Relief Act provided for members of the state military forces, including the right to postpone legal proceedings and a prohibition on nonjudicial foreclosures. Haw. Rev. Stat. §§ 657D-1 to 657D-63
Deficiency judgments	Allowed for judicial foreclosures
Cash exempted in bankruptcy	None. Under federal bankruptcy exemptions, $13,900 for one person, $27,800 for a married couple.
Notice to leave after house is sold	In a judicial foreclosure, new owner must get a court order (write of possession) to remove former homeowner after the sale.
Foreclosure statutes	Haw. Rev. Stat. §§ 667-1 through 667-20.1 (judicial); §§ 667-21 through 667-41 (nonjudicial)

Idaho

Foreclosure laws change! Check for updates at www.nolo.com/legal-updates.

Topic	State Rule
Most common type of foreclosure process	Nonjudicial under power of sale in deed of trust
Notice of the foreclosure	Foreclosing party must mail homeowner a notice of default and a 120-day notice of sale before the date set for sale. Foreclosing party must also make attempt to personally serve occupant with notice of sale and post notice of sale on property at least 30 days before the sale, as well as publish notice of sale over four consecutive weeks at least 30 days before sale. The notice of default must be accompanied by a modification request form. The lender must respond to a request for modification within 45 days and may not proceed to a foreclosure sale until it has responded to the modification request.
Reinstatement of loan before sale	Available within 115 days after notice of default is filed with county recorder
Redemption after sale	Not available after a nonjudicial foreclosure
Special protections for foreclosures involving high-cost mortgages	None
Special state protections for service members	Idaho law extends protections of federal Servicemembers Civil Relief Act to National Guard ordered to state active duty by governor in certain circumstances. Idaho Code § 46-409
Deficiency judgments	May be obtained in a lawsuit brought within three months after sale. Amount of deficiency is limited by fair market value at time of sale.
Cash exempted in bankruptcy	None
Notice to leave after house is sold	New owner is entitled to possession of the property on the tenth day following sale but must go to court to evict former owner. An eviction trial must be scheduled within 12 days after the filing of the complaint.
Foreclosure statutes	Idaho Code §§ 45-1505 to 45-1515

Illinois

Foreclosure laws change! Check for updates at www.nolo.com/legal-updates.

Topic	State Rule
Most common type of foreclosure process	Judicial
Notice of the foreclosure	Borrower has 30 days to respond after being served with summons and complaint. After court issues a judgment of foreclosure, a notice of sale must be published three times between 45 and seven days before sale. Notice of sale must be mailed to borrower at least ten business days before the sale.
Reinstatement of loan before sale	Available within 90 days after foreclosure complaint is served on borrower. Under High-Risk Home Loan Act, foreclosing party must serve notice of right to reinstate at least 30 days before starting foreclosure lawsuit.
Redemption after sale	Available for seven months after the complaint is served or three months after foreclosure judgment entered, whichever is later. If the mortgage holder is the purchaser at the sale, property sold below a certain value may be redeemed for 30 days after confirmation of sale by paying sales price plus costs and interest.
Special protections for foreclosures involving high-cost mortgages	Special defenses to foreclosure lawsuit. High-Risk Home Loan Act, 815 Ill. Comp. Stat. §§ 137/1 to 137/175
Special state protections for service members	Certain service members may apply to the court for a 90-day stay of foreclosure proceedings or, in some cases, a reduction in the monthly payments for up to 90 days. 735 Ill. Comp. Stat. §§ 5/15-1501.5, 5/15-1501.6. Court can postpone proceedings if state or federal military service directly results in failure to meet pre-service obligations. 330 Ill. Comp. Stat. § 60/5.1
Deficiency judgments	May be sought as part of the foreclosure lawsuit. Allowed only if borrower is served personally (unless borrower enters an appearance in the action).
Cash exempted in bankruptcy	Using the wildcard exemption, up to $4,000 for one person, $8,000 for a married couple.
Notice to leave after house is sold	Purchaser is entitled to possession 30 days after the court confirms the sale. New owner must file a complaint for forcible entry and detainer to remove any occupant who wasn't personally named in the foreclosure case.
Foreclosure statutes	735 Ill. Comp. Stat §§ 5/15-1501 to 5/15-1605

Indiana

Foreclosure laws change! Check for updates at www.nolo.com/legal-updates.

Topic	State Rule
Most common type of foreclosure process	Judicial
Notice of the foreclosure	Foreclosing party must give borrower 30 days' notice before filing foreclosure complaint. Borrower generally gets 20 days to respond to complaint. After the complaint is filed, house can't be sold for three months (a waiting period) in most cases (longer for certain older mortgages). Foreclosing party must publish notice of sale once a week for three consecutive weeks with the first publication occurring at least 30 days before the scheduled sale, and mail a copy to homeowner at the time of the first advertisement. Notice of sale must also be posted at courthouse.
Reinstatement of loan before sale	If the borrower reinstates before the court enters judgment, the foreclosure must be dismissed. If the borrower reinstates after judgment, but prior to the sale, the foreclosure must be stayed (postponed). Reinstatement also available for high-cost home loans (defined in Ind. Code § 24-9-2-8) any time before title is transferred by means of foreclosure.
Redemption after sale	Not available after sale
Special protections for foreclosures involving high-cost mortgages	Borrower in foreclosure may raise violations of the high-cost home loan statute as a claim, counterclaim, or defense to foreclosure. Ind. Code § 24-9-5-1. Borrower may cure the default and reinstate a high-cost home loan at any time until title is transferred by means of foreclosure. Ind. Code § 24-9-5-2
Special state protections for service members	Protections under the federal Servicemembers Civil Relief Act extended to National Guard members ordered to state active duty for 30 or more consecutive days. Ind. Code § 10-16-7-23
Deficiency judgments	Allowed if borrower does not waive applicable waiting period. (Borrower may agree to waiver in exchange for lender's agreeing not to seek a deficiency judgment.)
Cash exempted in bankruptcy	$400 for one person, $800 for a married couple.
Notice to leave after house is sold	Foreclosing party (if it is the purchaser at the sale) may proceed with an eviction against the former owners as an extension of the foreclosure action.
Foreclosure statutes	Ind. Code §§ 32-30-10-1 to 32-30-10-14, 32-29-1-1 to 32-29-1-11, 32-29-7-1 to 32-29-7-14

Iowa

Foreclosure laws change! Check for updates at www.nolo.com/legal-updates.

Topic	State Rule
Most common type of foreclosure process	Judicial
Notice of the foreclosure	Foreclosing party must mail notice of default and right to cure (reinstate) to borrower at least 30 days before filing suit (or 45 days if the property is agricultural) and a demand for payment of the accelerated balance 14 days before filing suit in order to qualify for an award of attorneys' fees. Borrower also gets a notice about the availability of counseling and mediation. To officially start the foreclosure, the lender files a lawsuit in court and serves borrower a summons and complaint. Notice must be posted publicly and published twice, with the first publication being at least four weeks before the sale date.
Reinstatement of loan before sale	Available within 30 days after notice of default if the land is nonagricultural (or 45 days if the land is agricultural)
Redemption after sale	If foreclosure is judicial with redemption, the borrower can redeem the home within one year, six months or three months (if the lender waives the deficiency in the foreclosure action and other criteria are met), or 60 days (if the borrower abandons the home and other criteria are met). If the lender elects to foreclose without redemption, the borrower can demand a delay of sale and redeem before the sale (no post-sale right of redemption). Post-sale redemption not available for alternative nonjudicial voluntary foreclosures.
Special protections for foreclosures involving high-cost mortgages	None
Special state protections for service members	If the service member entered into the mortgage to purchase real estate prior to military service, nonjudicial foreclosure is prohibited. Iowa Code § 29A.103
Deficiency judgments	Generally allowed, but prohibited under certain circumstances. (Consult with an attorney to find out if a deficiency judgment is permitted in your situation.)
Cash exempted in bankruptcy	Using the wildcard exemption, up to $1,000 for one person, $2,000 for a married couple.
Notice to leave after house is sold	If the foreclosure is judicial, the foreclosing party may generally include the eviction as part of the foreclosure action. If the foreclosure is nonjudicial, the new owner must file a separate eviction lawsuit.
Foreclosure statutes	Iowa Code §§ 654.1 to 654.26, 655A to 655A.9, 628.26, 628.27

Kansas

Foreclosure laws change! Check for updates at www.nolo.com/legal-updates.

Topic	State Rule
Most common type of foreclosure process	Judicial
Notice of the foreclosure	Borrower who is personally served with the complaint has 21 days to respond; if notice is only by publication in a local newspaper of general circulation, borrower has 41 days to respond. After court issues a foreclosure judgment, foreclosing party must publish a notice of sale at least three times; last publication must be between seven and 14 days before sale date.
Reinstatement of loan before sale	Not available (except as permitted by the terms of the mortgage)
Redemption after sale	Available for 12 months from the sale date (less if homeowner abandoned premises). Available for three months if borrower defaulted on mortgage before one-third of original debt was repaid. Court may extend three-month redemption period by another three months if homeowner loses his or her job after the sale and during the initial three-month period. Available for 12 months if all mortgage debt on property totals less than one-third of the house's market value.
Special protections for foreclosures involving high-cost mortgages	None
Special state protections for service members	None
Deficiency judgments	Allowed if court confirms that the price paid for property at sale is adequate compared to its fair market value. Sales price that covers foreclosing party's judgment, taxes, interest, and costs is considered adequate.
Cash exempted in bankruptcy	None
Notice to leave after house is sold	New owner (usually the foreclosing bank) does not have to send former owner a notice to terminate. After the redemption period, the bank can get a writ of assistance as part of the foreclosure action commanding the sheriff to forcibly remove the former owner.
Foreclosure statutes	Kan. Stat. Ann. §§ 60-2410, 60-2414, and 60-2415

Kentucky

Foreclosure laws change! Check for updates at www.nolo.com/legal-updates.

Topic	State Rule
Most common type of foreclosure process	Judicial
Notice of the foreclosure	Borrower has 20 days to respond after being served with the complaint. If court issues a foreclosure judgment, foreclosing party must post notice on courthouse door (and three other places) and publish notice in a newspaper.
Reinstatement of loan before sale	Generally, no right to reinstate (except as permitted by the terms of the mortgage). If loan is a high-cost home loan (under Ky. Rev. Stat. Ann. § 360.100), foreclosing party must provide a notice of default giving the borrower at least 30 days to reinstate before filing the foreclosure complaint.
Redemption after sale	Available six months after sale, if sale amount is less than two-thirds of property's appraised value.
Special protections for foreclosures involving high-cost mortgages	Before foreclosing a high-cost home loan, the foreclosing party must provide a notice of default to the borrower that gives 30 days to cure the default and reinstate the mortgage. Ky. Rev. Stat. Ann. § 360.100
Special state protections for service members	Protections under the federal Servicemembers Civil Relief Act extended to state National Guard ordered to state active duty by governor for a period of 30 days or more. Ky. Rev. Stat. Ann. § 38.510
Deficiency judgments	Allowed generally
Cash exempted in bankruptcy	Using the wildcard exemption, up to $1,000 for one person, $2,000 for a married couple. Under federal bankruptcy exemptions, $13,900 for one person, $27,800 for a married couple.
Notice to leave after house is sold	New owner is entitled to possession upon ten days' notice. If former owner does not move out, purchaser can get a writ of possession issued by the court.
Foreclosure statutes	Ky. Rev. Stat. Ann. §§ 426.005, 426.200, 426.260, 426.530, 426.560

Louisiana

Foreclosure laws change! Check for updates at www.nolo.com/legal-updates.

Topic	State Rule
Most common type of foreclosure process	Judicial, but most common process is an "executory" proceeding. In the mortgage document, the borrower will typically have "confessed to judgment" in case of a default. Upon default the foreclosing party files a foreclosure petition with the mortgage attached, and the court summarily orders the property seized and sold unless the borrower appeals or brings a lawsuit asking the court to stop (enjoin) the proceeding.
Notice of the foreclosure	The sheriff must serve the borrower a written notice of seizure. Notice of sale is published at least twice and not less than three days after the debtor has been served with the notice of seizure.
Reinstatement of loan before sale	Not available (unless permitted by the terms of the mortgage)
Redemption after sale	Not available
Special protections for foreclosures involving high-cost mortgages	None
Special state protections for service members	None
Deficiency judgments	Allowed. Can be obtained in an ordinary proceeding or in a separate suit after an executory proceeding (or by converting executory proceeding into an ordinary proceeding) if the property was properly appraised.
Cash exempted in bankruptcy	None
Notice to leave after house is sold	New owner can get writ of possession from court and the sheriff will remove former owners from the premises.
Foreclosure statutes	La. Code Civ. Proc. Ann. Arts. 3721 to 3753, 2631 to 2772

Maine

Foreclosure laws change! Check for updates at www.nolo.com/legal-updates.

Topic	State Rule
Most common type of foreclosure process	Judicial
Notice of the foreclosure	Foreclosing party must send a notice of right to cure 35 days before starting foreclosure. Borrower has 20 days to respond after being served with summons and complaint. After the redemption period expires (see below), the foreclosing party must publish notice of public sale for three consecutive weeks. Sale must be held 30 to 45 days after date of first publication. Foreclosing party must also mail a notice of sale at least 30 days before sale date to all parties who appeared in the foreclosure action.
Reinstatement of loan before sale	Borrower has the right to reinstate within 35 days after receiving the notice of right to cure. Also, lender, in its sole discretion, may let borrower reinstate the loan any time before the sale.
Redemption after sale	Redemption period is 90 days from the date the foreclosure judgment is entered, unless borrower appeals.
Special protections for foreclosures involving high-cost mortgages	Creditor cannot charge a prepayment penalty and cannot engage in flipping. If the creditor violates the law, the borrower can get damages. Me. Rev. Stat. tit 9-A, § 8-506
Special state protections for service members	Certain military service members (including state military forces on active state service) get the opportunity to stay (postpone) court proceedings. Me. Rev. Stat. Ann. tit. 37-B, § 389-A
Deficiency judgments	Allowed, but limited to the difference between the fair market value of the property at the time of the sale and the total outstanding debt if the foreclosing party buys the home at the foreclosure sale.
Cash exempted in bankruptcy	Using the wildcard exemption, $400 for one person, $800 for two ($6,400 and $12,800 depending on amount of homestead exemption used).
Notice to leave after house is sold	Foreclosing party can get a writ of possession against the foreclosed homeowners as part of the foreclosure action.
Foreclosure statutes	Me. Rev. Stat. Ann. tit. 14, §§ 6101 to 6325

Maryland

Foreclosure laws change! Check for updates at www.nolo.com/legal-updates.

Topic	State Rule
Most common type of foreclosure process	Nonjudicial under power of sale in deed of trust, but a court must ratify the sale
Notice of the foreclosure	Foreclosing party must serve borrower with notice of intent to foreclose at least 45 days before starting foreclosure, along with mediation information if applicable. Service must be by first-class and certified mail, return receipt requested. The foreclosing party officially starts the foreclosure by filing an Order to Docket with the court and serving a copy to the borrower along with mediation information, if applicable. Foreclosing party must also publish notice for three consecutive weeks, with the last publication not more than one week before sale. In addition, person authorized to make the sale must serve (by certified mail, return receipt requested) a notice of sale on homeowner at least 10 days but not more than 30 days before sale.
Reinstatement of loan before sale	Available until one day before sale date
Redemption after sale	Redemption available until the court ratifies the sale
Special protections for foreclosures involving high-cost mortgages	None
Special state protections for service members	Protections provided under the federal Servicemembers Civil Relief Act extended to members of the National Guard or Maryland Defense Force ordered to state military duty for a period of 14 consecutive days or longer. Md. Code Ann. [Pub. Safety] § 13-704
Deficiency judgments	Foreclosing party may file a motion for a deficiency judgment within three years after ratification of the auditor's report.
Cash exempted in bankruptcy	Using the wildcard exemption, $6,000 for one person, $12,000 for a married couple.
Notice to leave after house is sold	After the court ratifies the sale, the new owner (usually the foreclosing party) can obtain an order of possession from the court to evict the foreclosed homeowners.
Foreclosure statutes	Md. Code Ann. [Real Prop.] §§ 7-105 to 7-105.8

Massachusetts

Foreclosure laws change! Check for updates at www.nolo.com/legal-updates.

Topic	State Rule
Most common type of foreclosure process	Nonjudicial under power of sale
Notice of the foreclosure	Prior to accelerating the loan and initiating foreclosure proceedings, the foreclosing party must mail (or serve) to the borrower a 90-day notice of the right to reinstate the mortgage and that borrower may be eligible for state agency assistance. After loan is accelerated, the foreclosing party must mail a notice of sale to homeowner at least 14 days before the sale date, and publish notice for three consecutive weeks before the sale date.
Reinstatement of loan before sale	90-day right to cure (the terms of the mortgage may provide additional time)
Redemption after sale	Not available after a nonjudicial foreclosure
Special protections for foreclosures involving high-cost mortgages	If the original lender (or its assignee) violates Massachusetts' high-cost home loan law, the borrower can rescind the loan and use rescission as a defense to the foreclosure. Mass. Gen. Laws ch. 183C §§ 18, 15. Lender is required to attempt to modify certain high-cost and predatory loans. Mass. Gen. Laws ch. 244 § 35B
Special state protections for service members	The foreclosing party typically files a Servicemembers Civil Relief Act (SCRA) action with the land court separate from the actual foreclosure. The only purpose is to determine whether a borrower is entitled to the protections of the SCRA. The foreclosing party serves a copy of the complaint to the borrower, which gives the borrower the opportunity to file an answer if he or she is in the military.
Deficiency judgments	Can be obtained in separate lawsuit if a notice of intent to seek a deficiency is mailed to borrower at least 21 days before sale date.
Cash exempted in bankruptcy	$2,500 for one person, $5,000 for a married couple (plus an additional $6,000 using the wildcard exemption). Under federal bankruptcy exemptions, $13,900 for one person, $27,800 for a married couple.
Notice to leave after house is sold	The new owner must first give a notice to quit (leave) and then can begin eviction proceedings by filing a complaint in court.
Foreclosure statutes	Mass. Gen. Laws ch. 244, § 14, 17A, 17B, 18, 35A

Michigan

Foreclosure laws change! Check for updates at www.nolo.com/legal-updates.

Topic	State Rule
Most common type of foreclosure process	Nonjudicial under power of sale in a mortgage
Notice of the foreclosure	Foreclosing party must publish notice once a week for four consecutive weeks before sale and post a notice on property within at least 15 days of first publication. No notice need be mailed or served to borrower, however the mortgage contract might require the foreclosing party to mail a breach letter (typically giving 30 days to cure the default) prior to starting foreclosure proceedings.
Reinstatement of loan before sale	Not available (except as permitted by the terms of the mortgage)
Redemption after sale	If property is not abandoned and more than two-thirds of the original mortgage is still owed, redemption allowed for six months. If less than two-thirds is owed, the redemption period is one year. If the property is abandoned, redemption period is 30 days (or until the 15-day notice that the lender considers the premises abandoned expires, whichever is later).
Special protections for foreclosures involving high-cost mortgages	None
Special state protections for service members	The notice of foreclosure must include a statement to military service members. Mich. Comp. Laws § 600.3212. Michigan law provides special protections against foreclosure to certain military service members, including members of the Michigan National Guard. So long as either the mortgagor entered into the mortgage before becoming a service member or the mortgagor is deployed in overseas service, the lender can"t foreclose nonjudicially during the service member's period of military service (or within six months thereafter) unless a court ordered the sale or foreclosure. Mich. Comp. Laws § 600.3285
Deficiency judgments	Allowed after a nonjudicial foreclosure. But if the mortgage holder buys the property at the foreclosure sale, then borrower can contest the amount of the deficiency if the property was fairly worth the amount of the debt at the time of the sale or the foreclosure sale price was substantially less than the fair market value of the property.

Michigan (continued)

Topic	State Rule
Cash exempted in bankruptcy	None. Under federal bankruptcy exemptions, $13,900 for one person, $27,800 for a married couple.
Notice to leave after house is sold	New owner may start court proceedings to evict the former owner after the redemption period expires, unless former owners unreasonably refuse to allow the new owner to inspect the home, cause damage, or damage is imminent during the redemption period. Then eviction proceedings can be started earlier.
Foreclosure statutes	Mich. Comp. Laws §§ 600.3101 to 600.3185, 600.3201 to 600.3285

Minnesota

Foreclosure laws change! Check for updates at www.nolo.com/legal-updates.

Topic	State Rule
Most common type of foreclosure process	Nonjudicial under power of sale in a mortgage
Notice of the foreclosure	In most cases, foreclosing party must mail the borrower a notice of default giving 30 days to cure before officially starting a foreclosure, along with a notice about foreclosure prevention counseling. Foreclosing party must serve notice of sale on the occupant of the home, along with a foreclosure advice notice, at least four weeks before the sale and must publish the notice six weeks before the sale.
Reinstatement of loan before sale	Available any time before the foreclosure sale
Redemption after sale	For most borrowers, available for six months after the sale. In some cases, redemption period is 12 months (for example, the amount due is less than two-thirds of the original principal amount of the loan) or five weeks (abandoned homes or if the borrower postpones the sale under Minn. Rev. Stat. § 580.07). Former owner may stay in the house during this period.
Special protections for foreclosures involving high-cost mortgages	None
Special state protections for service members	Protections under the federal Servicemembers Civil Relief Act extended to service members called to state active service. Minn. Stat. § 190.055
Deficiency judgments	Not allowed in nonjudicial foreclosure with six-month redemption period (most common type of foreclosure) or five-week redemption period (applicable to abandoned properties)
Cash exempted in bankruptcy	None. Under federal bankruptcy exemptions, $13,900 for one person, $27,800 for a married couple.
Notice to leave after house is sold	New owner may file an eviction lawsuit after the redemption period expires.
Foreclosure statutes	Minn. Stat. §§ 580.01 to 580.30 (nonjudicial foreclosures)

Mississippi

Foreclosure laws change! Check for updates at www.nolo.com/legal-updates.

Topic	State Rule
Most common type of foreclosure process	Nonjudicial under power of sale in deed of trust
Notice of the foreclosure	Foreclosing party must publish notice of sale three consecutive weeks before sale date and post notice on the courthouse door. No notice need be mailed to borrower under state law, though most deeds of trust require the foreclosing party to send a 30-day notice of default prior to acceleration.
Reinstatement of loan before sale	Available at any time before the sale
Redemption after sale	Not available
Special protections for foreclosures involving high-cost mortgages	None
Special state procedures for service members	None
Deficiency judgments	May be obtained if lawsuit filed within one year of the sale. To get a deficiency judgment, the winning bid at the foreclosure sale must be reasonable based on the fair market value of the property, particularly if the lender is the high bidder.
Cash exempted in bankruptcy	Using the wildcard exemption, $50,000 for one person aged 70 or older, $100,000 for a married couple aged 70 or older.
Notice to leave after house is sold	The new owner must go to court to get an eviction order, usually after making a demand for possession.
Foreclosure statutes	Miss. Code. Ann. §§ 89-1-55 to 89-1-59

Missouri

Foreclosure laws change! Check for updates at www.nolo.com/legal-updates.

Topic	State Rule
Most common type of foreclosure process	Nonjudicial under power of sale in deed of trust
Notice of the foreclosure	Foreclosing party must send a notice of sale by registered or certified mail to the borrower not less than 20 days before the sale and publish notice in a newspaper.
Reinstatement of loan before sale	Not available (except as permitted by the terms of the deed of trust)
Redemption after sale	Available for one year after sale if borrower gives a notice of intent to redeem at the sale or within ten days before sale, satisfies bond requirement, and the holder of the debt being foreclosed buys the property at foreclosure sale.
Special protections for foreclosures involving high-cost mortgages	None
Special state protections for service members	None
Deficiency judgments	May be obtained in a separate lawsuit
Cash exempted in bankruptcy	Using the wildcard exemption, $600 for one person, $1,200 for a married couple, additional $1,250 for head of family plus $350 per child.
Notice to leave after house is sold	New owner files an unlawful detainer (eviction) lawsuit against the foreclosed homeowner.
Foreclosure statutes	Mo. Rev. Stat. §§ 443.290 to 443.440

Montana

Foreclosure laws change! Check for updates at www.nolo.com/legal-updates.

Topic	State Rule
Most common type of foreclosure process	Nonjudicial under power of sale in deed of trust (a trust indenture under the Small Tract Financing Act of Montana)
Notice of the foreclosure	Under the Small Tract Financing Act, foreclosing party must mail a notice to the borrower at least 120 days before sale and publish in a newspaper prior to the sale.
Reinstatement of loan before sale	Any time prior to sale under the Small Tract Financing Act
Redemption after sale	No right of redemption after a nonjudicial foreclosure under the Small Tract Financing Act
Special protections for foreclosures involving high-cost mortgages	None
Special state protections for service members	Courts may stay civil proceedings related to a service member's nonpayment on a mortgage for their primary residence or adjust the payment due. Mont. Code Ann. § 10-1-903. Applicable to any member of the Montana army or air National Guard serving on active duty ordered by the governor or full-time National Guard duty. Mont. Code. Ann. § 10-1-902
Deficiency judgments	Not allowed under the Small Tract Financing Act
Cash exempted in bankruptcy	None
Notice to leave after house is sold	Under the Small Tract Financing Act, the purchaser at the trustee's sale is entitled to possession of the property on the 10th day following the sale. If the former owner does not leave, the purchaser may initiate a lawsuit to evict the former homeowner after giving notice to quit (leave).
Foreclosure statutes	Mont. Code Ann. §§ 71-1-221 to 71-1-235 and §§ 71-1-301 to 71-1-321

Nebraska

Foreclosure laws change! Check for updates at www.nolo.com/legal-updates.

Topic	State Rule
Most common type of foreclosure process	Nonjudicial under power of sale in deed of trust
Notice of the foreclosure	Foreclosing party must record a notice of default at least one month before giving notice of sale (two months if the property is agricultural) and, in most cases, mail a copy to the borrower within ten days after recordation, notice of sale is then published once a week for five consecutive weeks; the last publication must be made at least ten days but not more than 30 days prior to the sale. Notice of sale must also be sent to the borrower 20 days prior to sale (in most cases).
Reinstatement of loan before sale	Borrower may reinstate by paying amount due within one month after recordation of notice of default (two months if the property is agricultural).
Redemption after sale	Not available
Special protections for foreclosures involving high-cost mortgages	None
Special state protections for service members	None
Deficiency judgments	May be obtained by filing separate lawsuit within three months after foreclosure sale. Judgment cannot exceed the difference between the indebtedness and the property's fair market value or the difference between the indebtedness and the sale price, whichever is less.
Cash exempted in bankruptcy	Using the wildcard exemption, $5,000 for one person, $10,000 for a married couple.
Notice to leave after house is sold	New owner may begin an eviction action after the foreclosure sale.
Foreclosure statutes	Neb. Rev. Stat. §§ 76-1005 through 76-1018 (nonjudicial)

Nevada

Foreclosure laws change! Check for updates at www.nolo.com/legal-updates.

Topic	State Rule
Most common type of foreclosure process	Nonjudicial under power of sale in deed of trust
Notice of the foreclosure	Foreclosing party records a three-month notice of default and election to sell and mails a copy to the borrower. The notice of default must also be posted on the property. Foreclosing party must also serve a notice stating borrower is in danger of losing the home to foreclosure at least 60 days before sale, and mail a notice of sale at least 20 days before sale. Notice of sale must also be posted on the property, in several public places, and published.
Reinstatement of loan before sale	Borrower may reinstate up to five days prior to sale.
Redemption after sale	12 months for judicial foreclosure. Not available after nonjudicial foreclosure.
Special protections for foreclosures involving high-cost mortgages	For a mortgage loan on or after October 1, 2003, that is subject to the Home Ownership and Equity Protection Act of 1994 (HOEPA), Nevada law requires the lender to serve the borrower a notice at least 60 days prior to the foreclosure. Nev. Rev. Stat. § 107.85. Violations of high-cost home loan statutes support a defense to foreclosure. Nev. Rev. Stat. § 598D.110
Special state protections for service members	None
Deficiency judgments	Foreclosing party may obtain deficiency judgment by filing a separate lawsuit within six months of foreclosure sale, but not if: loan was made on or after October 1, 2009; lender is a financial institution; the property is a single-family home owned by the borrower at the time of sale; the borrower has continuously occupied the property as a principal residence since getting the loan; the borrower used the proceeds of the loan to purchase the property; and the borrower has not refinanced the loan. Amount of deficiency is limited to the lesser of the difference between the total debt and fair market value of the home, or the difference between the total debt and foreclosure sale price.

Nevada (continued)

Topic	State Rule
Cash exempted in bankruptcy	$10,000 for one person, $20,000 for a married couple.
Notice to leave after house is sold	New owner must give former owner a notice to quit (leave) before filing an eviction lawsuit.
Foreclosure statutes	Nev. Rev. Stat. §§ 107.0795 through 107.130; 40.451 through 40.463

New Hampshire

Foreclosure laws change! Check for updates at www.nolo.com/legal-updates.

Topic	State Rule
Most common type of foreclosure process	Nonjudicial under power of sale in a mortgage
Notice of the foreclosure	Foreclosing party must either personally serve borrower or mail notice 45 days (as of January 1, 2016) before the sale, and publish the notice once a week for three consecutive weeks, with the first publication at least 20 days before the sale.
Reinstatement of loan before sale	Not available (except as permitted by the terms of the mortgage contract)
Redemption after sale	Not available after a nonjudicial foreclosure
Special protections for foreclosures involving high-cost mortgages	None
Special state protections for service members	Federal Servicemembers Civil Relief Act protections extended to members of the state guard, or militia called to active duty by the governor for a period of 30 days or more. N.H. Rev. Stat. Ann. § 110-C:2
Deficiency judgments	May be obtained by filing separate lawsuit after the foreclosure sale, provided lender exerts every reasonable effort to obtain a fair and reasonable price at the sale.
Cash exempted in bankruptcy	Using the wildcard exemption, up to $8,000 for one person, $16,000 for a married couple. Under federal bankruptcy exemptions, $13,900 for one person, $27,800 for a married couple.
Notice to leave after house is sold	New owner must give former owner a 30-day notice to quit (leave) before bringing an eviction lawsuit.
Foreclosure statute	N.H. Rev. Stat. Ann. § 479:25

New Jersey

Foreclosure laws change! Check for updates at www.nolo.com/legal-updates.

Topic	State Rule
Most common type of foreclosure process	Judicial
Notice of the foreclosure	Foreclosing party must send notice of intention to foreclose, including notice of the right to cure, by registered or certified mail and with a copy to the Department of Community Affairs, to the borrower 30 days but not more than 180 days before starting a foreclosure action. Foreclosing party then serves borrower summons and complaint. The foreclosing party must mail the borrower a notice 14 calendar days before applying for final judgment giving one final chance to cure the default. If the borrower provides notice of the intention to cure within 10 days after receipt of the judgment notice, the foreclosing party must wait another 45 days (after the effective date of the judgment notice) before requesting a final judgment. Notice of sale must be mailed to homeowner (and all parties who appeared in the action) at least ten days before sale, as well as posted on the property and in the sheriff's office, and published in two newspapers for four weeks.
Reinstatement of loan before sale	Available up to date of final judgment of foreclosure. Judgment may be delayed for 45 days if borrower needs extra time to reinstate.
Redemption after sale	Within the ten-day period after the sale, and up until the court issues an order confirming the sale if objections to the sale are filed. Also, if mortgage holder obtains a deficiency judgment, borrower can bring action for redemption within six months after deficiency judgment is entered. However, if you file an answer to the deficiency judgment lawsuit to dispute the deficiency, you lose the right to redeem.
Special protections for foreclosures involving high-cost mortgages	Foreclosure must be filed in court. Home Ownership Security Act, N.J. Stat. Ann. § 46:10B-26(k)

New Jersey (continued)

Topic	State Rule
Special state protections for service members	New Jersey law provides protections similar to the federal Servicemembers Civil Relief Act. For example, a service member can potentially stay (postpone) court proceedings and the period of military service is not included in the redemption period. The law applies to service members on federal duty or in state military service pursuant to the governor's orders. N.J. Stat. Ann. §§ 38:23C-1 to 38:23C-26
Deficiency judgments	May be obtained by filing a separate lawsuit within three months of sale or, if confirmation of the sale is required, from the date of the confirmation of the sale; court can limit amount to difference between loan debt and fair market value.
Cash exempted in bankruptcy	$1,000 for one person, $2,000 for a married couple. Under federal bankruptcy exemptions, $13,900 for one person, $27,800 for a married couple.
Notice to leave after house is sold	If the foreclosed homeowners do not leave after the foreclosure, the new owner (usually the foreclosing party) applies for writ of possession from the court.
Foreclosure statutes	N.J. Stat. Ann. §§ 2A:50-1 to 2A:50-21, 2A:50-53 to 2A:50-63

New Mexico

Foreclosure laws change! Check for updates at www.nolo.com/legal-updates.

Topic	State Rule
Most common type of foreclosure process	Judicial, but nonjudicial foreclosures are also possible
Notice of the foreclosure	**Judicial:** Borrower has 30 days to respond after being served with summons and complaint. After the court issues a foreclosure judgment, sale may not occur for 30 days. Foreclosing party must publish notice of sale four consecutive weeks before sale in a newspaper and also post notices in six of the most public places in the county. **Nonjudicial:** Foreclosing party must record notice of sale at least 90 days before the sale date and mail a copy to the borrower within five days of recording. Foreclosing party must also publish notice in a newspaper.
Reinstatement of loan before sale	Borrower usually gets a 30-day opportunity to reinstate before the foreclosing party initiates foreclosure. Some borrowers may also reinstate at any time prior to the time title is transferred by means of foreclosure sale.
Redemption after sale	For both judicial and nonjudicial foreclosures, New Mexico law gives a borrower nine months to redeem the home after a foreclosure sale. However, the terms of the mortgage or deed of trust can reduce the redemption period to not less than one month. (Most mortgages and deeds of trust contain a provision stating that the redemption period will be one month.)
Special protections for foreclosures involving high-cost mortgages	Assignees of high-cost loans may be held responsible for acts of lenders and mortgage originators and violations may be used to defend against the foreclosure. Home Loan Protection Act, N.M. Stat. Ann. § 58-21A-1
Special state protections for service members	The rights, benefits, and protections of the federal Servicemembers Civil Relief Act extended to members of the National Guard ordered to state active duty for a period of 30 or more consecutive state duty days or to any federally funded duty performed in an operational role for homeland security. N.M. Stat. Ann. § 20-4-7.1
Deficiency judgments	**Judicial:** Allowed. **Nonjudicial:** May be obtained by filing a separate lawsuit within six years of foreclosure sale; may not be recovered against a low-income household.

New Mexico (continued)

Topic	State Rule
Cash exempted in bankruptcy	Using the wildcard exemption, $500 for one person, $1,000 for a married couple ($5,500 and $11,000 if homestead exemption isn't used).
Notice to leave after house is sold	New owner (usually the foreclosing party) can get a writ of assistance to evict the former owner as part of the foreclosure action (judicial foreclosures) or file a separate lawsuit (nonjudicial foreclosures).
Foreclosure statutes	N.M. Stat. Ann. §§ 48-7-1 to 48-7-24, 39-5-1 to 39-5-23 (judicial); 48-10-1 to 48-10-21 (nonjudicial)

New York

Foreclosure laws change! Check for updates at www.nolo.com/legal-updates.

Topic	State Rule
Most common type of foreclosure process	Judicial
Notice of the foreclosure	New York law requires a servicer to make reasonable and good-faith efforts to give borrowers information about appropriate loss mitigation options. Lender or servicer must provide notice to the borrower at least 90 days before filing a foreclosure complaint. The complaint must be accompanied by a notice with information about the foreclosure process and sources of information and assistance. Borrower has 20 or 30 days to respond to the complaint, depending on whether served personally or by another method. Notice of sale must be published in a newspaper and posted publicly, in some cases. Under New York law, a servicer is prohibited from engaging in unfair, deceptive, or abusive business practices or misrepresenting or omitting any material information in connection with the servicing of a mortgage loan.
Reinstatement of loan before sale	Available any time before final foreclosure judgment (foreclosure will be dismissed) and any time after judgment, but before sale (foreclosure will be stayed).
Redemption after sale	Not available
Special protections for foreclosures involving high-cost mortgages	If lender violated provisions that apply to high-cost loans, borrower may use this as a defense against foreclosure. N.Y. Banking Law § 6-l; N.Y. Real Prop. Acts. Law § 1302
Special state protections for service members	New York has a law that is similar to the federal Servicemembers Civil Relief Act that applies to those on federal active duty or state duty pursuant to an order of the governor. Among other things, it provides that a service member may apply to the court for a stay of proceedings (postponement) in a foreclosure action under certain circumstances. N.Y. Mil. Law §§ 301 through 328
Deficiency judgments	Allowed if borrower is personally served or appears in the lawsuit. The deficiency amount is the amount of the debt less the higher of the fair market value or the sales price.
Cash exempted in bankruptcy	$6,000 for one person, $12,000 for a married couple if not using homestead exemption (up to $11,975 and $23,950 depending on amount of other personal property exemptions used).

New York (continued)

Topic	State Rule
Notice to leave after house is sold	New owner can evict by summary proceeding after giving a ten-day notice to leave or by getting an order of possession from the court as part of the foreclosure action.
Foreclosure statutes	N.Y. Real Prop. Acts Law §§ 1301 to 1391

North Carolina

Foreclosure laws change! Check for updates at www.nolo.com/legal-updates.

Topic	State Rule
Most common type of foreclosure process	Nonjudicial under power of sale in deed of trust. Property cannot be sold until the court clerk holds a hearing, reviews foreclosing party's paperwork, and certifies sale.
Notice of the foreclosure	A notice of hearing must be filed with the court to initiate the foreclosure. Foreclosing party must send borrower a notice including amount needed to cure the default and resources that are available to avoid foreclosure at least 45 days before filing a notice of hearing, as well as a notice of default within 30 days before the date of the notice of hearing. After the notice of hearing is filed, it must be served to the borrower not less than ten days before the hearing (20 days if served by posting). The hearing may be continued (postponed) for up to 60 days if loss-mitigation efforts may help avoid foreclosure. If foreclosure approved at hearing, borrower must be mailed a notice of sale at least 20 days before the sale, which must also be published in a newspaper and posted publicly.
Reinstatement of loan before sale	Not available (except as permitted by the terms of the mortgage or deed of trust)
Redemption after sale	Yes, during the upset bid period (initial upset-bid period lasts for 10 days after the report of sale is filed)
Special protections for foreclosures involving high-cost mortgages	None
Special state protections for service members	Nonjudicial foreclosure prohibited during or within 90 days after a borrower's period of military service if the mortgage or deed of trust originated before the period of military service. N.C. Gen. Stat. §§ 45-21.12A, 45-21.16
Deficiency judgments	Deficiency judgments are generally allowed, but not in foreclosures of purchase money (seller financed) mortgages and deeds of trust. Lender might also be barred from seeking a deficiency judgment if the mortgage is nontraditional or is a rate spread home loan, and the mortgage secures borrower's principal residence.
Cash exempted in bankruptcy	Using the wildcard exemption, up to $5,500 for one person, $11,000 for a married couple.
Notice to leave after house is sold	New owner must give former owner a 10-day notice to quit (leave) before getting an order of possession from the court.
Foreclosure statutes	N.C. Gen. Stat. §§ 45-21.1 to 45-21.33, 45-100 to 47-107

North Dakota

Foreclosure laws change! Check for updates at www.nolo.com/legal-updates.

Topic	State Rule
Most common type of foreclosure process	Judicial
Notice of the foreclosure	Foreclosing party must serve (usually by mail) borrower with a notice at least 30 days and not more than 90 days before starting the foreclosure. Foreclosing party gives notice of the foreclosure lawsuit by serving the borrower with the complaint and summons. Borrower has 21 days to respond. Notice of sale must be published in a newspaper for three weeks, and, in some cases, mailed to interested parties.
Reinstatement of loan before sale	Available within 30 days after service of the notice before foreclosure
Redemption after sale	Available within 60 days after foreclosure sale except for abandoned property and agricultural land. Agricultural land may be redeemed within 365 days after the filing of the summons and complaint in the office of the clerk of district court or the time of the first publication of the notice by advertisement. The final date for redemption of agricultural land may not be earlier than 60 days after the sheriff's sale.
Special protections for foreclosures involving high-cost mortgages	None
Special state protections for service members	None
Deficiency judgments	Not allowed in foreclosures of residential property of four or fewer units, one of which is occupied by the owner as his or her primary residence, on up to 40 contiguous acres.
Cash exempted in bankruptcy	$3,750 for one person without dependents, $7,500 for the head of household, $10,000 for one person (cannot use the homestead exemption), $20,000 for a married couple (cannot use the homestead exemption).
Notice to leave after house is sold	Former owner can stay in the house until redemption period ends. In the foreclosure judgment, the court can order the homeowner to turn possession over to the purchaser once the redemption period expires.
Foreclosure statutes	N.D. Cent. Code §§ 32-19-01 to 32-19-41

Ohio

Foreclosure laws change! Check for updates at www.nolo.com/legal-updates.

Topic	State Rule
Most common type of foreclosure process	Judicial
Notice of the foreclosure	After foreclosing party files lawsuit, borrower has 28 days to respond. After the court issues a foreclosure judgment, foreclosing party files the notice of sale with the court at least seven days prior to the sale and sends a copy to the debtor and parties who appeared in the action. Foreclosing party must publish notice of sale in a newspaper for three weeks before sale date.
Reinstatement of loan before sale	Not available (except as permitted by the terms of the mortgage)
Redemption after sale	Available until the court confirms the sale
Special protections for foreclosures involving high-cost mortgages	None
Special state protections for service members	Protections under the federal Servicemembers Civil Relief Act extended to National Guard ordered by the governor into active duty or training. Ohio Rev. Code Ann. §§ 5919.29, 5923.12
Deficiency judgments	Allowed, but judgment is void two years after confirmation of the sale by the court. Property cannot be sold for less than 2/3 of appraised value at the foreclosure sale.
Cash exempted in bankruptcy	Using the wildcard exemption, up to $1,825 for one person, $3,650 for a married couple.
Notice to leave after house is sold	After the sale is confirmed, the new owner can ask the court for a writ of possession and have the sheriff remove the foreclosed homeowners from the home.
Foreclosure statutes	Ohio Rev. Code Ann. §§ 2323.07, 2329.26

Oklahoma

Foreclosure laws change! Check for updates at www.nolo.com/legal-updates.

Topic	State Rule
Most common type of foreclosure process	Judicial (the foreclosure can be nonjudicial if the mortgage contract includes a power of sale clause; however, the borrower can force the lender to foreclose judicially by taking certain steps)
Notice of the foreclosure	After foreclosing party files lawsuit, borrower usually has 20 days to respond. After the court issues a foreclosure judgment, foreclosing party must serve a notice of sale on borrower by mail and publish notice of sale in a newspaper at least 30 days before the sale.
Reinstatement of loan before sale	Not available (except as permitted by the terms of the mortgage)
Redemption after sale	Allowed until court confirms sale
Special protections for foreclosures involving high-cost mortgages	None
Special state protections for service members	Federal Servicemembers Civil Relief Act protections extended to members of the Oklahoma National Guard when ordered to state active duty or full-time National Guard duty. Okla. Stat. tit. 44, § 208.1
Deficiency judgments	Allowed, but limited to the difference between the total debt and the fair market value of the property, or the difference between the total debt and the foreclosure sale price, whichever is less. Lender must ask the court for deficiency judgment at the same time it makes a motion for an order confirming the foreclosure sale or within 90 days after sale.
Cash exempted in bankruptcy	None
Notice to leave after house is sold	If the foreclosed homeowners don't leave the home, the court may (in the order confirming the sale) order the clerk of the court to issue a writ of assistance to the sheriff to give the purchaser possession of the home.
Foreclosure statutes	Okla. Stat. tit. 12, §§ 686, 764 to 765, 773; Okla. Stat. tit. 46, §§ 41 to 49

Oregon

Foreclosure laws change! Check for updates at www.nolo.com/legal-updates.

Topic	State Rule
Most common type of foreclosure process	Probably nonjudicial. In 2012, lenders switched from using the nonjudicial process to judicial foreclosures for various reasons that are no longer applicable. Lenders now typically use the nonjudicial process.
Notice of the foreclosure	Before filing a notice of default, foreclosing party provides notice about a resolution conference (mediation) to the borrower. Foreclosing party must record a notice of default in the county records and serve a notice of sale on borrower 120 days before the sale, either by personal service or mail, along with a "danger" notice that warns of the impending foreclosure mailed on or before the date the notice of sale is served or mailed. Notice of sale must also be published in a newspaper for four weeks.
Reinstatement of loan before sale	Available up to five days before sale. The law limits the amount borrower can be charged in attorney or trustee fees.
Redemption after sale	Not available after a nonjudicial foreclosure
Special protections for foreclosures involving high-cost mortgages	None
Special state protections for service members	Violations of the Servicemembers Civil Relief Act are an unlawful practice under Oregon law. Or. Rev. Stat. §§ 646.605, 646.608(LLL). The lender can't initiate a suit to foreclose a mortgage if the land covered by the mortgage is owned by a service member called into active service during war. Or. Rev. Stat. § 408.440. The "danger" notice must include information on how veterans can obtain assistance. Or. Rev. Stat. §§ 86.756, 408.515.
Deficiency judgments	Not allowed after a nonjudicial foreclosure or a judicial foreclosure of a residential trust deed.
Cash exempted in bankruptcy	Using the wildcard exemption, $400 for one person, $800 for a married couple.
Notice to leave after house is sold	New owner entitled to possession ten days after the sale; after which the purchaser may start an eviction action to remove former owner from the home.
Foreclosure statutes	Or. Rev. Stat. §§ 86.726 to 86.815, 88.010 to 88.106

Pennsylvania

Foreclosure laws change! Check for updates at www.nolo.com/legal-updates.

Topic	State Rule
Most common type of foreclosure process	Judicial
Notice of the foreclosure	For most borrowers, at least 30 days before starting the foreclosure, foreclosing party must mail the borrower a notice of intention to foreclose and send a notice about financial assistance under the Homeowner's Emergency Mortgage Assistance Program. After foreclosing party files foreclosure lawsuit, homeowner borrower has up to 30 days to respond. A notice of sale must be posted on the property and served to the borrower at least 30 days before the sale, as well as published in a newspaper once a week for three weeks.
Reinstatement of loan before sale	Available until one hour before the bidding at the foreclosure sale, but a maximum of three times in a calendar year.
Redemption after sale	Not available
Special protections for foreclosures involving high-cost mortgages	None
Special state protections for service members	Pennsylvania National Guard members on active state service (and 30 days thereafter) are exempt from civil process. Pa. Cons. Stat. Ann. tit. 51, § 4105
Deficiency judgments	Allowed if foreclosing party files separate lawsuit within six months after sale. If the foreclosing party was the purchaser at the sale, the deficiency is limited by the fair market value of the property.
Cash exempted in bankruptcy	$300 for one person, $600 for a married couple. Under federal bankruptcy exemptions, $13,900 for one person, $27,800 for a married couple.
Notice to leave after house is sold	New owner may start a separate ejectment action after foreclosure to evict former owner from the premises.
Foreclosure statutes	Pa. Stat. Ann. tit. 35, §§ 1680.402c to 1680.409c; Pa. Stat. Ann. tit. 41, §§ 403 to 404; Pa. R. Civ. P. §§ 1141 to 1150

Rhode Island

Foreclosure laws change! Check for updates at www.nolo.com/legal-updates.

Topic	State Rule
Most common type of foreclosure process	Nonjudicial under power of sale in mortgage
Notice of the foreclosure	Foreclosing party must provide a mediation notice to borrower prior to initiating foreclosure. Notice of sale must be mailed by certified mail to borrower at least 30 days before first publication and published in a newspaper for three consecutive weeks before sale.
Reinstatement of loan before sale	Not available (except as permitted by the terms of the mortgage)
Redemption after sale	Not available after a nonjudicial foreclosure
Special protections for foreclosures involving high-cost mortgages	Borrower can ask court to stop (enjoin) the foreclosure if the lender violated the Rhode Island Home Loan Protection Act, which forbids certain activities (such as balloon payments and negative amortization) related to high-cost home loans. R.I. Gen. Laws §§ 35-25.2-1 to 35-25.2-11
Special state protections for service members	Protections under the federal Servicemembers Civil Relief Act extended to all National Guard members on state active duty for a continuous period over 90 days. R.I. Gen. Laws § 30-7-10
Deficiency judgments	Allowed if foreclosing party files separate lawsuit after sale.
Cash exempted in bankruptcy	Using the wildcard exemption, up to $6,500 for one person, $13,000 for a married couple. Under federal bankruptcy exemptions, $13,900 for one person, $27,800 for a married couple.
Notice to leave after house is sold	After foreclosure, the purchaser may send a notice to vacate (leave) and then file an eviction lawsuit.
Foreclosure statutes	R.I. Gen. Laws §§ 34-27-1 to 34-27-5; 34-25.2-1 to 34-25.2-15

South Carolina

Foreclosure laws change! Check for updates at www.nolo.com/legal-updates.

Topic	State Rule
Most common type of foreclosure process	Judicial
Notice of the foreclosure	After foreclosing party files lawsuit, borrower has 30 days to respond. After court issues a foreclosure judgment, foreclosing party must publish notice of sale in a newspaper and also post it in three public places three weeks before the sale.
Reinstatement of loan before sale	Not available (unless the mortgage terms allow reinstatement)
Redemption after sale	Not available (though borrower can make an upset bid during the 30-day period following sale, if lender demands a deficiency judgment)
Special protections for foreclosures involving high-cost mortgages	If the court finds a violation of the high-cost home loans statute, it may refuse to enforce the agreement, or the term or part that was unlawful, or it may rewrite the agreement to eliminate the unlawful part. In an action to collect a debt, a borrower may assert a violation of the statute as a matter of defense by recoupment or set-off in such action. S.C. Code Ann. § 37-23-50
Special state protections for service members	None
Deficiency judgments	Allowed as part of the foreclosure lawsuit
Cash exempted in bankruptcy	$6,325 for one person, $12,650 for a married couple if not using homestead exemption.
Notice to leave after house is sold	The foreclosing party (typically the purchaser at the sale) may include an eviction as part of the foreclosure action and get a writ of assistance from the court.
Foreclosure statutes	S.C. Code Ann. §§ 15-39-610, 29-3-630 to 29-3-790

South Dakota

Foreclosure laws change! Check for updates at www.nolo.com/legal-updates.

Topic	State Rule
Most common type of foreclosure process	Nonjudicial under power of sale in a mortgage (but homeowner borrower may choose judicial foreclosure)
Notice of the foreclosure	Foreclosing party must publish notice of sale in a newspaper once a week for four weeks (including a statement about the right to insist on judicial foreclosure) and must serve borrower with written copy of the notice of foreclosure sale at least 21 days before sale.
Reinstatement of loan before sale	Not available in a nonjudicial foreclosure (unless allowed by the mortgage contract)
Redemption after sale	Generally, foreclosed homeowners in South Dakota get one year to redeem the property after a foreclosure sale. But if the mortgage is a short-term redemption mortgage, there is a 180-day redemption period after the purchaser records a certificate of sale in the land records.
Special protections for foreclosures involving high-cost mortgages	None
Special state protections for service members	State law extends legal protections under the federal Servicemembers Civil Relief Act to members of the South Dakota National Guard ordered to active duty service by the Governor or the President of the United States. SDCL § 33A-2-9
Deficiency judgments	Allowed, but if mortgage holder buys property at foreclosure sale, amount of deficiency is limited to difference between house's actual market value at time of sale and amount still owing on mortgage.
Cash exempted in bankruptcy	$5,000 for one person (not head of family), $7,000 for head of family, $12,000 for married couple.
Notice to leave after house is sold	If the foreclosed homeowner doesn't leave the home after the redemption period, the purchaser must give a three-day notice to quit (leave) before initiating an eviction action.
Foreclosure statutes	S.D. Cod. Laws Ann. §§ 21-48-1 to 21-48-26, 21-47-1 to 21-47-25

Tennessee

Foreclosure laws change! Check for updates at www.nolo.com/legal-updates.

Topic	State Rule
Most common type of foreclosure process	Nonjudicial under power of sale in deed of trust
Notice of the foreclosure	Foreclosing party must publish notice of sale in a newspaper at least 20 days before sale or post notice in several public places 30 days before sale (if there is no newspaper in the county). Foreclosing party must mail the borrower a copy of the notice of sale on or before the first publication.
Reinstatement of loan before sale	Not available (except as permitted by the terms of the mortgage or deed of trust, or in the case of a high-cost home loan)
Redemption after sale	Available for up to two years after sale, unless redemption period is waived in mortgage or deed of trust
Special protections for foreclosures involving high-cost mortgages	In the case of a high-cost home loan, the lender must send a notice of right to cure to the borrower at least 30 days before publishing the notice of foreclosure. The borrower can reinstate prior to three business days before the sale by paying the amount due to the lender. This right to cure may be exercised only once in any 12-month period. Tenn. Code Ann. § 45-20-104
Special state protections for service members	If a member of a reserve or Tennessee National Guard unit entered into a mortgage or deed of trust to purchase a home, and is subsequently called into active military service outside the U.S. during hostilities, the lender cannot foreclose until 90 days after the service member returns to the state. Tenn. Code Ann. § 26-1-111
Deficiency judgments	Allowed, but if the borrower proves that the foreclosed property sold for an amount materially less than fair market value, the court will limit the deficiency judgment to the difference between the outstanding mortgage debt and the fair market value of the property.
Cash exempted in bankruptcy	$10,000 for one person, $20,000 for a married couple.
Notice to leave after house is sold	Former owner may be evicted through an ejectment procedure.
Foreclosure statutes	Tenn. Code Ann. §§ 35-5-101 to 35-5-118, 66-8-101 to 66-8-103

Texas

Foreclosure laws change! Check for updates at www.nolo.com/legal-updates.

Topic	State Rule
Most common type of foreclosure process	Nonjudicial under power of sale in deed of trust
Notice of the foreclosure	Foreclosing party must serve notice of default to borrower by certified mail 20 days before serving notice of sale. Notice of sale must be served (mailed) to borrower 21 days before sale. Foreclosing party must also post notice of sale on courthouse door and file it in the office of the county clerk.
Reinstatement of loan before sale	Available within 20 days after foreclosing party serves (mails) the notice of default
Redemption after sale	Not available
Special protections for foreclosures involving high-cost mortgages	None
Special state protections for service members	Statutes of limitations are tolled for those under a "legal disability" who are entitled to sue for the recovery of real property or entitled to make a defense based on the title to real property. (The definition of "legal disability" includes those serving in the United States Armed Forces during time of war.) Tex. Civ. Prac. & Rem. Code § 16.022
Deficiency judgments	Allowed after a nonjudicial foreclosure if foreclosing party brings separate lawsuit within two years of sale. Amount may be determined by fair market value of the property, if borrower requests it.
Cash exempted in bankruptcy	$50,000 for one person, $100,000 for a family. Under federal bankruptcy exemptions, $13,900 for one person, $27,800 for a married couple.
Notice to leave after house is sold	New owner must serve former owner with three-day notice to quit (leave) and then file eviction (forcible detainer) lawsuit.
Foreclosure statutes	Tex. Prop. Code Ann. §§ 51.002 to 51.003

Utah

Foreclosure laws change! Check for updates at www.nolo.com/legal-updates.

Topic	State Rule
Most common type of foreclosure process	Nonjudicial under power of sale in deed of trust
Notice of the foreclosure	Foreclosing party must mail a notice of intent to file a notice of default to the borrower giving 30 days to cure the default. Foreclosing party then records a notice of default at least three months before giving notice of sale and mails a copy to the borrower within ten days of recording. At least three months after the notice of default is recorded, the foreclosing party publishes a notice of sale in a newspaper for three weeks; the last date of publication must be at least ten days but not more than 30 days before the sale. The notice of sale must also be posted on the property and mailed to the borrower at least 20 days before the sale.
Reinstatement of loan before sale	Available for three months after notice of default is recorded
Redemption after sale	Not available after a nonjudicial foreclosure
Special protections for foreclosures involving high-cost mortgages	None
Special state protections for service members	Utah law extends protections similar to the federal Servicemembers Civil Relief Act to National Guard members serving full-time with a recognized military unit called into service by the governor for at least 30 days. Utah Code Ann. §§ 39-7-102, 39-7-115
Deficiency judgments	May be obtained in a separate lawsuit within three months after the sale. The amount is limited by the property's fair market value.
Cash exempted in bankruptcy	None
Notice to leave after house is sold	If the homeowner doesn't vacate the home after the sale, the purchaser must give the foreclosed homeowner a notice to quit (leave) before initiating an eviction action.
Foreclosure statutes	Utah Code Ann. §§ 57-1-19 through 57-1-34; 78B-6-901 through 78B-6-906

Vermont

Foreclosure laws change! Check for updates at www.nolo.com/legal-updates.

Topic	State Rule
Most common type of foreclosure process	Judicial (strict foreclosure or by judicial sale)
Notice of the foreclosure	After foreclosing party files lawsuit, borrower generally has 21 days to respond. In a foreclosure by judicial sale, the lender must mail a notice of sale to the borrower no fewer than 30 days before the sale date and publish the notice in a newspaper no fewer than 21 days before the sale. When the court issues a foreclosure judgment in a strict foreclosure, it may also transfer ownership to foreclosing party without a sale so long as there isn't significant equity in the house.
Reinstatement of loan before sale	Available upon agreement before sale
Redemption after sale	In a strict foreclosure, available six months from date of foreclosure decree unless the judge orders, or the borrower and lender agree to, a shorter period. In a foreclosure by judicial sale, the redemption period is six months from the date of the foreclosure decree, unless the court orders a shorter time. Redemption is also available before the sale takes place, even if the initial redemption period expired.
Special protections for foreclosures involving high-cost mortgages	None
Special state protections for service members	Statute of limitations tolled for those who are in military or naval service of the United States or a member of the Vermont National Guard and ordered to state active duty, and at the time of entering such service or duty, had a cause of action against another person, or another person had a cause of action against him or her. Vt. Stat. Ann. tit. 12, § 553
Deficiency judgments	May be requested in the foreclosure complaint and is waived if not requested prior to the confirmation order (foreclosure by judicial sale), or in a separate lawsuit (strict foreclosure). If the mortgage holder buys the property, the amount of the deficiency is limited by the property's fair market value.
Cash exempted in bankruptcy	Using the wildcard exemption, $1,100 for one person, $2,200 for a married couple (up to $8,100 and $16,200 depending on amount of other exemptions used).

Vermont (continued)

Topic	State Rule
Notice to leave after house is sold	In a strict foreclosure, after the judgment is issued and the redemption period has ended, the court will issue a writ of possession. The writ of possession has the same force and effect and is executed in the same manner as a similar writ issued after an ejectment (eviction) proceeding.
Foreclosure statutes	Vt. Stat. Ann. tit. 12, ch. 172, §§ 4931 to 4954

Virginia

Foreclosure laws change! Check for updates at www.nolo.com/legal-updates.

Topic	State Rule
Most common type of foreclosure process	Nonjudicial under power of sale in deed of trust
Notice of the foreclosure	Foreclosing party must serve or mail a notice of sale to homeowner no less than 60 days prior to the sale in the case of a deed of trust on owner-occupied residential real estate. Notice must be published in a local newspaper of general circulation once a week for four consecutive weeks or five days, unless deed of trust provides for a different interval (but not less than once a week for two weeks or once a day for three days). Sale can be held eight days after the first publication, and no more than 30 days after last publication.
Reinstatement of loan before sale	Not available (unless permitted by the loan documents)
Redemption after sale	Not available
Special protections for foreclosures involving high-cost mortgages	None
Special state protections for service members	Servicemembers Civil Relief Act protections extended to National Guard members called to state active duty by the governor for 30 or more consecutive days. Va. Code Ann. § 44-102.1
Deficiency judgments	May be obtained in a separate lawsuit after the sale.
Cash exempted in bankruptcy	$5,000 for one person, $10,000 for a married couple (and $500 per dependent). $10,000 for one person 65 years of age or older, $20,000 for married couple 65 years of age or older. Additional $10,000 available for a disabled veteran.
Notice to leave after house is sold	New owner does not have to give former owner notice before filing eviction lawsuit, though foreclosed owner may receive a five-day notice to vacate.
Foreclosure statutes	Va. Code Ann. §§ 55.1-320 to 55.1-345

Washington

Foreclosure laws change! Check for updates at www.nolo.com/legal-updates.

Topic	State Rule
Most common type of foreclosure process	Nonjudicial under power of sale in deed of trust
Notice of the foreclosure	Foreclosing party must contact (or meet the requirements for attempting to contact) borrower at least 30 days before issuing notice of default to inform him or her about the opportunity to meet with the lender to try to work out an alternative to the foreclosure. A notice of default must be served on borrower 30 days before notice of sale is recorded or served. The notice of default must be served by both first-class mail and by registered or certified mail, return receipt requested, and by either posting the notice on the premises in a prominent place or by personal service on borrower. Foreclosing party must mail a copy of the notice of sale to the borrower and post on the property (or serve the occupant a copy) at least 120 days (or 90 days in some cases) before sale date. The notice of sale must also be published in a newspaper. No sale may occur within 190 days after the date of default.
Reinstatement of loan before sale	Available up to 11 days before sale
Redemption after sale	Not available after a nonjudicial foreclosure
Special protections for foreclosures involving high-cost mortgages	None
Special state protections for service members	Similar to federal Servicemembers Civil Relief Act. Applies to any resident of Washington state who is a member of the National Guard or member of a military reserve component. Wash. Rev. Code §§ 38.42.010 to 38.42.904
Deficiency judgments	Not allowed after a nonjudicial foreclosure
Cash exempted in bankruptcy	$2,000 (no doubling for a married couple). Under federal bankruptcy exemptions, $13,900 for one person, $27,800 for a married couple.
Notice to leave after house is sold	New owner entitled to possession on 20th day after purchase of the foreclosure sale and may then file eviction (unlawful detainer) lawsuit. The purchaser has a right to summary proceedings to obtain possession.
Foreclosure statutes	Wash. Rev. Code §§ 61.24.020 to 61.24.140

West Virginia

Foreclosure laws change! Check for updates at www.nolo.com/legal-updates.

Topic	State Rule
Most common type of foreclosure process	Nonjudicial under power of sale in deed of trust
Notice of the foreclosure	Notice of default must be given to the borrower, giving ten days to cure. Notice of sale must be sent to the borrower by certified mail, return receipt requested, a reasonable amount of time before the sale takes place and published in a newspaper, generally once a week for two weeks.
Reinstatement of loan before sale	Notice of default must give the borrower ten days to cure the default and reinstate the loan. The borrower loses the right to reinstate after three defaults.
Redemption after sale	Not available
Special protections for foreclosures involving high-cost mortgages	None
Special state protections for service members	None
Deficiency judgments	Allowed
Cash exempted in bankruptcy	Using the wildcard exemption, $800 for one person, $1,600 for a married couple (up to $25,800 and $51,600 depending on amount of homestead exemption used).
Notice to leave after house is sold	After sending a notice to vacate, purchaser may initiate an unlawful detainer (eviction) lawsuit against the foreclosed homeowners to evict them from the property.
Foreclosure statutes	W.Va. Code §§ 38-1-3 to 38-1-15

Wisconsin

Foreclosure laws change! Check for updates at www.nolo.com/legal-updates.

Topic	State Rule
Most common type of foreclosure process	Judicial
Notice of the foreclosure	After foreclosing party files lawsuit, borrower has 20 days to respond. If foreclosure is granted, court issues judgment and order of sale. Sale can't be held until after the redemption period (see below). A notice of sale must be published in a newspaper (and online sometimes) and posted publicly for three weeks prior to sale.
Reinstatement of loan before sale	Available any time before judgment. Borrowers may reinstate after judgment, but if they subsequently default, the foreclosure will continue.
Redemption after sale	Not available after sale. In Wisconsin, the redemption period ranges from five weeks to 12 months depending on the circumstances and occurs prior to the sale. The property can be redeemed at any time during this period.
Special protections for foreclosures involving high-cost mortgages	Prohibition on certain things (such as interest rate increases after a default) for high-cost home loans. Wis. Stat. §§ 428.202 to 428.211
Special state protections for service members	Protections against foreclosure for members of the National Guard or state defense force who are ordered into state active duty for 30 days or more. Lender cannot foreclose during or within 90 days after the service member's period of state active duty unless a court approves it before active duty and after the foreclosure. Applies to mortgages taken out prior to active duty. Wis. Stat. § 321.62
Deficiency judgments	Must be requested in the foreclosure complaint. The foreclosing lender will often waive the deficiency in order to shorten the redemption period.
Cash exempted in bankruptcy	$5,000 for one person, $10,000 for a married couple. Under federal bankruptcy exemptions, $13,900 for one person, $27,800 for a married couple.
Notice to leave after house is sold	Foreclosed homeowner may remain in possession through the redemption period up until the confirmation of the sale. The order confirming the sale may also include a writ of assistance, which is an order from the court directing the sheriff to remove the foreclosed homeowner from the home.
Foreclosure statutes	Wis. Stat. §§ 846.01 to 846.25

Wyoming

Foreclosure laws change! Check for updates at www.nolo.com/legal-updates.

Topic	State Rule
Most common type of foreclosure process	Nonjudicial under power of sale in a mortgage
Notice of the foreclosure	Foreclosing party must send a notice of intent to foreclose to homeowner by certified mail with return receipt at least ten days before first publication of the notice of sale. Notice of sale must be published in a newspaper once a week for four weeks. Also, prior to the first date of publication, a notice of sale must be sent to the homeowner by certified mail.
Reinstatement of loan before sale	Not available (except as permitted by the terms of the mortgage)
Redemption after sale	Available for three months after sale (12 months after sale if the property is agricultural)
Special protections for foreclosures involving high-cost mortgages	None
Special state protections for service members	Legal protections under the federal Servicemembers Civil Relief Act are extended to members of the Wyoming National Guard ordered to active state service by the state or federal government for a period of more than 30 consecutive days. Wyo. Stat. Ann. § 19-11-122
Deficiency judgments	Allowed
Cash exempted in bankruptcy	None
Notice to leave after house is sold	New owner must provide a notice to quit (leave) before filing an eviction lawsuit.
Foreclosure statutes	Wyo. Stat. Ann. §§ 34-4-101 to 34-4-113; 1-18-101 to 1-18-115

Index

A

Abandoned homes. *See* Unoccupied homes; Walking away
Acceleration, 34, 39, 174, 227
Active military. *See* Servicemembers
Actual income and expenses test (Chapter 7 bankruptcy), 142
Adjustable-rate mortgages (ARMs), 88, 227, 239
Administrative expenses (Chapter 13 bankruptcy), 227, 242
Alabama law and programs, 98, 132, 249–250
Alaska law, 38, 251
Alimony. *See* Family support debts
American Rescue Plan Act Homeowner Assistance Fund, 100
Amortization, 227, 235
  negative amortization, 239
  reamortization, 89, 94, 229, 242–243
Amount financed, 227
Annual percentage rate (APR), 227
  APR test for high-cost mortgages, 169
  See also Interest rates
Answer (judicial foreclosures), 40, 148, 149–151
Appraisal fees, 160, 161
Appraisals, 42, 228
APR. *See* Annual percentage rate
Arizona law and programs, 98, 252
Arkansas law, 253
ARMs (adjustable-rate mortgages), 88, 227, 239
Arrears, 228
  capitalization of, 89, 90, 94, 229

in Chapter 13 bankruptcy, 111, 112–113
  See also Loss mitigation options; Missed payments; *specific mitigation options*
Assignee liability, for fair lending violations, 170, 228
Assignments, of mortgages/deeds of trust, 32, 157
Assumptions (VA loans), 96
Attorney fees, 124, 217–219
  charged by lenders/servicers, 161–162
Auctions. *See* Foreclosure sale
Automatic stay, 228
  Chapter 7 bankruptcy, 127, 128, 134
  Chapter 13 bankruptcy, 110
  motions to lift, 128, 135, 237, 239

B

Balloon payments, 88–89, 155, 170, 228
Bank accounts
  protecting savings in bankruptcy, 136–138
  state laws on cash exemptions, 249–308
Bankruptcy, 109–143, 178, 221
  automatic stay basics, 110, 127, 128, 228
  bad-faith filings, 116, 134, 234
  deficiencies and, 17, 30, 126, 178, 181, 187, 195, 197–198
  as delaying tactic, 12, 13, 66, 81, 181, 201, 208
  filing date and debt dischargeability, 233
  filing to stop a foreclosure sale, 74, 127, 134, 135
  hiring a lawyer, 12, 13, 214, 215, 217–218
  housing counselors and, 80, 81
  lenders'/servicers' legal duties to filers, 74
  postpetition counseling requirement, 241
  prepetition counseling requirement, 242

serial filings, 244
when to consider, 68, 81
your credit and, 19, 127, 185
See also Chapter 7 bankruptcy;
  Chapter 13 bankruptcy
Bankruptcy code, 228
Bankruptcy exemptions, 128, 132–133,
  136–137, 233
  state laws on exempting cash, 249–308
Bankruptcy petition preparers (BPPs), 228
Bankruptcy trustee, 245
  Chapter 7 cases, 128, 129, 131, 139, 141,
  143
  Chapter 13 cases, 113, 119, 120
Bond posting requirements (court
  challenges), 152
BPPs (bankruptcy petition preparers), 228
Breach letters. *See* Notice of default
Budgeting and budget counseling, 60–61,
  76, 118, 139, 140, 230, 241
Buying back your home
  after the foreclosure sale, 83, 206, 243
  lease and buy-back arrangements, 21–22,
  236
  See also Redemption

C

California law and programs, 254–255
  attorney payment, 213
  bankruptcy exemptions, 132, 137–138,
  255
  deficiency judgments, 186, 255
  dual tracking protections, 74, 188
  Hardest Hit Fund program, 98
  high-cost mortgage protections, 254
  notice requirements, 36, 254, 255
  reinstatement and redemption rights, 9,
  254
  servicemembers protections, 255

short sales, 186, 188
  typical foreclosure scenario, 44–46
Cancellation (rescission) rights, 167–171,
  243
Capital gains tax, 50
Capitalization, of arrears, 89, 90, 94, 229
CARES Act, 84–85. *See also* COVID-19
  pandemic
Car loan cramdowns (Chapter 13
  bankruptcy), 115
Cash, as exempt property (bankruptcy),
  137–138
  state laws, 249–308
CFPB (Consumer Financial Protection
  Bureau)
  help for disputing errors or requesting
  mortgage information, 166
  HOEPA rules, 168
  MARS (mortgage assistance relief
  services) rules, 26
  mortgage servicing rules, 70–74
  online research resources, 226
  submitting a complaint to, 26
Chapter 7 bankruptcy, 125–143, 221
  appropriate situations for, 81
  the automatic stay, 127, 128, 134
  basics and overview, 12, 13, 126–129,
  138–140, 229
  Chapter 13 filings after, 122
  conversions from Chapter 13, 121
  deficiency judgments and, 126, 187
  as delaying tactic, 13, 66, 81, 126, 127,
  134–138, 201, 208
  dischargeable/nonpriority debts, 13, 126,
  129, 130
  exempt property, 128–129, 131, 132–133,
  136–138, 232
  to help you keep your house, 12, 61, 68,
  69, 126, 130–134

lawyers and, 12, 13, 128, 142, 143, 213, 218

nondischargeable/priority debts, 13, 126, 129, 242

nonexempt property, 129, 131, 135, 240

second and third mortgages and, 122, 126, 133–134

time required for, 12, 13, 128, 135–136

timing your filing, 136

what happens to your property and debts, 13, 128–129, 139

who is eligible, 140–142

on your credit report, 19, 127

Chapter 12 bankruptcy, 229

Chapter 13 bankruptcy, 8, 109–124, 221

administrative expenses, 227, 242

after Chapter 7 bankruptcy, 122

the automatic stay, 110

bad-faith filings, 116, 234

basics and overview, 12, 13, 110–112, 118–122, 229

case dismissals, 116, 120, 121, 123

conversions to Chapter 7, 121

debts you can reduce or eliminate, 110, 111–112, 113–115, 116–117

deficiency judgments and, 187

as delaying tactic, 13, 66, 110, 201, 208

estimating your plan payment total, 114

to help you keep your house, 12, 61, 68, 69, 110, 111–112

if you are ineligible for Chapter 7, 142

lawyers for, 13, 119, 123–124, 217

nondischargeable and priority debts, 110, 113, 119, 121–122, 242

repaying your mortgage arrears, 111, 112–113, 118

repayment plan approval and completion, 110, 119, 120–121

repayment plan requirements, 110, 113, 114, 118–119

second and third mortgages and, 12, 13, 111, 116–117, 122, 133, 134

time required for, 13, 110, 113, 114, 118

what happens to your debts, 13, 110, 111–115, 121–122

when payments must begin, 120

on your credit report, 19

Child support debts, 113, 119, 121, 122, 129, 242

Closed-end loans, 229

Collateral, 229, 244

cramdowns, 111, 114–115, 230, 245

See also Secured debts; Security interests

Colorado law, 74, 256–257

Complaint (judicial foreclosures). See Summons and complaint

Compromise sales (VA loans), 96. See also Short sales

Conciliation conferences. See Mediation programs

Confirmation hearing (Chapter 13 bankruptcy), 120, 123, 229

Conforming loans, 230

Connecticut law and programs, 40, 97, 203, 258

Consumer Financial Protection Bureau. See CFPB

Contesting foreclosure in court, 8, 68, 145–176

appropriate situations for, 146, 154–171

basics, 15, 40, 146–147

bond posting requirements, 152

in Chapter 13 bankruptcy, 115

as delaying tactic, 15, 41, 204, 205

hiring a lawyer, 147, 151, 154, 160, 171, 205, 219

if you win your case, 40, 149

in judicial foreclosure states, 40, 41, 42, 146, 147–151, 173, 204, 205

lis pendens filings, 153

MERS foreclosures, 158–159

in nonjudicial foreclosure states, 146, 152–154, 173, 204

representing yourself, 147, 150–151, 160

servicemembers, 15, 155

suing for money, 174–176

time required for, 149, 154

See also Foreclosure defenses

Continuity of contact rule, 71

Conventional loans, 230

Coronavirus Aid, Relief, and Economic Security (CARES) Act, 84–85. *See also* COVID-19 pandemic

Court challenges. *See* Contesting foreclosure; Foreclosure defenses

Court foreclosures. *See* Judicial foreclosures

COVID-19 (coronavirus) pandemic, 2

American Rescue Plan Act Homeowner Assistance Fund, 100

communicating with your lawyer and, 216

COVID-19 National Emergency Standalone Partial Claims, 95

FHA loss mitigation options, 84–85, 95

forbearance programs, 11, 72, 84–85

foreclosure moratoriums, 9, 58, 76, 180

Cramdowns, 111, 114–115, 230, 245

Credit bids (foreclosure sales), 42, 46

Credit bureaus, 230

Credit card debt, 110, 113–114, 126, 130, 241. *See also* Unsecured debts

Credit/debt counseling, 60–61, 65, 118, 139, 140, 230, 242. *See also* Housing counselors

Creditors, 230

Chapter 7 bankruptcy and, 127, 128, 131, 132–133, 139

Chapter 13 bankruptcy and, 110, 123, 129

motions to lift automatic stay by, 128, 135, 237, 239

See also Lenders and servicers

Creditors' meeting (bankruptcy), 119, 139, 140, 231

Credit report and credit scores, 19, 230

bankruptcy and, 19, 127, 185

credit repair, 222

delinquency reporting suspensions for disaster victims, 107

evictions and, 46, 208

impact of foreclosure, 19, 20–21, 185

modifications and, 89

obtaining a new mortgage after foreclosure, 20–21

requests for information to servicers and, 166

SCRA benefits and, 105

short sales and, 19, 185

Criminal fines and penalties. *See* Fines and penalties

Curing default. *See* Reinstatement

Current monthly income, under bankruptcy law, 231

D

Damages. *See* Money judgments

Debt consolidation, 231

Debt/credit counseling, 60–61, 65, 118, 139, 140, 230, 242. *See also* Housing counselors

Debtor, defined, 231

Deceleration, 173–174

Deeds in lieu of foreclosure, 2, 8, 66, 80
  basics, 18, 178, 193–194, 231
  deficiencies and, 18, 96, 193–194, 195, 232
  government loans and, 16, 96, 194
  your credit and, 19
Deeds of trust
  basics, 31, 43, 231
  determining whether you have one, 38
  judicial vs. nonjudicial foreclosures and, 37, 38
  as security instruments, 157, 172
  transfers of, and legal authority to foreclose, 157–160
  See also Nonjudicial foreclosures
Default
  defined, 231
  See also Missed payments; Notice of default
Default interest rate, 232
Default judgments, 40, 42, 103–104, 148–149
Deficiencies and deficiency judgments, 1, 194–198
  bankruptcy and, 17, 30, 126, 178, 181, 187, 195, 197–198
  basics, 30, 49–50, 194–195, 232
  deeds in lieu of foreclosure and, 18, 96, 193–194, 195, 232
  if you walk away from your house, 17, 65
  judicial vs. nonjudicial foreclosures and, 38, 49
  market value and, 50, 237
  potential tax liability for deficiency write-offs, 17, 18, 50, 65, 81, 181, 186–187, 195–198
  reverse mortgages and, 64
  short sales and, 18, 81, 185, 186–187, 190, 191, 195

state laws, 49–50, 186, 194–195, 249–308
vehicle repossessions, 130
your credit and, 19
Delaware law, 259
Delaying foreclosure
  by applying for a modification, 89, 180, 202–203
  by challenging the foreclosure in court, 15, 41, 204, 205
  by filing for bankruptcy, 12, 13, 66, 81, 181, 201, 208
  by participating in mediation program, 97, 154
  RESPA information requests and, 166
  servicemembers, 15
  See also Bankruptcy; Contesting foreclosure; Staying in your house payment-free during foreclosure
Delinquent payments. See Arrears; Default; Missed payments
Department of Housing and Urban Development. See HUD
Disaster-related mortgage relief, 3, 105–107
Discharge, 232. See also Chapter 7 bankruptcy; Chapter 13 bankruptcy
Dischargeable debts, 232. See also Chapter 7 bankruptcy; Chapter 13 bankruptcy
Discovery, 150, 155
Disposable income (Chapter 13 bankruptcy), 114, 117, 118, 119, 232, 242
District of Columbia law, 260
Dodd-Frank Wall Street Reform and Consumer Protection Act, 70, 168
Drunk driving debts, 129
Dual tracking and dual tracking protections, 69–71, 74, 80, 165, 188
Due-on-sale clause violations, 33, 71

E

Emotional issues, 4, 20, 52–56, 181

Endorsements (promissory notes), 32, 157, 159

Enhanced Relief Refinance program, (Freddie Mac loans), 11, 68, 92

Equity stripping, 232

Evictions, 42, 46, 53, 206–208, 241
  evictions moratoriums, 180

Exempt property, exemption rules (Chapter 7 bankruptcy), 128–129, 131–133, 135, 136–138, 232–233, 245
  nonbankruptcy exemptions, 240
  state laws on exempt cash, 249–308

Extended rescission rights, 167–171, 243

F

Fair Debt Collection Practices Act (FDCPA), 35, 71

Fair lending laws and violations. *See* Federal law; State law; Unfair lending practices

Fair market value. *See* Market value

Family support debts, 113, 119, 121, 122, 129, 242

Fannie Mae and Fannie Mae loans, 233, 244
  basic assistance options, 90, 92–93
  COVID-19 foreclosure moratorium, 9, 76, 180
  deed in lieu programs, 16, 194
  determining who owns your loan, 91, 92
  disaster-related mortgage relief, 105, 106–107
  Flex Modification program, 1, 61, 90, 92–93
  High Loan-to-Value Refinance Option, 11, 68, 92

limits on attorney fees charged by lenders/servicers, 161–162
loan eligibility after foreclosure, 20–21
pandemic-related forbearance option, 84–85

FDCPA (Fair Debt Collection Practices Act), 35, 71

Federal bankruptcy exemptions, 132, 136–137, 233

Federal Emergency Management Agency (FEMA), 105, 107

Federal Home Loan Mortgage Corporation. *See* Freddie Mac

Federal Housing Administration. *See* FHA

Federal Housing Finance Agency. *See* FHFA

Federal law
  American Rescue Plan Act, 100
  bankruptcy code, 228
  CARES Act, 84–85
  Dodd-Frank Wall Street Reform and Consumer Protection Act, 70, 168
  dual tracking protections, 69–71, 80
  Fair Debt Collection Practices Act (FDCPA), 35, 71
  Home Ownership and Equity Protection Act (HOEPA), 167–171, 232, 235
  Mortgage Forgiveness Debt Relief Act, 186, 196
  mortgage servicing rules and requirements, 33–35, 70–74, 75, 163–166, 188, 226
  Real Estate Settlement Procedures Act (RESPA), 70, 163–166, 226, 242
  regulating foreclosure consultants, 26
  researching online, 74, 226
  Servicemembers Civil Relief Act (SCRA), 101–105, 155
  Truth in Lending Act (TILA), 70, 167–171, 246

Federally-backed mortgages. *See* Government-backed mortgages; *specific agencies and loan programs*

Federal National Mortgage Association. *See* Fannie Mae

Federal nonbankruptcy exemptions, 240

Federal Reserve Foreclosure Resource Centers, 220

Federal Trade Commission. *See* FTC

Fees
excessive or inaccurate fees as foreclosure defense, 160–166
fee-based foreclosure assistance, 26, 48, 87, 211
for force-placed insurance, 162
HOA fees, 100, 129, 183, 184
late fees, 11, 85, 163, 170
points and fees test for high-cost mortgages under HOEPA, 169
points (loan origination fees), 236, 241
for property inspections, 160–161, 242

FEMA (Federal Emergency Management Agency), 105, 107

FHA and FHA loans, 233, 234
assistance resources, 221, 222
determining whether your loan is FHA-guaranteed, 91
disaster-related mortgage relief, 105, 106
FHA-HAMP, 94, 95
HECM reverse mortgage program, 14, 63–65
limits on attorney fees charged by lenders/servicers, 161–162
loss mitigation options, 61, 84–85, 93–96

FHFA (Federal Housing Finance Agency), pandemic-related relief, 9, 76, 84–85, 180

FICO scores, 89, 230. *See also* Credit and credit scores

Field service companies. *See* Property preservation companies

Finances
evaluating your situation, 56–61
See also Bankruptcy; Budgeting; Credit/ debt counseling; Home equity

Fines and penalties owed, 122, 129, 163

Fines and penalties recoverable from lenders, 235, 241

First mortgages, 31. *See also* Mortgage *entries*

Flex Modification program (Fannie Mae/ Freddie Mac), 1, 61, 90, 92–93

Florida law and programs, 98, 174, 261

Forbearances, 10, 68, 78
basics, 10, 82–85, 233
for disaster victims, 106, 107
FHA loans, 93, 94, 106
pandemic-related forbearance programs, 11, 72, 84–85
payment deferral programs after, 72, 83, 84–85
VA loans, 96, 106

Force-placed insurance, 162–163

Foreclosure alternatives. *See* Deeds in lieu of foreclosure; Keeping your house; Loss mitigation options; Short sales

Foreclosure basics, 5–28, 233
avoiding scams, 21–26, 47, 48, 101, 192
current filing statistics, 58
emotional issues, 4, 20, 52–56, 181
ensuring your home is not treated as vacant, 26–28
getting help, 7, 76–81, 210–219
impact on your credit, 19, 20–21, 185
recent legal changes, 2
tax issues, 17, 18, 50, 186–187, 195–198

terminology, 31–32, Glossary
what to expect, 7–8
your options summarized, 8–18
See also Foreclosure process
Foreclosure by possession, 37
Foreclosure defenses, 15, 146, 154–176, 222
active-duty servicemembers, 101, 104, 155
basics, 146
expired statute of limitations, 172–174
foreclosure based on false information, 115, 146, 151
improper notarization, 146
inaccurate/excessive lender fees, 160–166
no legal authority to foreclose, 135, 146, 151, 157–160
procedural defects, 88, 135, 146, 150–151, 154, 156–157, 165, 205
promissory estoppel claims, 175–176
robosigning, 146, 151
uncommon defenses, 155
unfair lending practices, 15, 146, 154, 167–171, 174–175
See also Contesting foreclosure
Foreclosure moratoriums, 9, 58, 75, 76, 105, 106, 180
Foreclosure notices. *See* Notice of default/notice of foreclosure; Notice of foreclosure sale
Foreclosure process, 29–48
basics, 6, 7–8
completion of, 182–184
concurrent loss mitigation applications (dual tracking), 69–71, 74, 80, 156, 165, 188
dos and don'ts during, 46–48
foreclosure by possession, 37
how much time and notice you'll have before a sale, 30, 33–36, 52–53, 180–181, 202–205

judicial foreclosure basics, 30, 37, 39–41, 236
nonjudicial foreclosure basics, 30, 37, 43–46, 240
procedural defects by lender/servicer, 88, 135, 146, 150–151, 154, 156–157, 165, 205
stopping mortgage payments during, 1, 6, 16, 19–20, 46, 136, 179–180
typical scenarios, 41–42, 44–46, 179–180
when lenders/servicers may begin, 33–35, 39, 41, 70–71, 188, 202
See also Foreclosure basics; Judicial foreclosures; Nonjudicial foreclosures; Staying in your house
Foreclosure relief
foreclosure avoidance mediation programs, 47, 97–98, 154, 213
Hardest Hit Fund programs, 2, 47, 98–101
hiring a lawyer, 212–213
for natural disaster victims, 3, 105–107
pandemic-related assistance programs, 2, 11, 72, 84–85, 95, 100
paying private companies for assistance, 26, 48, 87, 211
working with a housing counselor, 7, 47, 68, 76–81
See also Foreclosure moratoriums; Foreclosure rescue scams; Government assistance programs; Loss mitigation options
Foreclosure rescue scams, 7, 36, 220, 236
basics, 21–26, 234
legal protections, 26, 48
types of, 21–25, 192, 236, 237
what to watch out for, 25, 47, 48, 101

Foreclosure sale
  bankruptcy filing and, 74, 127, 134, 135
  court confirmation and title transfer, 41, 42
  how soon it may be held, 30, 33–36, 70–71
  if the lender never holds the sale, 182–184
  if you have submitted a loss mitigation application, 73
  lenders as bidders/purchasers, 42, 43, 49, 207
  lis pendens filings and, 153
  notice of sale, 9, 35–36, 42, 43, 45, 203
  the redemption period, 11, 206
  redemption rights after, 83, 206, 243
  staying in your house after, 20, 179, 181, 206–208, 241
  stopping an imminent sale, 74
  typical scenarios, 42, 45–46
  See also Foreclosure moratoriums
Foreclosure strategies, 3, 51–66, 67–107
  basics, 1–2, 8–18
  basing your decision on economics, 52, 53
  emotional issues and, 4, 20, 52–56, 181
  evaluating your financial situation, 56–61
  if you decide to give up your house, 1–2, 66
  if you decide to keep your house, 1, 7, 68
  stopping your mortgage payments, 1, 6, 16, 19–20, 46, 136, 179–180
  time constraints and, 30, 34, 69–70, 74
  See also Bankruptcy; Contesting foreclosure; Delaying foreclosure; Giving up your house; Keeping your house; Loss mitigation options
Forensic loan audit scams, 24–25

Forgiven debt, 234
  Hardest Hit Fund loan forgiveness, 99
  as taxable income, 17, 18, 50, 65, 81, 186–187, 195–198, 234
Form 1099, for forgiven debt, 195, 196, 198, 234
Formal forbearances (FHA loans), 93, 94
Fraud, 25, 122, 129, 146
Freddie Mac and Freddie Mac loans, 234, 244
  basic assistance options, 90, 92–93
  coronavirus-related forbearance option, 84–85
  deed in lieu programs, 16, 194
  determining who owns your loan, 91, 92
  disaster-related mortgage relief, 105, 106–107
  Enhanced Relief Refinance program, 11, 68, 92
  Flex Modification program, 1, 61, 90, 92–93
  limits on attorney fees charged by lenders/servicers, 161–162
  loan eligibility after foreclosure, 20–21
  pandemic-related foreclosure moratorium, 9, 76, 180
FTC (Federal Trade Commission)
  foreclosure fact sheets, 220
  mortgage assistance relief services (MARS) rules, 26

G

Georgia law and programs, 98, 262
Ginnie Mae, 234
Giving up your house, 177–196
  advantages of staying until the sale, 6, 20, 179–180, 185, 200, 202
  basics, 1–2, 15–18, 65–66
  Chapter 7 bankruptcy and, 12, 81

Chapter 13 bankruptcy and, 66, 110
the deed in lieu of foreclosure option,
    178, 193–194
emotional issues, 4, 20, 52–56, 181
how long you may be able to stay, 30,
    33–36, 52–53, 180–181, 200–205
moving out too early, 48, 182
the short sale option, 178, 184–192
stopping your mortgage payments, 1, 6,
    16, 19–20, 46, 136, 179–180
walking away (strategic default), 8,
    16–17, 178, 181
your credit and, 19
your options summarized, 8, 66, 178
See also Bankruptcy; Deeds in lieu of
    foreclosure; Deficiencies; Delaying
    foreclosure; Short sales; Staying in your
    house payment-free
Good-faith bankruptcy filings, 134, 234
Government assistance programs, 61, 221,
    222
    disaster-related mortgage relief, 105–107
    foreclosure avoidance mediation
        programs, 47, 97–98, 154, 213
    Hardest Hit Fund programs, 2, 47,
        98–101
    overview, 90–97
    pandemic-related foreclosure
        moratoriums, 9, 58, 76, 180
    pandemic-related programs, 2, 11, 72,
        84–85, 95, 100
    See also Government-backed mortgages;
        Housing counselors; *specific agencies
        and loan programs*
Government-backed mortgages
    disaster-related mortgage relief,
        105–107
    HECM reverse mortgages, 14, 63–65

identifying your loan's owner/guarantor,
    91
loss mitigation options overview, 90–97
pandemic-related foreclosure
    moratoriums, 9, 58, 76, 180
pandemic-related loss mitigation options,
    2, 11, 72, 84–85, 95, 100
refinance programs, 11, 68, 92
See also specific agencies and loan programs
Government mortgage guarantors, 234.
    See also Government-backed mortgages
Government National Mortgage
    Corporation (Ginnie Mae), 234

H

HAMP (Home Affordable Modification
    Program), 94, 95
Hardest Hit Fund programs, 2, 47, 98–101
Hardship discharges (Chapter 13
    bankruptcy), 121
Hawaii foreclosure timelines, 205
Hawaii law, 263
Hazard insurance. *See* Insurance
HECM program (reverse mortgages), 14,
    63–65
HELOCs. *See* Home equity lines of credit;
    Second and third mortgages
High-cost mortgages
    HOEPA protections, 167–171, 232, 235
    state protections, 171, 249–308
High Loan-to-Value Refinance Option
    (Fannie Mae loans), 11, 68, 92
HOA fees, 100, 129, 183, 184
HOEPA (Home Ownership and Equity
    Protection Act), 167–171, 232, 235
Holiday evictions moratoriums, 180
Home Affordable Modification Program
    (HAMP), 94, 95

Home equity, 232
bankruptcy and, 12, 116, 128, 130, 131–133, 135, 137, 138
estimating, 56–57
foreclosure strategies and, 17, 53, 56, 62–65
reverse mortgages, 8, 14, 62–65, 244
scams that target, 21–23
See also Negative equity
Home equity conversion mortgage (HECM) program, 14, 63–65
Home equity lines of credit, 31, 168, 191. *See also* Home equity loans; Second and third mortgages
Home equity loans, 235, 240
rescission rights under TILA, 168
short sales and, 191–192
See also Junior liens and mortgages; Second and third mortgages
Home mortgages. *See* Mortgage *entries*
Homeowner Assistance Fund (American Rescue Plan Act), 100
Homeowner assistance programs. *See* Foreclosure relief; Government assistance programs; Loss mitigation options
Homeowners' association fees, 100, 129, 183, 184
Home ownership
emotional issues, 4, 20, 52–56, 181
See also Title transfers
Home Ownership and Equity Protection Act (HOEPA), 167–171, 232, 235
Homeownership Preservation Foundation, 211, 220
Homestead declarations, 235
Homestead exemptions, 128, 132–133, 137, 138, 235

Homestead laws, 30
Home values, 57, 58. *See also* Market value
Housing counselors, 8, 47, 68
bankruptcy filings and, 80, 81, 127
basics, 7, 76–81
for budgeting help, 61, 76
finding a counselor, 7, 77, 210–211, 220
for Hardest Hit Fund information, 101
help for servicemembers, 102
for help with deeds in lieu of foreclosure, 193
for help with short sales, 189
for loss mitigation options and applications, 7, 10, 68, 76–81, 127, 202–203
NFCC counseling, 211, 221
HUD (Department of Housing and Urban Development)
HECM reverse mortgage program, 14, 63–65
pandemic-related foreclosure moratoriums, 9, 76, 180
website resources, 221
See also Fannie Mae; FHA; Freddie Mac; Housing counselors

I

Idaho law, 264
Illegal lending practices, 166, 213
procedural defects, 88, 135, 146, 150–151, 154, 156–157, 165, 205
robosigning, 75, 146, 151
TILA and HOEPA violations, 170, 232, 235
See also Foreclosure defenses; Mortgage servicing rules; Unfair lending practices
Illinois law and programs, 98, 265

Impound accounts, servicer failures to make payments from, 163, 164

Income
Chapter 7 bankruptcy eligibility and, 140–142
Chapter 13 bankruptcy and, 118–119, 121

Income taxes. *See* Tax *entries*

Indiana law and programs, 98, 266

Informal forbearances (FHA loans), 93, 94

Inheritors, federal rules protecting, 73

Injunctions, 235
in nonjudicial foreclosure challenges, 152–153, 161, 204
See also Automatic stay

Insolvency, 181, 187, 197, 234, 236

Inspection fees, 160–161, 242

Insurance
failure to pay premiums from impound accounts, 164
force-placed by lender, 162–163
Homeowner Assistance Fund for insurance expenses, 100
mortgage insurance, 91
reverse mortgages and, 14, 63, 64

Interest, 235
on missed payments, 8, 9, 41, 45, 83, 228
See also Amortization

Interest-free loans, 99
partial claims (FHA loans), 93, 95, 96

Interest-only loans, 235–236

Interest rates
adjustable-rate mortgages (ARMs), 88, 227, 239
default rate, 232
high-cost mortgages, 169
jumbo loans, 236
loan term and, 237
rate reductions, 10, 88, 89, 100, 104–105

required disclosures, 170
subprime loans, 245

Investment properties
bankruptcy and, 12, 13
foreclosure strategies and, 17, 53
tax liability for deficiency write-offs, 197
See also Rental properties

Investors (mortgage owners), 32. *See also* Lenders and servicers

Iowa law, 267

IRS. *See* Tax *entries*

J

Joint debtors, 236

Judgment liens. *See* Judicial (judgment) liens

Judgment proof status, 236

Judgments. *See* Default judgments; Deficiencies and deficiency judgments; Money judgments; Summary judgments

Judicial foreclosures, 31, 39–42
for active-duty servicemembers, 36, 101–104, 155
basics, 30, 37, 39–41, 236
contesting, 40, 41, 42, 146, 147–151, 173, 204, 205
default judgments, 40, 42, 103–104, 148–149
deficiency judgments and, 38, 49
evictions and, 206–207
excessive lender fees and, 161
if you don't respond, 40
in nonjudicial foreclosure states, 43
notice requirements, 35, 39, 41, 70, 203
states with, 40
strict foreclosure, 40, 41, 203, 236, 245
summary judgments, 40, 149, 150
time required for, 35, 37, 41, 42, 204–205

time to respond to the lender's
complaint, 35, 147, 204
typical scenario, 41–42
when lenders/servicers may begin the
process, 33–35, 41, 70–71, 188, 202
zombie foreclosures in judicial
foreclosure states, 182
See also Contesting foreclosure;
Foreclosure defenses
Judicial (judgment) liens, 236
bankruptcy and, 112, 121, 126, 130
Jumbo loans, 236
Junior liens and mortgages
COVID-19 National Emergency
Standalone Partial Claims, 95
foreclosure actions by subordinate
lienholders, 34, 71
negative equity and, 111, 116–117, 126,
133–134, 240
short sales and, 191–192
See also Second and third mortgages

K

Kansas law, 268
Keeping your house, 67–107
appropriate situations for, 56, 62–65
bankruptcy and, 12, 61, 68, 69, 110,
111–112, 126, 130–134
evaluating your financial situation, 56–61
mortgage relief for natural disaster
victims, 3, 105–107
protections for active-duty
servicemembers, 101–105
your options summarized, 8, 68
See also Bankruptcy; Contesting
foreclosure; Housing counselors; Loss
mitigation options; *specific options*
Kentucky foreclosure timelines, 205
Kentucky law and programs, 98, 269

L

Late fees, 11, 85, 163, 170
Late payments
impact on your credit, 19
See also Missed payments
Lawsuits
mass joinder lawsuit scams, 24
to recover deficiencies, 49, 195
suing lenders or servicers, 25, 102, 166,
174–176
See also Contesting foreclosure;
Evictions; Judicial foreclosures; Money
judgments; Settlements
Lawyers, 212–219
attorney fees charged to you by lenders/
servicers, 161–162
for Chapter 7 bankruptcy filings, 12, 13,
128, 142, 143, 213, 218
for Chapter 13 bankruptcy filings, 13,
119, 123–124, 217
fees, 124, 217–219
to fight foreclosure in court, 147, 151,
154, 160, 171, 205, 219
finding the right lawyer, 75, 197, 214–217
how they can help, 87–88, 212–213
if sale is imminent, 74
remote communications with, 216
to represent servicemembers, 103
for tax advice, 196, 197
when you may need, 212, 213
Lease and buy-back arrangements, 21–22,
236
Leaving your house. *See* Giving up your
house
Legal aid services, 151, 154, 214
Legal challenges. *See* Contesting
foreclosure; Foreclosure defenses
Legal citations, 224–225, 226

Legal research and resources, 33, 47, 220, 221–226. *See also* State laws

Legal updates, 2, 4, 7, 10, 58, 83, 100

Lenders and servicers
  authority to foreclose, 135, 146, 151, 157–160
  basics, 32, 238
  contacting to identify your loan's owner/ guarantor, 91
  correspondence from, 47, 48, 88
  deed in lieu of foreclosure agreements, 193–194
  excessive/inaccurate fees charged by, 160–166
  failure to complete foreclosure process, 182–184
  federal mortgage servicing rules, 33–35, 70–74, 75, 163–166, 188, 226
  foreclosure delays by, 75
  as foreclosure sale bidders/purchasers, 42, 43, 49, 207
  ignoring notices from, 48, 54
  keeping records of communications, 47, 88
  legal duties to borrowers, 35, 45, 70–74, 88, 167–171
  loss mitigation applications and processing, 70–73, 74, 79–80
  mortgage relief for disaster victims, 105
  negotiating a short sale, 189, 190, 191–192, 211
  notifying lender of rescission, 171
  notifying that you still occupy the home, 28
  reinstatement option and, 10
  requesting information about improper fees or misapplication of payments, 163–166
  right to secure your vacant home, 26–27
  servicers' authority to approve loss mitigation, 78, 82
  third-party offers to negotiate with, 23–24
  third-party offers to review legal compliance, 24–25
  when to contact, 47
  See also Creditors; Foreclosure defenses; Loss mitigation options; Mortgage *entries*

Lenders and services, in-house (proprietary) modifications, 1, 61, 86

Library of Congress legal research site, 226

Lien avoidance/reductions (lien stripping), 237, 245
  Chapter 7 bankruptcy and, 122, 133–134
  in Chapter 13 bankruptcy, 111, 112, 114–115, 116–117, 122, 134, 240
  cramdowns, 111, 114–115, 230, 245

Liens, 236
  types of, 236, 237, 245
  See also Junior liens; Second and third mortgages

Lis pendens filings, 153

Loan modifications. *See* Loss mitigation options; Modifications

Loan term, 237
  extensions of, 88, 90, 94

Loss mitigation applications, 70–73, 79–80
  acceleration and, 174
  applying for a modification, 86–88
  as delaying tactic, 89, 180, 202–203
  if you are giving up your house, 178

Loss mitigation guidelines, 80

Loss mitigation options, 81–97, 222
  bankruptcy filings and, 74
  basics, 8, 10, 81–89
  Chapter 13 bankruptcy and, 110, 112

deed in lieu of foreclosure basics, 18,
178, 193–194, 231
failure to grant promised modifications,
162, 175–176
forbearance basics, 10, 82–85, 233
for government-backed mortgages,
90–97
lawyers for help with, 87–88, 212–213
modification basics, 10, 61, 68, 85–89,
238
refinancing basics, 68, 92, 212
reinstatement or redemption basics, 8,
9–10, 83
repayment plan basics, 10, 68, 78, 82,
243
servicemembers' rights and options,
101–105, 155
servicers' authority to approve, 78, 82
short sale basics, 18, 178, 184–185, 190,
244
third-party offers to negotiate, 23–24
time constraints, 69–74
working with a housing counselor, 7, 47,
68, 76–81
your rights under federal rules, 35, 45,
70–74, 88
See also Government assistance
programs; Government-backed
mortgages; *specific mitigation options*
Louisiana law, 270

M

Maine law, 158, 271
Making Home Affordable website, 77, 220
Malicious acts, debts arising from, 121, 129
Market value, fair market value, 231, 237
appraisals, 42, 228
deficiencies and, 50, 237
estimating your equity, 57

MARS (mortgage assistance relief services)
rules, 26
Maryland law, 272
Massachusetts foreclosure timelines, 205
Massachusetts law, 37, 132, 138, 273
Mass joinder lawsuit scams, 24
Materialmen's liens, 237
Means test (Chapter 7 bankruptcy),
140–142, 238
Mechanic's liens, 237, 245
Median family income, bankruptcy and,
118, 140, 141, 142, 238
Mediation programs, 47, 97–98, 154, 213
Medical debts, 126, 130
MERS (Mortgage Electronic Registration
Systems), 91, 158–159, 238
Michigan law and programs, 98, 274–275
Military personnel. *See* Servicemembers
Minnesota law, 74, 132, 158, 276
MIP (FHA mortgage insurance), 91
Misapplied mortgage payments, 115, 162,
163, 164
Missed payments, 228
Chapter 7 bankruptcy and, 13, 130, 136
how lenders/servicers may deal with, 27
if you've missed just a few, 6
interest on, 8, 9, 41, 45, 83, 228
lenders'/servicers' duty to discuss loss
mitigation, 35, 45
negotiating a repayment plan, 10, 68, 78
notifying lender/servicer that you still
occupy the property, 28
reamortization, 89, 94, 229, 242–243
when lenders/servicers may begin
foreclosure, 33–35, 39, 41, 70–71, 188,
202
See also Arrears; Loss mitigation options;
specific options
Mississippi law and programs, 36, 98, 277

Missouri law, 278

Modifications, 1, 85–89
  after forbearance, 85
  appeal rights if a modification is denied, 73
  to avoid strategic default label, 178
  bankruptcy filings and, 112, 127, 130
  basics, 10, 61, 68, 85–89, 238
  concurrent foreclosure process (dual tracking), 69–71, 74, 80, 156, 165, 188
  for disaster victims, 106, 107
  Fannie Mae/Freddie Mac Flex Modification program, 1, 61, 90, 92–93
  FHA loans, 93, 94, 95, 96, 106
  Hardest Hit Fund programs, 98–101
  how to apply, 86–88
  in-house (proprietary), 1, 61, 86
  lawyers for help with, 213
  promised, failure to grant, 162, 175–176
  stopping payments during eligibility assessment, 19–20
  third-party offers to negotiate, 23–24
  trial periods, 86, 93, 175
  VA loans, 96, 106
  working with a counselor, 7, 47, 68, 76–81
  See also Government assistance programs; Loss mitigation options

Money judgments
  bankruptcy and judgment debts, 112, 121, 126, 130
  judgment proof status, 236
  suing lenders/servicers for money, 174–176
  See also Deficiencies and deficiency judgments

Montana law, 279

Mortgage arrears. *See* Arrears; Missed payments

Mortgage assistance relief services (MARS) rules, 26

Mortgage assumptions (VA loans), 96

Mortgage-backed securities, 239

Mortgage brokers, 212, 238

Mortgagee, 239

Mortgage Electronic Registration Systems (MERS), 91, 158–159, 238

Mortgage Forgiveness Debt Relief Act, 186, 196

Mortgage holder, 32, 238. *See also* Lenders and servicers

Mortgage lenders. *See* Lenders and servicers

Mortgage modifications. *See* Modifications

Mortgage payments. *See* Arrears; Missed payments; Payments

Mortgage refinancing. *See* Refinancing

Mortgage reinstatement. *See* Reinstatement

Mortgage releases. *See* Deeds in lieu of foreclosure

Mortgages
  acceleration by lender, 34, 39, 174, 227
  bankruptcy and, 110, 111–114, 126, 130–134
  defined, 238
  determining whether you have one, 38
  obtaining a new mortgage after foreclosure, 20–21
  as security instruments, 157, 172
  terminology, 31–32, Glossary
  vs. deeds of trust, 31, 37, 38
  your rescission rights, 167–171, 243
  See also Lenders and servicers; Second and third mortgages

Mortgage servicers, 32, 238
  authority to approve loss mitigation, 78, 82
  See also Lenders and servicers

Mortgage servicing rules, 33–35, 70–74, 75, 163–166, 188, 226

Mortgage transfers, 32
  legal authority to foreclose and, 32, 157–160
  unfair lending practices liability and, 170

Mortgagor, 239

Motions to lift automatic stay, 128, 135, 237, 239

Moving out
  moving too soon, 48, 182
  offers to pay you to move, 207
  zombie foreclosures, 48, 178, 182–184
  See also Giving up your house; Staying in your house

N

National Consumer Law Center, 220, 222

National Foundation for Credit Counseling, 211, 221

Natural disaster victims, 3, 105–107

Nebraska law, 280

Negative amortization, 239

Negative equity, 239–240
  foreclosure strategies and, 17, 53, 65
  junior mortgages and, 111, 116–117, 126, 133–134, 240
  refinancing programs for, 68, 92
  See also Short sales

Negotiating with lenders/servicers, 80
  short sale negotiations, 189, 190, 191–192, 211
  See also Loss mitigation options

Nevada law and programs, 74, 98, 132, 281–282

New Hampshire law, 37, 283

New Jersey law and programs, 98, 284–285

New Mexico law, 286–287

Newspaper publication, notice by, 36, 42, 43, 203

New York foreclosure timelines, 205

New York law, 174, 225, 288–289

NFCC (National Foundation for Credit Counseling), 211, 221

Nonbankruptcy federal exemptions, 240

Nondischargeable debts, 240
  Chapter 7 bankruptcy, 126, 129
  Chapter 13 bankruptcy, 110, 113, 119, 121–122

Nonexempt property (bankruptcy), 113, 121, 129, 131, 135, 240. *See also* Unsecured debts

Nonjudicial foreclosures, 31, 37
  basics, 30, 37, 43–46, 240
  challenging in court, 146, 152–154, 173, 204
  deficiency judgments and, 38, 49
  excessive lender fees and, 161
  judicial foreclosures in nonjudicial foreclosure states, 36, 38, 43
  lis pendens filings, 153
  mortgage assignments and, 159
  notices and notice requirements, 36, 43, 45, 70, 203, 204
  states with, 44
  staying after you receive notice of, 203, 204
  time required for, 36, 204
  typical scenario, 44–46
  when lenders/servicers may begin the process, 33–35, 70–71
  See also Foreclosure defenses

Nonpriority debts, 240

Non–purchase-money security interests, 240

Non-recourse loans, 49

North Carolina law and programs, 98, 290

North Dakota law, 291

Notarization, improper, 146

Notice of deemed vacancy, 28

Notice of default/notice of foreclosure, 8, 203

  basics, 33–36

  how long you may be able to stay in your home after, 53, 203–205

  how much time you have to respond, 30, 35–36, 40

  ignoring notices, 48, 54

  inaccurate/excessive fee statements in, 160–166

  judicial foreclosures, 35, 39, 41, 70, 147, 203

  nonjudicial foreclosures, 36, 43, 45, 70, 203, 204

  procedural errors by lenders, 156–157

  reinstatement rights and, 9, 43

  state laws, 35, 36, 179, 249–308

Notice of error, sending to servicers, 163–166

Notice of force-placed insurance, 162

Notice of foreclosure sale, 9, 35–36, 42, 43, 45, 203

Notice of motion to lift automatic stay (bankruptcy), 135

Notice of rescission, to lenders, 171

Notice to quit (after foreclosure), 207, 241

  state laws, 249–308

  staying after you receive, 20, 208

O

Ohio law and programs, 98, 225, 292

  typical foreclosure scenario, 41–42

Oklahoma, 293

Online resources

  bankruptcy exemptions, 128, 133

  budgeting, 60

  Chapter 7 bankruptcy, 139, 141, 143

  complaints about foreclosure consultants, 26

  disaster-related assistance, 107

  federal mortgage servicing rules, 74, 226

  foreclosure and debt counseling, 7, 60, 210–211, 220, 221

  foreclosure mediation programs, 98

  foreclosure rescue scams, 220

  general foreclosure information, 220–221

  Hardest Hit Fund programs, 101

  home values, 57

  identifying your loan's owner/guarantor, 91

  lawyer referrals, 75, 197, 215

  legal aid programs, 151, 154

  legal research and resources, 220, 222, 223–226

  legal updates, 2, 4, 7, 10, 58, 83, 100

  letters for disputing errors or requesting mortgage information, 166

  Making Home Affordable website, 77, 220

  median income by state, 141

  mortgage affordability calculators, 59

  pandemic-related foreclosure moratoriums, 9, 76, 180

  pandemic-related legal information, 2, 84

  reverse mortgages, 14

  Rural Housing Service loans, 97

  tax liability for canceled debt, 196

  VA loans, 97

Open-ended loans, 241

Oregon law and programs, 97, 98, 294

Origination fees (points), 236, 241

Originator, 241

P

Pandemic-related assistance. *See* COVID-19 (coronavirus) pandemic

Partial claims (FHA loans), 93, 95, 96

Partially secured debts, 241. *See also* Cramdowns; Undersecured debts

Payment-Option ARMs, 239

Payments
  evaluating affordability of, 58–61
  late payments and your credit, 19
  misapplied or uncredited, 115, 162, 163, 164
  potential to reduce, 88–89
  reamortization and, 89, 229, 242–243
  waivers for disaster victims, 107
  See also Arrears; Forbearances; Missed payments; Modifications; Refinancing; Staying in your house payment-free

Payoff statements, inaccurate, 163, 165

Peaceful entry (foreclosure by possession), 37

Penalties. *See* Fines and penalties

Pennsylvania foreclosure timelines, 205

Pennsylvania law, 295

Permanent injunctions (nonjudicial foreclosures), 152

Personal financial management counseling (bankruptcy), 118, 139, 140, 241. *See also* Budgeting and budget counseling

Personal injury debts, 121, 129

Personal property
  defined, 241
  See also Bankruptcy exemptions; *specific types of property*

Points, 236, 241

Points and fees test (high-cost mortgages), 169

Possession, foreclosure by, 37

Posted notice of foreclosure, 36, 39, 43, 203

Postpetition counseling (bankruptcy), 118, 139, 140, 241

Power of sale foreclosures. *See* Nonjudicial foreclosures

Predatory lending, 241. *See also* Illegal lending practices; Unfair lending practices

Preforeclosure sales (FHA loans), 93, 96. *See also* Short sales

Preliminary injunctions (to stop nonjudicial foreclosures), 152–153, 161, 204

Prepayment penalties, 169

Prepetition counseling (bankruptcy), 118, 138, 140, 230, 242

Principal balance
  capitalization of missed payments, 89, 90, 94, 229
  reductions of, 99, 100

Priority debts (bankruptcy), 13, 110, 119, 121, 129, 242

Projected disposable income (bankruptcy), 114, 117, 118, 119, 232, 242

Promissory estoppel, 175–176

Promissory notes, 31, 172
  endorsements of, 32, 157, 159
  loan transfers and authority to foreclose, 157–160

Proof of service, 242

Property damage, as breach of agreement, 34

Property inspection fees, 160–161, 242

Property insurance. *See* Insurance

Property preservation companies, 26–28

Property taxes
    failure to pay, as breach of agreement,
        34, 64
    reverse mortgages and, 14, 63, 64
    servicers' failure to pay, 163
    zombie foreclosures and, 183, 184
Proprietary modifications, 1, 61, 86
Public notice of foreclosure, 36, 42, 43

Q

Qualified Principal Residence
    Indebtedness exclusion (tax-free debt
    forgiveness), 196, 234

R

Real estate professionals, 189, 190, 211
Real Estate Settlement Procedures Act
    (RESPA), 70, 163–166, 226, 242
Real property, defined, 242
Reamortization, 89, 94, 229, 242–243
Recording
    checking your mortgage/deed of trust,
        38
    confirming completion of foreclosure
        process, 184
    of homestead declarations, 235
    of lis pendens notices, 153
    of money judgments, 236
    of mortgage assignments, 32, 157, 158,
        159
    of mortgages/deeds of trust, 31
    of notice of default/foreclosure, 9, 33,
        36, 70, 156
Recoupment, 167
Redemption, 8, 11, 83, 206, 243
    state laws, 249–308
Redemption period, 11, 206

staying in your house during, 52–53,
    206
Refinancing, 68, 92, 212, 243
    debt consolidation, 231
    Fannie Mae and Freddie Mac programs,
        11, 68, 92
    refinance loan rescission rights, 168
Refunding (VA loans), 96
Regulation X, 70, 163, 226
Regulation Z, 70
Reinstatement, 8, 9–10, 43, 83, 100, 243
    inaccurate/excessive reinstatement fee
        quotes, 160–166
    state laws, 249–308
Relocation assistance, 194
Rental properties
    Chapter 13 bankruptcy and, 12, 13, 115
    See also Investment properties
Renters and renting, 55–56, 248
Repayment period extensions, 88
Repayment plans (missed mortgage
    payments), 10, 68, 78, 82, 243
    FHA loans, 93, 94
    VA loans, 96
    See also Chapter 13 bankruptcy
Rescission rights, 167–171, 243
RESPA (Real Estate Settlement
    Procedures Act), 70, 163–166, 226,
    242
Reverse mortgages, 8, 14, 62–65, 244
Rhode Island law and programs, 37, 98,
    296
RHS (Rural Housing Service) loans, 91,
    97, 222. *See also* USDA loans
Robosigning, 75, 146, 151
Rural Housing Service (RHS) loans, 91,
    97, 222. *See also* USDA loans

S

Savings
  as advantage of staying in your home
    during foreclosure, 6, 20, 179–180,
    185, 200, 202
  protecting in bankruptcy, 136–138
SBA (Small Business Administration)
  loans, 107
Scams. *See* Foreclosure rescue scams
SCRA (Servicemembers Civil Relief Act),
  101–105, 155
Second and third mortgages, 31, 244
  Chapter 7 bankruptcy and, 122, 126,
    133–134
  Chapter 13 bankruptcy and, 12, 13, 111,
    116–117, 122, 133, 134, 240
  deeds in lieu of foreclosure and, 18
  elimination under Hardest Hit Fund
    programs, 99
  equity stripping, 232
  potential tax liability for writeoffs, 187,
    195–196
  rescission rights and, 168, 169
  short sales and, 18, 191–192
  See also Home equity loans; Junior liens
    and mortgages
Secondary loan market, 244
Second homes, Chapter 13 bankruptcy
  and, 12, 13, 115
Secured creditors, 244
Secured debts, 244
  in Chapter 7 bankruptcy, 128, 129
  in Chapter 13 bankruptcy, 111,
    114–115
  partially secured/undersecured debts,
    240, 241, 246
  See also specific loan types

Secured property. *See* Collateral; Secured
  debts
Securitization, 244
Security interests (secured interests), 244
  non–purchase-money security interests,
    240
  See also Collateral; Liens; Secured debts
Selling your house. *See* Short sales
Serial bankruptcy filings, 244
Servicemembers
  federal protections for, 15, 36, 101–105,
    155
  state protections for, 36, 105, 249–308
Servicers. *See* Lenders and servicers;
  Mortgage servicers
Set-asides, for property taxes and
  insurance (reverse mortgages), 14, 63
Short sales, 2, 8, 66, 80, 184–192
  appropriate situations for, 190
  avoiding scams, 192
  bankruptcy filings and, 187
  basics and benefits, 18, 178, 184–185,
    244
  deficiencies and, 18, 81, 185, 186–187,
    190, 191, 195
  disadvantages and potential problems,
    18, 81, 185–187
  FHA loans, 93, 96
  getting help with, 189, 190, 211
  multiple lenders and, 18, 191–192
  terms and timelines, 187–190
  your credit and, 19, 185
Single point of contact requirement
  (lenders), 71
Six-month gross income test (Chapter 7
  bankruptcy), 140–142
Small Business Administration (SBA)
  loans, 107

South Carolina law and programs, 98, 132–133, 297

South Dakota law, 298

Standing, to bring foreclosure suits, 157, 159–160

State assistance programs

  foreclosure avoidance mediation programs, 47, 97–98, 154, 213

  Hardest Hit Fund programs, 2, 47, 98–101

  pandemic-related programs, 11, 100

State law, 2, 247–308

  attorney fees charged by lenders/ servicers, 161–162

  attorney payment for foreclosure assistance, 213

  bankruptcy exemptions, 128, 132–133, 136–137, 245

  deceleration, 174

  deficiencies and deficiency lawsuits, 49–50, 186, 194–195

  dual tracking, 74, 188

  eviction after foreclosure, 42, 46

  fee-based foreclosure assistance, 26, 213

  foreclosure by possession, 37

  foreclosure notice requirements, 35, 36, 179

  high-cost mortgage protections, 171

  homestead laws, 30

  judicial foreclosure states, 40

  nonjudicial foreclosure states, 44

  reinstatement and redemption rights, 9, 11, 83, 243

  researching online, 33, 223–225, 248

  right to request judicial foreclosure, 38

  short sales, 186, 188

  special protections for servicemembers, 36, 105

standing to bring a foreclosure suit, 158, 159

state-by-state listing, 247–308

statute of limitations for foreclosures, 172

violations as foreclosure defenses, 15

See also specific states

Statute of limitations

  for foreclosure, 172–174

  for SCRA claims, 102

Statutory liens, 245

Stay. *See* Automatic stay

Staying in your house payment-free during foreclosure, 1, 66, 136, 199–208, 213

  advantages for lender, 201

  advantages of, 6, 20, 179–180, 185, 200, 202

  after foreclosure sale, 20, 179, 181, 206–208, 241

  after notice of intent to foreclose, 203–205

  after notice to quit, 20, 208

  bankruptcy filings and, 12, 136–138

  basics, 19–20, 179–181

  evictions, 42, 46, 53, 206–208, 241

  how much time you may have, 30, 33–36, 52–53, 180–181, 200–205

  notifying lender that you still occupy the home, 28

  offers to pay you to move out, 207

  vs. short sale, 81

  See also Delaying foreclosure

Strategic default, 16, 178. *See also* Walking away

Strict foreclosure, 40, 41, 203, 236, 245

Student loan debt, 110, 112, 129

Subordinate liens. *See* Junior liens and mortgages; Second and third mortgages

Subprime loans, 245

Successors in interest, federal rules protecting, 73

Summary judgments, 40, 149, 150

Summons and complaint, 41–42, 245

basics, 39, 203

how much time you have to respond, 35, 147, 204

See also Judicial foreclosures

Support debts, 113, 119, 121, 122, 129, 242

T

Tax debts

in Chapter 7 bankruptcy, 129

in Chapter 13 bankruptcy, 113, 119, 121

short sales and, 191

zombie foreclosures and, 183, 184

See also Tax liens

Taxes

capital gains tax, 50

forgiven debt as taxable income, 17, 18, 50, 65, 81, 186–187, 195–198, 234

See also Property taxes; Tax debts; Tax liens

Tax liens, 191, 245

Temporary restraining orders (TROs), 152–153, 161, 204. *See also* Contesting foreclosure

Tennessee law and programs, 98, 299

Termination notice. *See* Notice to quit

Texas law, 300

Third mortgages. *See* Second and third mortgages

TILA (Truth in Lending Act), 70, 167–171, 246

Title transfers

after foreclosure sale, 41, 42

confirming, if you move out before sale, 184

due-on-sale clauses and violations, 33, 71

to foreclosure rescue companies, 22–23

mortgage assumptions after (VA loans), 96

reverse mortgages and, 64

without a sale (strict foreclosure), 40, 41, 203, 236, 245

See also Deeds in lieu of foreclosure

Traffic tickets, 129

Trials. *See* Contesting foreclosure

TROs (temporary restraining orders), 152–153, 161, 204. *See also* Contesting foreclosure

Trustee (bankruptcy). *See* Bankruptcy trustee

Trustee (nonjudicial foreclosure administrator), 43

Truth in Lending Act (TILA), 70, 167–171, 246

Truth in lending disclosures, 170

U

U.C.C. (Uniform Commercial Code), 32, 157, 172

Undersecured debts, 246. *See also* Cramdowns; Partially secured debts

Underwater mortgages/properties. *See* Negative equity

Unemployment

FHA Special Forbearance-Unemployment program, 94

Hardest Hit Fund programs, 98–101

Unfair lending practices

assignee liability for, 170, 228

as foreclosure defense, 15, 146, 154, 167–171, 174–175

predatory lending defined, 241

See also Illegal lending practices

Uniform Commercial Code (U.C.C.), 32, 157, 172

Unlawful detainers. *See* Evictions

Unoccupied homes, 200, 201
  lender's right to secure, 26–27
  occupancy as mortgage requirement, 34
  zombie foreclosures, 48, 178, 182–184

Unsecured debts
  Chapter 7 bankruptcy and, 126, 130, 133–134
  Chapter 13 bankruptcy and, 110, 111, 113–114, 119, 240
  consolidating as secured debt, 231
  second and third mortgages as, 116–117, 133–134, 240
  See also specific types

Upside-down mortgages. *See* Negative equity

USDA loans, 222
  determining whether you have an RHS loan, 91
  loss mitigation options, 84–85, 97
  pandemic-related foreclosure moratorium, 9, 76, 180

U.S. Department of the Treasury, Hardest Hit Fund programs, 2, 47, 98–101

Utah law, 301

Utility costs, 100

V

Vacant homes. *See* Unoccupied homes

Vacation or second homes, Chapter 13 bankruptcy and, 12, 13, 115

Variable interest rates. *See* Adjustable-rate mortgages

VA (Veterans Administration) loans, 222, 234
  disaster-related relief, 105, 106
  identifying, 91
  loss mitigation options, 96–97
  pandemic-related relief, 9, 76, 84–85, 180

Vehicle loan cramdowns (Chapter 13 bankruptcy), 115

Vehicle repossessions, 130

Vermont law, 40, 203, 224, 302–303

Veterans Administration loans. *See* VA (Veterans Administration) loans

Virginia law, 304

W

Walking away from your house, 8, 16–17, 178, 181
  zombie foreclosures, 48, 178, 182–184

Washington, D.C. law and programs, 98

Washington state law, 305

Waste, as breach of agreement, 34

Waterfall process (FHA loss mitigation), 93–96

West Virginia law, 306

Wildcard exemptions (bankruptcy), 137–138

Willful acts, debts arising from, 121, 129

Wisconsin law, 183, 307

Workouts. *See* Loss mitigation options

Writ of possession or writ of assistance, 42, 207, 241

Wyoming law, 308

Z

Zombie foreclosures, 48, 178, 182–184